All My Relatives

All My Relatives

Community in Contemporary Ethnic American Literatures

Bonnie TuSmith

Ann Arbor

THE UNIVERSITY OF MICHIGAN PRESS

Copyright © by Bonnie TuSmith 1993
All rights reserved
Published in the United States of America by
The University of Michigan Press
Manufactured in the United States of America

1996   1995   1994   1993   4   3   2   1

Library of Congress Cataloging-in-Publication Data

TuSmith, Bonnie, 1951–
    All my relatives : community in contemporary ethnic American
literatures / Bonnie TuSmith.
        p.   cm.
    Includes bibliographical references and index.
    ISBN 0-472-10323-7 (alk. paper)
        1. American literature—Minority authors—History and criticism.
    2. American literature—20th century—History and criticism.
    3. United States—Literatures—History and criticism. 4. Ethnic
    relations in literature. 5. Community life in literature.
    6. Ethnic groups in literature. 7. Minorities in literature.
    I. Title.
    PS153.M56T87   1993
    810.9'920693—dc20   92-42423
                                                                    CIP

A CIP catalogue record for this book is available from the British Library.

This book is for my mother and sisters,
all Sisters of Color, Steve, and my partner Jerry.

Preface

The Lakota medicine man Lame Deer describes the typical sweat lodge experience thus:

> There is a great surge of power. You inhale that breath, drink in the water, the white steam. It represents clouds, the living soul, life. The heat is very great. Your lungs are breathing fire, and if you can't stand it you can say, "*Mitakuye oyasin*—all my relatives," and somebody will open the flap and let the cool air in for you. (*Lame Deer*, 180)

In this Indian purification ritual when someone is in trouble he or she calls on the extended family—the ancestors, the tribe, the rocks and trees, the birds and animals, the world, the universe—for help. The expression "all my relatives" leaves out nothing and no one and serves as the ultimate concept of community in many works by ethnic American writers.

Within this framework the term *community* refers to the relatedness and dynamic interdependence of all life-forms rather than the stagnant, conformist vision that the term tends to evoke in a capitalist society. From a nondualistic perspective the communal does not mean the negation of the individual. In fact, many writers discussed in this study insist that the individual necessarily comes before the communal. In other words, without a sense of individual self-worth one cannot attain true community with others. The ideology of individualism, on the other hand, operates outside the individual-and-communal framework in that it views the self as existing in a vacuum—the extended family having neither relevance nor worth—and it views self-interest as the ultimate value. It is this concept of individualism that pits the individual *against* the collective in North American society.

The hypothesis of my book is that, among the various cultures of ethnic Americans, communal values continue to inform the cultures' worldviews. From this premise the study seeks to critique the ideology of individualism in American society. Since any monolithic characterization of our variegated population makes me nervous, when studies since the civil rights era proclaim that "Americans have lost the language to express communal values" (Bellah) and that ours is a "culture of narcissism" (Lasch), I necessarily had to call the question "Which Americans?" Immediately coming to mind were the wealth of communal expressions embedded in ethnic American speech patterns, such as the "y'all" of Southern black folks, the "familia" of Latinos, and the expression for *everyone*, "dà jiā" (big family), of Chinese Americans. Surely, I reasoned, vernacular speech patterns among various groups of Americans do not reflect a loss of communal language. To explore this question I embarked on an adventure that resulted in this multicultural study with the ethnically identified title "All My Relatives."

As a first-generation Chinese American who grew up partly in the streets of Manhattan, I have known for a long time that American society is anything but homogeneous. My reality among marginalized African American, Puerto Rican, Italian American, and Jewish American kids taught me that survival required a willingness to cross cultures in a hurry. Beneath the color line bonds were formed according to our strengths and weaknesses—according to our ability to think on our feet. In such an environment I never had the time—or the luxury—to be a "model minority." It was not until my teenage years, as my family gradually moved into predominantly white residential neighborhoods such as the Flushing, Queens, of the mid-1960s, that I became a "model." Suddenly, my sisters and I were "exotic Orientals" and condemned to some preordained, immutable outsider status. Our newly acquired multiethnic identity could not stand up to such a wall of prejudice. Even as Anglos *preferred* us to black people because Asians were supposed to be "quieter" and "cleaner," we were tolerated but not invited to dinner. The silencing of my Asian American self began in those days and created a prison from which it took years to escape.

In celebration of my own liberation as well as the liberation of others like me I am committing my energies to the broadening of American literary discourse to include voices from ethnic cultures in the United States. To some academics claiming multiethnic knowledge or expertise means that the scholar is "asking for it," meaning that she or he can expect to be attacked from all sides for encroaching on others' "turfs." I am well aware of the risks and pitfalls of my critical approach. It might have been "safer" for me to have written a book on Asian American literature. After all, at this point in ethnic literary studies there is significant scholarship on the cultural productions of major non-European American groups. How ethnic cultures relate to one another—as well as to European American culture—is less clear. From my perspective, if we continue to overlook the relationships and connections among American cultures and persist in separatism, we scholars are guilty of perpetuating misunderstandings that even now have serious repercussions in educational institutions and in the larger society. Based on my own American experience, I felt that I had no choice but to undertake a multicultural study.

I have made a similar choice in my university teaching. By exploring literatures by non-European Americans in university undergraduate and graduate courses with the assumption that the four broad categories of African American, Asian American, Latino/a, and Native American are equally important, my students and I have gained significant insight, which would have escaped us had we studied one ethnic group exclusively. Given the dichotomization of American society into black and white, it is virtually impossible to perceive the larger whole without some strategy for a cross-cultural, multiethnic study. And without the larger picture we are all caught in partial constructs of what we assume is "*the* American reality."

It is important to warn the reader that this study is *not* literary history. Rather, it is a critical analysis of a handful of significant prose works by ethnic writers in relation to the specific theme of individualism and community. The scope of a multicultural study must by its nature be wide-ranging. For the chapter on the literature of an ethnic group to be "representative" of that group would be an impossible task. In an attempt to be somewhat more inclusive, however, a final section is appended to each chapter that provides selective commentary on additional authors from each ethnic group. It is also necessary to add that this study is not meant to be a one-on-one comparative analysis of various texts. While the final chapter does make comparisons in a more cross-cultural dialogue, throughout most of the analyses intertextual connections are left to the reader. My approach is to offer as balanced a presentation as possible in terms of gender and ethnicity and to trust the reader to make relevant comparisons among the texts discussed. The hope is that, by my including an array of ethnic literary voices in a study with a central focus, the reader will be able to connect the individual critiques and come up with meaningful cross-cultural, cross-gender interpretations.

In pursuing this project I have been privileged to encounter several people who care enough to insist on keeping us honest. Rather than name individuals who have supported me through the writing of this book, I would like to state here that, without the key people in my life—that is, my friends and families (including students, university colleagues, editors, writers, and community activists)—I could not have accomplished my goal. You are all my relatives, and I am honored to be part of such a dedicated tribe.

Contents

Chapter 1

Ethnicity and Community

The Issue of Ethnicity in America

The 1960s witnessed what some scholars labeled an "ethnic revival" in America. Previously, the civil rights movement of the late 1950s had made visible the nation's most identifiable "other": the African Americans. As thousands of protesters marched across television screens, middle America experienced a shock—these people, too, resided in America. With the potential emergence of a Third World coalition in this country the observation that "the fault lines of conflict in America are invariably ethnic" became more than an academic cliché for viewers at home (Boelhower, *Through a Glass Darkly*, 20). But why are the fault lines "ethnic" rather than "racial"? In America the two terms have been more or less synonymous until recent times. Perhaps *ethnic* now sounds less discriminatory, since it implies cultural diversity, than *race*, which usually reduces the issue to the color of one's skin. Terminology, or naming, can be problematic when we discuss who or what is "an American." The image of black versus white encapsulates what Gunnar Myrdal identified four decades ago as "an American dilemma."

The significance of the 1960s movement for civil rights—and what makes the era a watershed for all Americans—is the assertion by excluded citizens that second-class status by virtue of one's race, creed, or national origin is unacceptable. The visibility of black protesters inspired other historically excluded groups to demand a hearing. By the early 1970s culturally distinct groups such as Native Americans, Asian Americans, and Chicano/as began to speak for themselves. What these groups have to say about American values, as presented in their emerging literatures, is the focus of this study. Before we can take the category of "ethnic writers" for granted, however, it is necessary to explore the complex question of ethnicity in

America. This chapter addresses some major issues in the ethnic debate.

What Does *Ethnicity* Mean?

There are two sources from which the word *ethnic* is derived. From the Greek *ethnos* we get "nation" or "people." In this context we have the sense of peoplehood or community. Another Greek word, *ethnikos*, however, has the explicit designation of "heathen" or "other." In *Beyond Ethnicity* Werner Sollors attributes this second connotation to American usage. Tracing the etymology one step further, Sollors finds that the contrast between *heathen* and *chosen people* in traditional Christianity, when used in the American context, becomes *ethnic* versus *American*. An "ethnic," then, is "nonstandard, or, in America . . . not fully American" (25). This definition makes it difficult for WASPs (white Anglo-Saxon Protestants) to be considered ethnics. After all, in order to have an "other" there must first be a self. In other words, WASPs are the norm to whom ethnics are "other." Various terms used to describe the Americanization process—from *melting pot* to *assimilation*—presuppose, in the above context, the shedding of one's ethnic culture to conform to the WASP standard. When scholars use terms such as *host society, core culture, mainstream,* or *dominant culture* in contrast to *ethnic culture,* the unstated assumption is that the only nonethnic culture is that of WASPs. It is important not to confuse WASP culture with the broader culture, which includes the contributions of all Americans. For the purposes of this study, *ethnic* will consistently refer to people of color. The four literary groupings used here belong under this general rubric (a rationale for this terminology follows). When referring to the broader white culture I will use various terms (WASP, Anglo-American, Anglo, European American, white), depending on the context of the discussion and the common usage of the specific ethnic group being considered. The most general term for white culture, however—and the one that is sometimes the most useful for purposes of contrast with ethnic Americans—is *European American*, which can include WASPs and other white Americans of European origin.

According to Sollors, the term *ethnicity* first appeared in 1941 in a five-volume community study (23). For the target Massachusetts community the authors Warner and Lunt designated eight groups (all non-WASP white) plus "Negro" as ethnic in contrast to "Native" or "Yankee." The other traits studied were age, sex, and religion. While Sollors does not make the connection here, this initial use of *ethnicity* seems a conscious substitution for the previously prevalent use of *race*. Since the researchers grouped both white and black people as ethnics, culture rather than color determined ethnicity. Another often cited source, David Riesman's 1953 *American Scholar* essay (which was mistakenly credited with the coinage of the word *ethnicity*), identifies as "ethnic victims" Indians, Mexicans, Spaniards, and Japanese (Sollors, *Beyond Ethnicity*, 22). It is important to note here that these first references to ethnicity *did* include people of color. Since contemporary usage of the term *ethnic* implies identification with a group that is different in specific aspects from WASP culture, the present study's target groups of writers (African American, Asian American, Native American, and Chicano/a) are certainly ethnic. The prevalent practice among scholars of labeling people of color in America "racial minorities" while labeling white non-WASPs "ethnics" or "immigrants" reflects certain assumptions that are value-based. This point will be argued more fully later in the chapter.

In discussing the issue of ethnicity and race Sollors refers to a keen observation made by Oscar Handlin in the 1957 essay "What Happened to Race?" In Sollors's words:

> . . . before the rise of the word "ethnicity," the word "race" was widely used to refer to larger and smaller groupings of mankind: for example, the Irish race or the Jewish race. In fact, the National Socialist genocide in the name of "race" is what gave the word a bad name and supported the substitution of "ethnicity." (38)

By pointing out that *ethnicity* replaced *race* in postwar American usage, Handlin suggests that the two terms had been considered interchangeable. From this observation Sollors concludes that, since *race* is a "heavily charged term," it is better to view it as "one aspect of ethnicity" (39). As the present discussion will show, although this might be a suitable position in relation to white ethnics, it is evasive and inadequate when applied to people of color in America.

"Ethnic Fever"

That a new ethnic awareness seemed to be surfacing in the 1960s came as a shock to many social theorists. The expectation that various immigrant groups in America would assimilate into the larger urban industrial society did not take place. Nathan Glazer and D. Moynihan's 1963 study, *Beyond the Melting Pot*, documents the tenacity of ethnic cultures in New York City. Ethnic groups are not just products of the "Old Country" transplanted in America but are continually being recreated by their new American experiences. According to the study, not only are there self-selected groupings by ethnicity; these "Negroes, Puerto Ricans, Jews," etc., have become identifiable "interest groups" as well (17). Another key work published a year later confirms the persistence of ethnic groups in America (although the author claims "structural" rather than "cultural" ethnicity): "As though with a wily cunning of its own, as though there were some essential element in man's nature that demanded it . . . the sense of ethnic belonging has survived" (Gordon, *Assimilation*, 25). This mysterious ethnic force manifested itself everywhere. Native Americans, Latino/as, Asian Americans—racially visible groups that had been politically and economically invisible—identified themselves as members of viable communities with specific needs. Analogously for African Americans, the slogan Black is Beautiful challenged negative attitudes toward people of color. Then, in the midst of the movement for racial pride and roots seeking, another segment of American society proclaimed itself the "new ethnics."

In 1972 Michael Novak published *The Rise of the Unmeltable Ethnics*, a pivotal work that heralded the dawning of the "white ethnics" (Americans of eastern and southern European ancestry). In this work he makes an impassioned argument on behalf of ethnicity as a solution to the collective identity crisis experienced by his subject population: "People uncertain of their own identity are not wholly free. They are threatened not only by specific economic and social programs, but also at the very heart of their identity. The world is mediated to human persons through language and culture, that is, through ethnic belonging" (229).

After establishing the primacy of ethnicity Novak proceeds to detail instances of social, cultural, and religious community among the new ethnics. Appropriately, the first chapter claims the 1970s as "the decade of the ethnics." In identifying "individualism, competition, and merely rational interest" as prominent aspects of WASP culture, and in reminding the reader that seventy million white ethnics—who do not necessarily subscribe to this value system—mean an interest group of considerable clout, the book gave the ethnic revival a new twist. Novak's contentions seem plausible, even courageous and humane—until one examines those in the category of "enemies" in his view. Besides WASPs, Novak attacks young people, people of color, and intellectuals. Statements such as the following betray a chip-on-the-shoulder, me-too attitude: "The recent increase in black, Chicano, and Indian consciousness left other ethnic groups in a psychologically confused state. They are unable to be WASPS; they have lost confidence in being themselves" (*Rise of the Unmeltable Ethnics,* 7–8). The new ethnicity's position regarding blacks is especially damaging to its egalitarian claims. In a typical maneuver Novak explains white ethnic violence toward Martin Luther King, Jr., and his marchers by claiming that "the tactic of demonstration is inherently WASP and inherently offensive to ethnic peoples" (13). According to Novak, then, nonviolent black demonstrators were behaving like WASPs and therefore deserved to be stoned by ethnics. While this line of reasoning hardly requires serious consideration, Novak's claims concerning ethnic status do.

The "Myth" of Ethnicity

In a 1974 essay defending his position Novak itemizes what the new ethnicity does and does not include. Criteria such as a different language, a subculture, an ethnic neighborhood, etc., are out. Instead, there are sneaking suspicions such as "a growing sense of discomfort," "gut reactions," "a growing self-confidence," and "a sense of being discriminated against." We (southern and eastern European Americans) played by the rules, Novak appears to be lamenting. We were not, in his words, "'ethnic,' or even 'hyphenated,' but only 'American.' . . . And in the end, even then, they retain the power and the status" ("New Ethnicity," 19).

What the new creed consists of is a gut-level feeling of exclusion, which remains undocumented in Novak's work. Granted that ethnicity, like race, is an emotionally charged concept that too often gets people up in arms, white ethnicity Novak-style appears a blatant play

for the brass ring of power and status. Consequently, ethnic revival-
ists were accused of manipulation, duplicity, and racism. In *The Ethnic Myth* Stephen Steinberg sees the ethnic revival as a "dying gasp":
"symptomatic of the atrophy of ethnic cultures and the decline of
ethnic communities" (51). In identifying his purpose as being "to
exorcise ethnicity" Pierre Van den Berghe states in his recent book:
"I abhor its narrowness, its bigotry, its intolerance, its violence, and
its outbursts of irrationality" (*Ethnic Phenomenon*, xii). Irving Howe,
the author of a comprehensive study on immigrant Jews entitled *The
World of Our Fathers*, also looks askance at the ethnic craze. To him
seeking one's heritage is "sentimental" and boils down to "a last
hurrah of nostalgia." Rather than a "conquest of history," it is more
of an "improvisation of myth" ("Limits of Ethnicity," 18). Sollors
spells out his hostility in no uncertain terms: "The heart of the matter
is that in the present climate consent-conscious Americans are willing
to perceive ethnic distinctions . . . as powerful and as crucial; and that
writers and critics pander to that expectation" (*Beyond Ethnicity*, 13).
For the above writers, the emphasis on ethnicity is divisive, unethi-
cal, and potentially dangerous. Proving that ethnicity in America is
a myth has become the preoccupation of many a social theorist.

A recent study on worldwide ethnic revivals defines an ethnic
group as "a type of community, with a specific sense of solidarity and
honour, and a set of shared symbols and values." The rationale for
this type of community resides in the members' sense of shared
history and their "myths of group origins and group liberation." The
author, Anthony Smith, emphasizes the importance of mythology for
ethnic group cohesion: "The more striking and well-known these
myths of group formation and group deliverance, the greater the
chances for the ethnic group to survive and endure" (*Ethnic Revival*,
65). In this context "myths" refers to stories of a people's shared
experiences and is used in a positive sense. External factors may also
supply a group with its own myths, as in the case of African Americans. The cultural features thus forged serve as self-affirmation for
the group. Since the 1960s the word *black*, in contrast to the imposed
term *Negro*, has become a symbol for ethnic membership and pride
(De Vos and Romanucci-Ross, *Ethnic Identity*, 31). While Smith's
study encompasses ethnic revivals around the globe and focuses on
the new dimension of transformation toward nation-states, the significance of mythology in solidifying a group cannot be overlooked

(this point will be explored later in this discussion). The subjective, intangible aspect of a group's sense of identity becomes problematic, however, when one must quantify cultural content to prove one's ethnicity. Where an ethnic community does not have a present territorial base or a coherent past, as is the prevalent case with ethnic groups in America, the claim to ethnic status may appear more myth than reality. No wonder critics of the new ethnicity question its legitimacy.

Boundary Maintenance and Symbolic Ethnicity

Fredrik Barth's emphasis on boundary-formation and maintenance in the introduction to *Ethnic Groups and Boundaries* signals a major shift in the ethnic debate. The idea that it is the "ethnic *boundary* that defines the group, not the cultural stuff that it encloses" (15), provides critics of the ethnic revival with a formidable argument. Ethnicity, in this view, emerges only through social contact and confrontation. Self-identification and the perceptions of others determine group membership. Since cultural content changes over time, the "it" of an ethnic group is not an immutable core culture but, rather, is how members of one group distinguish themselves from others. This description has enabled at least one prominent sociologist to insist that "the ethnic status is conspicuously devoid of 'social content'" (Parsons, "Some Theoretical Considerations," 65). Glazer and Moynihan clarify this point of view: "The cultural *content* of each ethnic group, in the United States, seems to have become very similar to that of others, but the emotional significance of attachment to the ethnic group seems to persist" (*Beyond the Melting Pot,* 8). The present study will take issue with these broad generalizations when they are applied to cultures in America that are not of European origin. First, however, we should examine the claim that signs of ethnic identification are only "empty symbols" (Parsons, "Some Theoretical Considerations," 65).

While Parsons cites David Schneider's *American Kinship* (1968) as his source for the "no-content" thesis, a more recent work, Herbert Gans's article "Symbolic Ethnicity" (1979), claims the attention of ethnic theorists. Simply put, Gans sees no ethnic revival occurring. Instead, he attributes the commotion to (1) the increased visibility of upwardly mobile ethnics and (2) the new trend in ethnic behavior he calls "symbolic ethnicity" (198). Gans's description of ethnic practices emphasizes expedience: "Ethnicity, now that it is respectable and no longer a major cause of conflict, seems therefore to be ideally suited to serve as a distinguishing characteristic" (215). Symbols, such as Jewish rites of passage or certain ethnic foods, must not "take much time" or "upset the everyday routine" (205). To Gans this type of effortless third-generation ethnicity reinforces rather than negates the straight-line theory of acculturation-assimilation (in which the ethnic group is eventually absorbed by the larger culture).

At this point it is necessary to examine the confusion in terminology to which I have previously alluded. When theorists evoke ethnic boundaries and symbols to support the no-content thesis of ethnicity, which elements of the population are they describing? Sollors, for example, utilizes the above-cited studies and others to emphasize the ephemeral nature of ethnic claims and support his contention that America needs to progress "beyond ethnicity" (*Beyond Ethnicity*, 33–39). The populations observed and tested were Jewish for Gans and "Anglo-Saxon, Irish, and Italian" in a Greeley and McCready ethnicity study cited by Sollors (34). Sollors, however, includes Native Americans, blacks, and Chinese Americans (the latter with oblique references to the writers Frank Chin and Maxine Hong Kingston) in his book without distinguishing these groups from the test populations. The assumption is that ethnic theories developed from surveying white ethnics apply to the nonwhite population as well. But do they? How, one could well ask, do groups judged primarily by their race, and with American experiences manifestly different from those of "white ethnics," accommodate these theories? Are people of color "ethnic" in the same sense? Should theories such as symbolic ethnicity apply to them? The trouble is that, thus far, social scientists have not examined this question closely. Consequently, the term *ethnic* shifts with each theorist, betraying unidentified assumptions of inclusion and exclusion that are inaccurate at best. Let us explore a few of these assumptions.

"Racial Minorities" versus "Ethnics"

In Gans's essay "Symbolic Ethnicity," the distinction between "ethnics" and "racial minorities" seems clear in one passage:

At present, the costs of being and feeling ethnic are slight. The changes that the immigrants and their descendants wrought in America now make it unnecessary for ethnics to surrender their ethnicity to gain upward mobility, and today ethnics are admitted virtually everywhere . . . . Moreover, since World War II, *the ethnics have been able to shoulder blacks and other racial minorities with the deviant and scapegoat functions they performed in an earlier America,* so that ethnic prejudice and "institutional ethnism" are no longer significant. (214–15; emphasis added)

In this passage Gans's description of the changed climate for (white) ethnics in America is problematic when it is juxtaposed to "blacks and other racial minorities" because of its unstated assumptions and its unclear point of view. It summarily dismisses people of color as a foil for white ethnics. The phrase "have been able to shoulder . . . with" presents an unsavory image of exploitation and, perhaps due to its abruptness and unfortunate choice of words, might be construed as approval on the author's part. At the very least Gans seems to be making his point at the expense of "racial minorities."

In the same article Gans briefly broadens his use of *ethnic* to include nonwhites as well. This occurs in his conclusion: "All Americans, save the Indians, came here as immigrants and are thus in one sense ethnics." This momentary concession is made to show who is absolutely not an ethnic: namely, "people who arrived in the seventeenth and eighteenth centuries, and before the mid-nineteenth-century old immigration" (218). The problem is, if there are other people who are "in one sense ethnics," then why are they not included in Gans's definition of *ethnics?* This point is not addressed in the article. Unfortunately, the nonclarification of assumptions becomes insidious when other scholars use Gans's influential essay across the board—applying the concept of symbolic ethnicity to white and nonwhite Americans alike.

In a report on black Americans published in the 1978 *Annals of the American Academy of Political and Social Science* coauthors Barbara Carter and Dorothy Newman fault the 1976 *Annals* issue of *Social Indicator* for discussing almost exclusively the white immigration since 1891 under the topic "ethnic diversity." Blacks, Asian Americans, and Native Americans are hardly touched upon. This lapse occurs, the authors point out, in spite of the fact that "the main immigration of Japanese and Chinese, the largest of the Asian groups, was in the late nineteenth century and early in the twentieth" (188–89). Since the *Annals* is an official publication of the American Academy of Political and Social Science and might very well influence governmental policy, this exclusion seems ominous. The report also points out that, since the gains of the 1960s, the "white majority" no longer recognizes the continuing reality of racial discrimination in America. The issue resides in one's angle of vision: "Minorities define discrimination in terms of its consequences or effects. The white majority perceives it largely in terms of the intent of both our institutional practices and consequences" (191).

Good intentions do not always translate into positive results. When Gans claims that "ethnic prejudice and 'institutional ethnism' are no longer significant" he is projecting a majoritarian viewpoint that does not even recognize the experience of nonwhite Americans. The tendency not to see something that is there—whether it is a significant population of nonwhites when dealing with the ethnic diversity of America or the persistence of discrimination when it is not in the books—makes the research of some social scientists in the field of ethnic studies open to question.

One of the few studies that does distinguish "racial minorities" from "immigrant white minorities" states that its analysis deals exclusively with the latter population. Basically, says the author, "given the different economic and political dimensions of ethnicity in the two instances, it would not be correct to treat [the two] as variants of the same phenomenon" (Steinberg, *Ethnic Myth,* 50–51). The "ethnic myth" of the book's title, then, refers only to white ethnics. This coherent use of terms is rare among books and articles consulted for the present research.

The widespread practice of using *racial minorities* for people of color and *ethnics* or *immigrants* for Jews, Slovaks, Poles, Italians, etc., requires rethinking. Since the ethnic revival has touched both nonwhites and whites, why should the word *ethnic* suddenly apply only to descendants of immigrant whites? The term *immigrant* is also problematic when used generically to refer to the eastern and southern Europeans. The Japanese, for example, arrived in this country during the period of the "new immigration." Why are these people not "immigrants"? The dichotomization of race versus ethnicity along color lines (nonwhites identified by race, white non-WASPs identified by ethnicity) seems a mixing of apples and oranges. Were nonwhites responsible, as some claim, for forcing the race issue and identifying themselves solely in racial terms?

In his 1970 update of *Beyond the Melting Pot* Glazer rather peevishly faults "Negroes" for becoming "blacks." In 1963 black people had been treated in his New York study as one ethnic group among others, and "Negroes themselves saw their place in the city in these terms" (xiv). By 1969, however, "we seem to be moving to a new set of categories, black and white, and that is ominous." What is more, he says, blacks are now forming an alliance with the self-identified "internally colonized" groups of brown, yellow, and red.

Parsons also considers the new term detrimental. By utilizing color as their symbol of solidarity, he criticizes, blacks have "made it possible or easier to attribute biologically hereditary characteristics to the group" ("Some Theoretical Considerations," 76). In a footnote Parsons cites a black woman's explanation of the symbol. The emphasis on blackness, she had told him, was to counteract the black community's own stratification based on shades of color (lighter equals higher status). "In a sense," concludes Parsons, "this is a case of making a virtue of necessity" (75). While this comment is literally accurate, the positive spirit behind black symbolism is lost. It seems as if the entire history of black-white race relations in America were irrelevant—even nonexistent—for both men. By making blackness a positive attribute instead of the stigma it has always been, the theorists insist, black people have created an "[ominous] new set of categories." This type of argument tends to blame the victim for his or her oppression.

Glazer's complaint that black people had allowed themselves to be considered ethnic and later promoted racial identification instead really misses the point. This type of either/or status assignment does not reflect black reality. In the United States race and ethnicity have never been separable for people of color. If we say that race is one aspect of ethnicity, we must qualify this generalization when referring to nonwhite ethnics. For people who are judged by their physical characteristics *before* their group affiliations race is a given. Physical appearance would be an empty bond, however, without some sense of peoplehood based on cultural ties. A person who identifies herself as Chicana is making an ethnic reference with race as a forgone conclusion. A Chicana writer, therefore, is an ethnic writer in the sense generally used in the common culture: she is ethnically affiliated with the Mexican American heritage. Given this basic definition, a black writer is also ethnic if he or she identifies with a specifically African American culture. Since, as mentioned earlier in this chapter, the concept of ethnicity (whether real or imagined) has gained currency in America in the last three decades, we cannot exclude certain groups from ethnic considerations by lumping them under "racial minorities." While the designation itself might be value-free, users of the term often are not. At best, racial minorities tend to get dismissed in theoretical discussions on ethnicity. For this reason the present study claims the term *ethnic Americans* for its target groups of writers. How white ethnics became *the* ethnics is the topic of the following discussion.

Co-optation: Strategy for Legitimacy

In making a distinction between the sacred and the profane in American history, Sollors states: "Since the 1960s the sacred side of the antithesis has increasingly been the ethnic one. In contemporary usage ethnicity has largely been transformed from a heathenish liability into a sacred asset" (*Beyond Ethnicity*, 33). While the author of this statement might not approve of the transformation, the accuracy of his claim is corroborated by the flood of ethnic material at the library. This is why it is doubly disturbing when books with *ethnicity* in their titles overlook nonwhite ethnics. We might trace this development back to events of the late 1960s.

The political scientist Martin Kilson, in an analysis of the new ethnicity, discusses the American black-white conflict in terms of presidential administrations. Black Americans initiated ethnic awareness, says Kilson, to redress their "inferior ethnic characterization" by whites ("Blacks and Neo-Ethnicity," 237). From 1966 on the revitalization of black culture became militantly antiwhite. It took a while—until 1970—for black moderates to step in and redefine the movement along political, reformist lines. In the Kennedy-Johnson era black ethnic politicization worked due to federal support. This success, however, was "perceived by the majority white social groups as a premature consolidation of ethnicity" (242). Hence, a conservative backlash set in.

At the forefront of the antiblack crusade was the Nixon administration. By Nixon's second term, beginning in 1972, what many white Americans had considered legitimate political goals promoted by blacks were perceived as "intrinsically *Negro goals*" and, therefore, "un-American" (239). Kilson aptly calls this "the *ethnicization* of racial perceptions." Black ethnicity Nixon-style, then, was totally negative. What had ideologically represented group solidarity and affirmation backfired during this period. Ethnic status did not elevate blacks because "few whites accord Negroes those positive societal and cultural attributes associated with the term 'ethnic groups'—*attributes that attract historical celebration in time, ancestry, and heritage*" (240). The reification of ethnicity, and the accompanying exclusion of African Americans from its exalted domain, crystallized in 1972 with the "unmeltable ethnics."

From Kilson's description of the late 1960s political climate it is easy to identify Novak's place in the picture. Formerly stigmatized ethnic groups like "Irish, Poles, Italians, and Jews," Kilson informs us, were part of the white majority backlash against blacks (242). The proclamation of a "new ethnicity," therefore, seems like an appropriate political ploy. The issue is not who did it first or who did what to whom. Both blacks and whites utilized the ethnic revival to their advantage. The problem is, once a sufficient number of whites showed an interest in their cultural heritages nonwhites lost their ethnic status in political and social discourse. Then, when other whites wished to disprove the authenticity of white ethnic American cultures—labeling ethnic affiliations "voluntary," "symbolic," and "empty"—by indirect association nonwhite cultures were discredited as well. What got lost in the shuffle was the truism that "ethnicity is often a matter of choice for whites"; with nonwhites, however, "this was not possible, because their skin color, hair texture, and stature made them easily recognizable" (Woolbright and Hartmann, "The New Segregation," 146).

While ethnicity might prove a passing phase for the white population in America, it is here to stay for the easily identifiable other. Until racial discrimination ends people of color cannot—and do not necessarily wish to—assimilate and give up their ethnic identities. They are also not as prone to proving how unmeltably ethnic they really are. Novak's protestations of ethnicity are a bit too shrill.

In an eye-opening essay on insiders and outsiders in American history R. Laurence Moore makes the important observation that people who have claimed outsider status have often been "at the center of the American experience" ("Insiders and Outsiders," 399). There are definite advantages to playing the outsider, including the reverence accorded cultural heroes (who are often outlaws) in the popular imagination. Moore views Novak's "new ethnicity" as an insider's pitch for the benefits of outsiderhood and a means of "cutting WASP America down to size" (409). While Novak's outsider rhetoric seems to turn the tradition of American jeremiads on its head (given the consensus function of jeremiads, according to Sacvan Bercovitch), it is a specifically political strategy for legitimation through co-optation. By claiming ethnicity as the special realm of "new immigrants," Novak appropriates a key term from America's historical outsiders—the people of color, or "racial minorities."

The strategy of co-optation practiced by insiders on true outsiders can be located throughout American history. Sollors gives fascinating examples of how Indian-white relations resulted in co-optation of "indigenous Indian legitimacy" by whites (*Beyond Ethnicity*, 128). Through a combination of fantasy and projection, as in the legends of "lovers' leaps" and noble chieftains, whites were able to use their idealization of the Indian to legitimate their own romantic involvements (which did not fit the Puritan creed). The ultimate irony is that "the idealized imagery of Indians was produced at the height of the Indian removals" (129).

While all of this romanticizing was going on, labels such as "savage" and "uncivilized" served to dehumanize an entire race. Throughout *The Invasion of America* Francis Jennings emphasizes the ideological implications of semantic manipulation. The word *pioneers*, for example, evokes images of courageous, resourceful white men. Actually, says Jennings, Indians were the original pioneers. By attaching *pioneer* to *white*, European settlers and subsequent colonial historians made the enterprise of pioneering an exclusively white domain.

A contemporary example of white co-optation can be found in Alice Walker's essay *"One* Child of One's Own." Referring to an exchange between a white feminist student and herself, Walker quotes the student as asking, "What about Black *feminists? . . .* Shouldn't they work with women?" (133). In an explanatory note Walker makes the following observation:

It is, apparently, inconvenient, if not downright mind straining, for white women scholars to think of black women as women, perhaps because "woman" (like "man" among white males) is a name they are claiming for themselves, and themselves alone. Racism decrees that if they are now women (years ago they were ladies, but fashions change) then black women must, perforce, be something else. (While they were "ladies" black women could be "women," and so on.) (133–34)

Apparently the word *woman*, like the word *ethnic*, no longer applies to certain segments of the American population. It is against these subtle forms of co-optation that people of color in America are beginning to speak. And in the process their writers and theorists are legitimating themselves and their ethnic cultures within the broader context of American society.

Ethnic American Writers

The prevalent bias that ethnic identification is nothing more than a nostalgic clinging to the past—a tenacious resistance to the forces of modernization—operates from a stagnant model for ethnic cultures. It is rarely the case that a people exist in isolation without outside influences. Even the Native Americans, a people who have shown the most determination to maintain their cultures in this country, have sustained a significant amount of acculturation over three centuries. While cultures change and adapt to the group's social circumstances, however, there is still a sense of commonality among group members. In the case of nonwhite cultures in America ethnic group identification is partly a direct consequence of racial visibility and forced marginality. Writers who identify themselves with a nonwhite culture in America are necessarily engaged in some form of cross-cultural debate.

The writers discussed in this study are mostly first-generation college graduates. Since, except for those who are African American, non-European American writers only began to gain recognition in the late 1960s, they are also likely to be the first generation of professional writers identified with specific ethnic cultures. In considering their literary contributions it is important to keep in mind William Boelhower's warning: "There is no parthenogenesis of ethnic codes. One

ethnic novel or a particular ethnic encyclopedia does not account for
the production of another. In truth, there is no unilateral aesthetic
starting point for the multi-ethnic critic" (*Through a Glass Darkly*, 35).
While the second part of this chapter will clarify some methodological
assumptions for the present research, it is appropriate to address
Boelhower's point here. The debunking focus of the present discussion seems necessary given the confusion among scholars regarding
ethnicity and the consequent exclusion of non-European groups from
ethnic categories. The insistence on ethnic (separate culture) status
for non-European American writers, however, does not mean that
these writers can be lumped together and approached from a unilateral perspective. One must always keep in mind the different historical and cultural experiences of each ethnic group as well as the variations among individuals. Boelhower reminds us that it would be
self-defeating to promote a "rival myth," to replace an erroneous
monocultural paradigm with a multiethnic one that assumes "the
formal paradigm attributes of [its] melting-pot predecessors" (23).
To avoid this pitfall the present study utilizes theoretical approaches
that are specific and indigenous to each ethnic culture, writer, and
text.

Community and Individualism

Contemporary American Culture:
The Language of Individualism

In a collaboration entitled *Habits of the Heart: Individualism and Commitment in American Life* (1985), Robert Bellah and his four associates
conclude: "If there are vast numbers of a selfish, narcissistic 'me
generation' in America, we did not find them, but we certainly did
find that the language of individualism, the primary American language of self-understanding, limits the ways in which people think"
(290).[1] After a five-year study (1979–84) of over two hundred middle-
class whites from both coasts the sociologists found that Americans
have lost the language for expressing communal values. From interviewing and observing their test subjects the researchers determined
that, "in the language they use, their lives sound more isolated and
arbitrary than, as we have observed them, they actually are" (21).
This discrepancy suggests that, while middle Americans are ideologi-

cally and linguistically individualistic, they are more social in practice. Bellah's research group named the discourse of individualism
the "first language" and that of tradition/commitment the "second
language" of American culture.

That the individual is the sole arbiter of values is the common
position taken by Bellah's test subjects: "What is good is what one
finds rewarding. If one's preferences change, so does the nature of
the good" (6). This jargon of self-determination seems to corroborate the authors' understanding of American society: "But the
notion that one discovers one's deepest beliefs in, and through,
tradition and community is not very congenial to Americans. Most
of us imagine an autonomous self existing independently, entirely
outside any tradition and community, and then perhaps choosing
one" (65). According to the researchers, the image of the self-
sufficient American presented in their study confirms Alexis de
Tocqueville's worst fears (see *Democracy in America*, 36–38). As one
of the first to apply the term *individualism* to "the American
character"—a trait that threatened to outweigh the mores, or "habits of the heart," that made the new nation a success—Tocqueville
foresaw a major drawback to democracy. In his own words: "Thus,
not only does democracy make men forget their ancestors, but also
clouds their view of their descendants and isolates them from their
contemporaries. Each man is forever thrown back on himself alone,
and there is danger that he may be shut up in the solitude of his
own heart" (508). In Tocqueville's view this type of isolation generates strife and leaves a people vulnerable to despotism. Without
mediation, then, the first language of American individualism holds
dangers for self and society.

While Bellah and his associates claim that Americans are not
really narcissistic but only talk that way, their findings are not
comforting. For those who believe that language affects thought
patterns[2]—as the book itself suggests in its assessment that individualistic language "limits the way people think"—the ideology-action
distinction appears precarious. How long, the book seems to be asking, before Americans *are* completely narcissistic in thought and in
deed? Hence, the authors express a sense of urgency in reinstating
the second language of communal commitment as America's primary discourse. The study at once negates and validates earlier
warnings against individualistic values found in works such as

David Riesman's *The Lonely Crowd* (1950) and Christopher Lasch's *The Culture of Narcissism* (1978).

That individualism is more an American ideology than a way of life is also the hypothesis of a 1979 essay by Christopher Jencks. While American revolutionaries never bothered about fraternity, says Jencks, by Tocqueville's day there was a preponderance of voluntary associations ("Social Basis," 80). Despite Tocqueville's warnings against excessive isolation Jencks conjectures that individualism has probably been more ideology than practice in America since before the 1830s. Regarding contemporary American life he finds a lack of communitarian language which mirrors that noted in Bellah's study discussed above. Jencks observes that, in his college classroom, words like *fraternity* and *community* are alien concepts: "They [his students] do not seem to have even a basic vocabulary for discussing the ties that bind us all together, much less a developed ideology regarding the importance of these ties" (81). Between Bellah's study and Jencks's essay it appears that Americans are verbally isolating themselves from one another and have been creating ideological word barriers for some time.

As previously mentioned, *Habits of the Heart* is based on a specific test population. Since the researchers assumed that "the mobile middle classes define reality for most of us in the United States" (306), they focused their study on the white middle class. The terminology of their disclaimer in the preface makes a now familiar distinction: "Though we were able to include considerable ethnic diversity, we were not able to illustrate much of the racial diversity that is so important a part of our national life" (ix). In other words the study includes some white ethnics, does not include people of color, and is at root naive about issues of ethnicity and diversity in America. When we read that "Americans" have an individualistic language and ideology, therefore, we cannot help wondering whether Bellah's test subjects do in fact "define reality for most of us."

Given the restrictive focus of the Bellah study, when we are confronted with its central question—"Has the individualism that Tocqueville observed with anxiety become so all-pervasive that we are no longer citizens?" (*Individualism and Commitment*, 3)—we are tempted to consult other Americans as well. The present study, then, will address segments of the population not included in Bellah's inquiry. Since America's purported individualism operates on the level of language, an examination of literature by contemporary ethnic American writers contributes a necessary perspective to the individualism-versus-community debate.

Individualism in European American Literature

In "Melodramas of Beset Manhood" Nina Baym credits Americanists of the 1950s with the perpetuation of the rugged individualist myth in American literature.[3] In response to Lionel Trilling's 1947 accusation that American novelists were nonrealistic and antisocial, says Baym, these critics turned vice into virtue and found "romance" to be the crucial ingredient in American fiction. Baym points out that embedded in this version of American literature is the vision of the self-made man:

> Behind this promise [the idea of America] is the assurance that individuals come before society, that they exist in some meaningful sense prior to, and apart from, societies in which they happen to find themselves. The myth also holds that, as something artificial and secondary to human nature, society exerts an unmitigatedly destructive pressure on individuality. To depict it at any length would be a waste of artistic time; and there is only one way to relate it to the individual—as an adversary. (71)

From this point of view the fact that we find a prevalence of American fictional heroes operating in a vacuum—whether they are visualized as American Adams or Lone Rangers—reflects the bias of white male critics. Partly because critics play an influential role in *creating* literature, an individual-against-society stance has been equated with *the* American literary tradition. A brief discussion of one critic's position should indicate how this has come about.

In *The American Novel and Its Tradition* Richard Chase finds that the American novel "has been stirred . . . by the aesthetic possibilities of radical forms of alienation, contradiction, and disorder" (2). According to him, it is this "romantic" quality that identifies a work as essentially American. Efforts to impose unity and resolve contradictions, as in the case of William Dean Howells, inevitably produce "dull" and "mediocre" writing (10). From Chase's perspective, then, one must either impose order or revel in disorder. The critic points out that, whereas the British both need to and are good at creating a middle ground ("The English novel at its best is staunchly middle-brow" [10]), the Americans, due to the "Manichaean quality of New England Puritanism," are interested in the "melodrama of the eternal struggle of good and evil" (11). While Chase claims that critics like D. H. Lawrence have been too preoccupied with what is wrong with American literature to see what it is, his own description of the American novel is also one-sided.

According to Chase, Puritanism, the frontier, and democracy are the "historical facts" that led to the individualistic nature of American culture (11). While this is a standard position among Americanists, the glorification of these aspects of history serves to promote a mono-lithic myth of "American character." Chase contributes to the myth by stating that it is the inherent contradictions in our past that have "vivified and excited the American [literary] imagination." In Chase's estimation the desire to explore "dark and complex truths," in ac-cordance with the romantic rather than realistic model, leads Ameri-can fiction down seductive paths: "And the intense desire to drive everything through to the last turn of the screw or twist of the knife, which distinguishes American writers from English, often results in romantic nihilism, a poetry of force and darkness" (xi). In this formu-lation American literature has a distinctive character indeed. The only problem is, this monolithic "character" offers a static and narrow view of the broad American culture. Specifically, it does not account for the writings of women and ethnics.

The American myth promoted by critics such as Chase is mis-leading. As Baym puts it: "We are all very familiar with this myth of America in its various fashionings, and owing to the selective vision that has presented this myth to us as the whole story, many of us are unaware of how much besides it has been created by literary Ameri-cans" ("Melodramas," 72). The question is, when we turn our atten-tion to fictional writers other than Cooper, Hawthorne, Melville, James, Twain, Fitzgerald, Hemingway, and Faulkner, does the image of American individualism still apply? In the present study I will discuss a selection of prominent literary works by ethnic American men and women in an attempt to answer this question.

Ethnic American Literature: The Language of Community

In the wake of the late-1960s "ethnic revival" literature by people of color has gained public attention.[4] While tokenism is still practiced among publishers (various critics have commented on the one-prominent-black-writer-at-a-time phenomenon), there is at least a rising interest in African American, Asian American, Native American, and Latino/a culture and literature among educators. Given the long overdue inclusion of ethnic and women's writings into the curriculum, our understanding of American literary tradition—at least the version promoted in the 1950s and early 1960s—must be revised. That is, we can no longer take it for granted that the Bellah research group's "first language of American individualism" adequately characterizes the "American Way" in either life or art. At a minimum we must distinguish, as the writers in this study do, Eurocentric culture or literary tradition from ethnic traditions in this country. Since many of us agree that cultural diversity is an undeniable characteristic of American society, we must beware of applying monolithic terms to non-WASPS. Many times these terms simply do not fit.

With the emergence of ethnic literature there has been a growing body of ethnic scholarship in the past two decades. In various critical studies, whether referring to writers from one or more ethnic cultures, scholars have remarked on the collectivist or communal orientation of ethnic American literature. Thus, Mary Dearborn finds that ethnic women's writings are communal acts, Houston Baker insists on the "collectivistic ethos" of black culture, Elaine Kim claims that Asian American literature is community oriented, Kenneth Lincoln emphasizes the tribal aspects of Native American works, Tomás Rivera observes that Chicano/a writers exhibit a "hunger for community," and so on. In general terms historical group consciousness and ethnic cultural traits that emphasize connectedness claim the attention of writers and critics alike.

The concept of "community" can be quite ambiguous. In sociological parlance it generally refers to "an aggregate of people who share a common interest in a particular locality" (Bender, *Community and Social Change*, 5). This definition, however, does not account for the experiential, feeling level of what people mean by community. Thomas Bender suggests that we remove the structural requirements (e.g., "The New England town was a community, but it was not a definition of community") for the term and define *community* as "a network of social relations marked by mutuality and emotional bonds" (7). He also suggests that we change our attitudes toward community. Rather than community collapse, he says, we have actually experienced community transformation in our social history (145). He notes that such a transformation is described in Ferdinand Tönnies's 1887 typology of shift from *Gemeinschaft* ("community," or small town) to *Gesellschaft* ("society," or big city), which seems to him, however, much too simplistic for modern society (17–43). While Tönnies's contention that our nostalgia for "lost community" generates feelings of emptiness and futility might be accurate, his static, linear model suggests that Utopia once truly existed, which, of course, is not the case.

What should be clear at this point is that we have identified a myth of individualism *and* a parallel myth of community in the broad American culture. The main contention here is that the hegemonic critical establishment has considered the first myth romantic and heroic, while the second has had the negative connotation associated with "nostalgia." A further contention is that, with the Eurocentric penchant for polarities and given our society's white male structure, individualism often represents the strength of male power, while community becomes equated with female weakness. Among ethnic writers, these same cultural myths exist to varying degrees, depending on the background and consciousness of the writer. In addition to and often in spite of this prevalent point of view, however, there is the possibility of an alternative vision gleaned from a different reality. Bender's "network of social relations marked by mutuality and emotional bonds" often reflects the ethnic writer's vision of community. For many writers who identify with their ethnic cultures community is a continuously evolving possibility that they strive to capture in literary discourse.

This quest for alternative visions of community through literature means reevaluating the forms as well as the aims of art. When, for example, the controversial Chicano educator/writer Richard Rodriguez claims that the novel cannot capture Chicano communal life, or, in a critic's words, "Rodriguez argues that the novel is best capable of depicting a solitary existence against a large social background"

(Vallejos, "Ritual Process," 5), he seems to have a rigid notion of what a novel is. On the other hand, he might be considered one ethnic writer who has not artistically explored the possibilities of his ethnicity. For those writers who are not overly concerned with genre restrictions (Silko says, for example, that genre distinctions such as poetry versus prose do not interest her at all ["Silko Interview," 98]), the "novel" can capture a great deal. The writers in the present study have successfully utilized various genres (the novel in particular) to convey a sense of the ethnic community.

In a 1982 essay entitled "Chicano Literature: The Establishment of Community" Tomás Rivera traces the community-building mind-set of Chicano writers in the 1970s (he notes that "the idea of community has imposed itself on the action and theme of literary works" [12]). Rivera interprets this literary penchant, this "hunger . . . in the Chicano writer to create a community" as a positive act to decolonize the "colonized mind[s]" of Mexican Americans (17, 10). While the author/critic's analysis of community is somewhat misleading in its emphasis on newness,[5] it does present a significant contrast to the Bellah group's belief that Americans lack the language to express communal values. In other words, while Bellah's research group found one thing among white middle-class Americans, a completely opposite phenomenon was occurring among nonwhites in the same period. The question then becomes, how should we interpret the apparent communal emphasis among multiethnic literatures?

When reading ethnic texts an important point to keep in mind is the mediating function performed by the writer. We cannot ignore, as John Reilly reminds us, "the sequence of choices an author makes in creating a narrative" ("Criticism," 8). Ethnic content is filtered through the author's imaginative and linguistic skills, and the product is a work of art. The writer may incorporate communal elements into a work—using principles derived from the oral tradition, for example—without actually advocating communal values. What is more, the ethnic form itself may cause a work to appear more community oriented than the author implicitly intends. We must, therefore, consider an individual work in its cultural and literary context in assessing its contribution to and position on the issue of community.

A second point to bear in mind is that writers from ethnic American cultures are often several generations removed from their ancestors' places of origin. What makes the ethnic culture identifiable is the group experience, a historical past forged out of "colonization" and "invisibility," in America. Therefore, a particular ethnic writer's position regarding individualism and community stems from a combination of historical and social factors as well as personal choice. In other words, we cannot analyze an occasional work of ethnic literature and expect it to be representative of an entire group. As quoted from Boelhower earlier, "There is no parthenogenesis of ethnic codes."

Indeed, such "codes" change over time. Critics are finding that ethnic literature published in the 1940s and 1950s differs significantly from contemporary works (late 1960s on). Partly in response to ethnic awareness movements stemming from the 1960s revival (e.g., Black Power and Aesthetics movements, American Indian movement [AIM], Chicano movement, Asian American Student movement), even writers who portray self-sufficient individuals are presenting them in a social context. In "The Heirs of Ralph Ellison," an essay that analyzes the novels (written between 1970 and 1975) of six contemporary black male writers,[6] Elizabeth Schultz concludes: "Ellison's heirs insist that they be not only contemplative individuals but also active social beings; they insist upon their characters' relationship with others, in particular other Afro-Americans" (122). The "not only/but also" suggests a shift among black writers. According to Schultz, the "paralysis and alienation" that can be found in *Invisible Man* and other modernist fiction has disappeared from the contemporary scene.

Not only has African American literature shifted from the alienated individual to the individual *in* society, but it also contrasts with the fiction of European American postmodernists. In a recent full-length study on African American literature Bernard Bell states: "Unlike their white contemporaries, black American postmodernists are not merely rejecting the arrogance and anachronism of Western forms and conventions, but also rediscovering and reaffirming the power and wisdom of their own folk tradition" (*Afro-American Novel*, 284). While both Schultz and Bell studied black writers, their main point—that contemporary African American fiction affirms culture and tradition—applies to other ethnic groups as well.

Ethnic Literary Strategy and Vernacular Theory

As one of the pioneers in the field of multiethnic literature, Dexter Fisher makes the following observation:

> Minority writers, in particular, draw substantially on the oral traditions of their cultures, perhaps because they are more intimately connected with their groups than "mainstream" writers and more intent on countering the effects of assimilation by asserting what is uniquely theirs. Whatever the reason, the importance of folklore and the oral tradition to minority literature is paramount. (*Third Woman*, 568)

A prominent aspect of oral culture, one that every writer in the present study explores, is the art of storytelling. By its very nature an oral performance is a communal act. Since the interaction between teller and audience is participatory, the language utilized by the teller must be both relational and accessible. The combining of oral traditions with written ones results in a cross-pollination process. Contemporary ethnic writers seem particularly interested in conveying the qualities of orality in their stories.

To make words come alive, to see words change on the page, to get the story across—these are some of the concerns ethnic writers have stressed in personal interviews. An important goal, it seems, is to transcend the limitations of literary language. One major strategy for accomplishing this goal is to utilize vernacular speech patterns in the main narrative. By doing this the author generates an ambience of folk culture that, through communal voices, conveys a sense of shared experience and group destiny. The specific motivation behind such a strategy is, of course, the artistic validation of one's ethnic culture and value system against a hegemonic European American standard in literature.

The American Heritage Dictionary offers two main definitions for *vernacular*: "(1) The native language of a country or region, esp. as distinct from literary language. (2) The nonstandard or substandard everyday speech of a country or region." The concepts of "native language" and "everyday speech" are both important to ethnic writings. Although the word *colloquial* contrasts with *literary* as informal, conversational speech, it assumes participation in a monoculture.

Vernacular, however, is culture specific and nonassimilative. As a form of expression, the implications of *vernacular* extend beyond spoken language. In Houston Baker's understanding the term signals "arts native or peculiar to a particular country or locale" (*Blues*, 2). The broader definition of *language* as "arts" incorporates various forms of cultural expression, such as stories (sermons, legends, myths), song (chants, field hollers, the blues), and dance. The vernacular in ethnic literary terms becomes "the ways in which folks communicate" or folklore *as* serious literature.

In sociolinguistics it is generally believed that "*all* languages, and correspondingly *all* dialects, are equally 'good' as linguistic systems" (Trudgill, *Sociolinguistics*, 20). There are no formal, linguistic grounds for the contention that "standard" English is "better" than other language varieties. The long-standing historical and class-bound stigma of "substandard" status, with its concomitant judgment of racial inferiority for creoles such as black vernacular English (BVE), has no doubt affected ethnic literary output. In the works I will be discussing—by Chin, Walker, and Wideman, for example—the literary exploration of vernacular speech instills a sense of authentic, convincing voice in the narrative. In reading these texts one no longer gets the sense of disjuncture—of a language (standard English) inappropriately superimposed on ethnic subjects. As Celie puts it in *The Color Purple*, "Look like to me only a fool would want you to talk in a way that feel peculiar to your mind" (Walker, 194).

In various ways, then, ethnic writers seek to create literary forms that are more harmonious with their cultural experience. We should understand that many contemporary writers are engaged in exploration and innovation. Not every attempted strategy works, and not everyone has the same agenda. Techniques such as juxtaposition, circular structure, linguistic register shifts, deliberate ambiguity, communal voice, and repetition are utilized in conjunction with more traditional literary conventions. The product often requires active audience participation in a listening posture. Approaching the text with an open mind helps. In a review of Henry Louis Gates's recent critical work entitled *The Signifying Monkey* John Wideman makes a depressing observation: "Rather than growing closer, standard English and black vernacular seem to be splitting farther apart. Blacks and whites find it increasingly difficult to understand one another"

(3). Ethnic writers are actively seeking ways to bridge this gap by broadening the linguistic fields found in American literature.

During the Harlem Renaissance the use of dialect was rejected by black critics and writers. According to Gates James Weldon Johnson objected to the use of dialect in black poetry due to its popular association with the "head-scratching, foot-shuffling, happy-go-lucky fool" (*Figures in Black*, 179). Johnson, says Gates, characterized the limitations of dialect as "an instrument with but two full stops, humor and pathos." From Gates's point of view, however, the removal of dialect from African American literature was detrimental to the Harlem Renaissance: "With the passage of dialect went a peculiar sensitivity to black speech as music, poetry, and distinct means of artistic discourse on the printed page" (181). This example illustrates that it is not the inherent qualities in a linguistic system but, rather, general attitudes toward the system by its users that determines a particular language's value. Among contemporary ethnic writers the poetry inherent in dialect or vernacular speech is utilized to full advantage. The result is often stunning and enlivens the written word.

Houston Baker's characterization of the vernacular as "a slave born on his master's estate" brings up issues of class, power, and oppression (*Blues*, 2). While Baker uses the image to support his "blues matrix," here I am borrowing it to illustrate the difference between an "elite" versus a "folk" approach to culture. William Clements makes the distinction between an "elitist historical sense"—which he equates with Eliot's use of *tradition*—and a "folk historical sense" in ethnic writers like Silko and Momaday ("Folk Historical Sense," 65–66). Basically, the elitist appropriates aspects of folk culture and incorporates them into the Eurocentric literary tradition. A writer from the folk viewpoint, however, perceives him- or herself as an integral part of a "continuing artistic heritage" (66). Instead of dealing with folklore as a commodity, folk writers enhance and contribute to the culture from within. In reference to the theme of individualism and community the elitist writer builds on his or her "individual talent" (in Eliot's sense), while the folk writer builds on the community. Baker's master/slave analogy—in which the master exploits and the slave is the commodity being exploited—can be reversed to affirm the value of slave culture and its vernacular.

Validation of folklore in literary discourse is what makes ethnic literary strategies unique. The distinctions that writers and critics of the Eurocentric tradition continue to make between the oral and the written (with their accompanying value judgments) contribute to Wideman's point about the distance between black versus white language. Are ethnic authors, in order to be recognized as writers in American culture, obligated to write away from their people? Can vernacular usage be considered valid art? The present study seeks to take ethnic texts on their own terms without preconceived notions of which "language" is more appropriate for literary production. While the writers I will be discussing are careful artists who appreciate the power of the written word, ultimately their purpose is to "get the story told." When ethnic American writers strive for accessibility in their art, they are emphasizing the communicative value of language. The orientation is communal rather than esoteric. This attitude can be paralleled with their people's experience of an earlier America. In a study on the social aspects of American English J. L. Dillard informs us:

> Indians found Pidgin English useful in a contact situation with the Chinese who came in from around the time of the gold rush and who, like the Blacks, were more successful in relating to the Indians as peers than to Europeans. (*Toward a Social History*, 126)

If "Indians," "Chinese," and "Blacks" in their early contacts in America were able to communicate with one another when their languages were so different, then it is obviously not language barrier per se that keeps people apart.

Examining Community in Literature:
A Pluralistic Approach

The handful of works examined here hardly covers the field of multiethnic literatures today. This study is merely a beginning and serves a specific purpose. As mentioned earlier, it seeks to consult neglected voices in the population on a classic moral issue: namely, what do ethnic Americans think about the issue of individualism versus community, and how are these viewpoints portrayed in their written art? The assumption here is that the analysis of serious literature is a valid means of tapping an individual's value system. While social scientists can interpret their subjects' words more or less literally, however, critics of literature confront a verbal artifact whose meaning is essentially figurative. Ethnic literatures should not be treated as showcase windows to exotic cultures.

The study features a male and a female writer from each of four broad ethnic American groups: African American, Asian American, Native American, and Chicano/a. The selection criteria were as follows:

1. The writers view themselves and are viewed by their ethnic communities as writing from their ethnic experience.
2. Each work appeared on the literary scene since the civil rights movement.
3. Each work is a sustained prose narrative.
4. Each work is a central document within its respective field of ethnic literary studies.
5. Each text is a serious work of art.
6. Each work raises issues concerning community and individualism in some manner (thematically, technically, etc.).
7. Each work appropriately fits the intended balance of male and female writers in the study.
8. Each work is available and accessible to the general public.

I do not view these eight writers as representative of their cultures but, rather, as writers who have made the conscious choice of drawing from their ethnic backgrounds. For some, as in the case of John Wideman, the choice is made after the writer has proven him- or herself in a predominantly Eurocentric literary tradition. Given the historical bias against ethnic literature in academia, this situation is not unusual. Until very recent times the curricula of higher education in America have been exclusively European American in the "Great Western Tradition." For these writers to be consciously "ethnic" often requires exploration of traditions outside academia. Since all eight of the principal writers in the study have university degrees, this road has taken some longer than others to travel. Thus, the works under discussion must be viewed in terms of a writer's own process of development rather than as a final and fixed articulation of his or her position.

In addition to the eight texts studied in some depth I also discuss other works at the end of each chapter. My purpose here is to broaden the discourse so that the eight writers do not carry undue weight as being somehow representative of their cultures. While the previously stated selection criteria apply to the additional texts and writers as well, I have made an attempt to include more recent works and to place each text in relation to literature from other cultures within a specific ethnic category. In this way I hope to remind the reader that there is a wealth of ethnic literature available and not just the token few that are actively being promoted at any given time.

While I do make an occasional cross-textual reference in these analyses, my main strategy is to allow the eight individual studies to exist side-by-side without extensive comparison. In this way the reader is free to make connections both cross-culturally and intertextually. Since there is no agreed-upon canonical approach to multiethnic literary criticism, I have the flexibility and the responsibility to explore various alternative approaches. In other words my approach is deliberately pluralistic and eclectic, and borrows from different disciplines and theoretical schools of criticism. Whenever possible I have consulted theorists from within the specific ethnic culture under discussion. I must note here that, in particular, these include the writers themselves. In critical essays and personal interviews all eight writers are contributing to a greater understanding of ethnic literatures and cultures. Given that there is at times no clear delineation between critic and author within the multiethnic literary community, it is necessary to consult the writers' scholarly statements and, to a limited extent, their biographical experiences. Whenever there is a discrepancy between what the writer says outside the text and the point of view promoted in the work itself, however, I have opted to privilege the literary work. After all, I am investigating what the writer is saying through literature.

In current criticism the "trickster" role that ethnic writers play in the text is almost a cliché. Mary Dearborn's study on ethnic women writers shows, for example, that there is a "subtext," an insiders' language, in classic ethnic literature mediated by white editors and publishers. This phenomenon leads the feminist critic Judith Fryer to conclude: "This problem of uncovering the subtext, of identifying the inside language, is a complicated one, and one for which contemporary literary theory, which reduces texts to significations and authors to irrelevant entities, is counter-productive" ("Tending the

Language," 662). I agree with Fryer that the author cannot be left out of an interpretation of the ethnic text. Furthermore, as this analysis will show, an ethnic writer's operating historical context cannot be ignored. It is important to correct the impression, however, that ethnic literature automatically resorts to a covert subtext strategy. Ethnic writers today are a lot less likely to permit the type of mediation and "midwiving" of their works that Dearborn found for an earlier period. It is more accurate to say that the ethnic writer has become the mediator. Therefore, the subterfuge to which the Indian writer Mourning Dove had to resort in 1927 or the African American writer Zora Neale Hurston in 1937 is no longer all-pervasive in ethnic texts. As will be shown in the case of Maxine Hong Kingston, tricksterism is as much a conscious artistic technique as it is the result of an oppressive publishing environment.

In discussing these writers, I have often disagreed with prevalent critical interpretations. Although I did not undertake this project to argue with critics but, rather, to explore how specific writers engage the issue of community, it has proven impossible to ignore some of the myopic positions that have been imposed on ethnic literatures. When a critical analysis is blatantly biased or inadequately sensitive to contextual or literary issues it perpetuates stereotypes and degrades understanding of the text. When the reader lacks basic knowledge of a work's specific cultural, historical, and social context, he or she tends to filter the narrative through a single lens; usually, this frame of reference stems from the reader's Eurocentric assumptions about American culture. Such myopia has been a major, continuing problem for ethnic writers. It has, for example, driven craft-conscious artists to list pages of straight ethnic history in their creative works (Wideman prefaces his novel with twenty pages of lynching records in *The Lynchers*; Kingston presents eight pages of Chinese immigration laws in the middle of *China Men*).

While ethnic American writers must deal with the difficult issue of providing context within the text in order to communicate with the general reader, literary critics have the obligation to be adequately informed before undertaking criticism. Because they are in a position to mediate between the literary text and its readership, critics bear the burden of risk and responsibility involved in adding their voices to the multifaceted dialogue between ethnic writers and their audiences. If the critic's contribution is to be constructive, he or she must simultaneously respect and acknowledge communal differences and values, recognize participation in a common enterprise, face the fact that all interpretation is ideologically grounded, and take the risks inherent in being an informed audience for ethnically and individually diverse works. Given the relatively recent admission of multiethnic literatures into American literary studies, the situation is particularly fragile. Responsible criticism is a necessity if the diverse traditions of ethnic cultures are to have their say in the general discourse of American society.

Chapter 2

Asian American Writers

Stigmatized as "model minorities" since the early 1960s,[1] Asian Americans today have to combat the insidious stereotype of being "successful" in America. Along with the new wave of anti-Asian sentiments that this image has engendered,[2] there is also the classic mystique of the "exotic and inscrutable Oriental." As artists born in this country with Asian features and surnames, both Frank Chin and Maxine Hong Kingston have been forced to write against the Oriental mystique. The burden becomes apparent when we observe that Chin's first play, *The Chickencoop Chinaman* (1972), was criticized for featuring a protagonist who "doesn't talk or dress or act like an Oriental" (Kim, *Asian American Literature*, 174).

Since model minorities are supposed to be self-effacing and compliant (as opposed to African Americans, whom the term is meant to denigrate), their literature should not expose raw nerves. The radical anthology *Aiiieeeee!*, edited by Chin and others, was therefore not mainstream enough for publication: "Some publishing companies rejected the book because it was 'too ethnic,' advising the editors to become better acquainted with white ethnic writers' attempts to 'mold . . . "difference" to enrich the society.' . . . The ethnicity of yellow writing embarrasses white publishers" (Kim, *Asian American Literature*, 174). That Asian American literature can be "too ethnic," which means it is not sufficiently assimilated into European American culture, is really cause for celebration rather than condemnation. Given the little known histories of Chinese, Japanese, Korean, Filipino, Asian Indian, and Southeast Asian populations in the United States, writing from an ethnic perspective can only be a step forward—an educational process for both the writer and his or her audience. Publishers and critics alike, however, tend to resist writings by Asian Americans that do not comply with their notions of the exemplary text (such as *Flower Drum Song* by Chin Yang Lee, *American in Disguise* by Daniel Okimoto, and *Fifth Chinese Daughter* by Jade Snow Wong).

Chin's *Year of the Dragon* and Kingston's *Woman Warrior* are radical in their own ways. The first thing one should say about these works is that they are the creations of Chinese Americans. That is, they stem from an ethnic culture in the United States that is approximately one-and-a-half centuries old. Given that "about 80 percent of the forebears of the Chinese in mainland United States were from Ssu Yi" in Kwangtung province (Hsu, *Challenge*, 42), as were the ancestors of both writers, we are dealing with a specific population of Americans with an identifiable myth of origin. Since Kwantung is only one out of the eighteen provinces that constitute China proper, the concept of "Chinese" in this context has its obvious limitations. When Chin's or Kingston's protagonist says "the Chinese" he or she is using an adulterated term, which has been filtered through a specific historical experience in America. Therefore, the writers discussed in this chapter are by no means representative of other Asian American writers, do not speak for the Chinese in China, and certainly cannot be equated with "white" ethnics.

What makes Kingston and Chin radical for the early 1970s is that neither plays into American society's model minority expectations. Both writers insist on being themselves in as unflattering a light as warranted by the stories they tell. To accomplish this each writer employs a particular linguistic/literary strategy. Kingston assumes the trickster role of artful ambiguity to convey *her* truth, and Chin conveys the complexities of ethnic family dynamics through a bold use of pidgin and vernacular speech patterns. Both draw from the Chinese American culture in narrative technique and subject matter. Although the works under discussion reflect only one phase of the writers' development, they capture the primacy of individual/communal concerns among specific Asian American authors. Given our relative inexperience with reading authentic, unmediated texts by Chinese Americans, we could easily misinterpret *The Woman Warrior* and *The Year of the Dragon* based on our unexamined assumptions. At this point an example of one scholar's misreading should illustrate the problem.

In William Boelhower's thought-provoking monograph on ethnic semiotics in American literature one finds the following reference to Kingston:

> In an attempt to march in step with the American Way, the majority of immigrants, blacks, and Indians were at least superficially willing to let go of their unique patrimony, as Maxine Hong Kingston explains in *The Woman Warrior*: "The Chinese I know hide their names; sojourners take new names when their lives change and guard their real names with silence." (*Through a Glass Darkly*, 82)

As we will see in this chapter, the practice of evasiveness—the refusal to name names—to which the author alludes is purely pragmatic within the context of the experience of Asians in America and has its historical basis in anti-Chinese laws. It has little to do with conforming to the "American Way" or relinquishing one's "unique patrimony," superficially or otherwise. To remain in this country, until recent times, Chinese individuals—and, consequently, their families—who immigrated under assumed names have had to hide their real names. Boelhower makes the common error of equating the situation of Asian immigrants with that of eastern Europeans. Even if an Asian person is willing to change names, his or her physical features are still unassimilated. Unlike the white ethnic examples Boelhower draws from American literature (e.g., Fitzgerald's protagonist changes his name from Gatz to Gatsby), people of color cannot "pass" in white America through a simple name change.

As Boelhower himself has pointed out, the reading of ethnic texts requires special skills (he speaks of "the lack of reader competence in ethnic semiotics" and the "complicity required by speaker and listener if they wish to communicate" [85]). It is especially dangerous to read Kingston literally and out of context. If nothing else, the two Chinese American writers studied here might teach us something about the art of suspending one's cultural assumptions in an effort to meet the "other" halfway.

"Chinaman Word Strategy": Frank Chin's *Year of the Dragon*

> It has often been pointed out that traditional Asian societies demand the subordination of the individual to the family and community, while the individual is supreme in modern Western societies. Asian American literature expresses the need for balance between these two emphases.
> —Elaine H. Kim, *Asian American Literature*

To discuss Frank Chin's art in relation to the above quote by Elaine Kim we must first take into account Chin and his fellow editors' position as stated in the preface of the 1974 anthology *Aiiieeeee!* Better yet, if we view the title of the work as an "ethnic sign"[3] derived from a culture-specific environment, the editors' intent becomes apparent. The stringing together of several vowels is foreign to English; visually, the sign serves to disturb readers' expectations. What is the significance of such an unusual symbol? Repetition of vowels and an exclamation point—from these visual clues, the reader might postulate that strong emotion is involved. Vowels are "soft," however, as opposed to consonants. Does the word suggest ease, comfort, or even pleasure?

When we vocalize *aiiieeeee,* our mouths gradually close from the initially open *ah* position while the tongue contracts toward the palate. The extension of the long *e* sound, in conjunction with the emotive force of the exclamation point, requires holding this closed, contracted position for several seconds. This forced constriction of the vocal chords and tightening of facial muscles results in discomfort. By voicing what appears to be a meaningless grouping of vowels, the reader literally *experiences* something of the pain signified by a vernacular onomatopoeia more intense and prolonged than *ouch.* In other words, for meaning to emerge an ethnic sign like *aiiieeeee* must be vocalized. At the outset, then, ethnic insiders are placing specific demands on the general reader: only those who are willing to participate and experience discomfort need apply. The anthology is strategically directed at cultural insiders, namely Asian Americans, for other Americans to overhear.

According to the editors, the "pushers of American culture" have historically used *aiiieeeee*—an Asian expression of distress—to stereotype the "yellow man" (as caricatured in movies, comics, etc.). By emblazoning the sign on the cover of one of the first Asian American anthologies since the civil rights era,[4] therefore, the editors are reclaiming their cultural heritage: what had been stigmatized is now being affirmed and celebrated. As the preface states, "It [*aiiieeeee!*] is more than a whine, shout, or scream. It is fifty years of our whole voice" (viii). The pain of exclusion produces a collective cry: Asian American writers are inserting their *aiiieeeee* into American culture. This show of solidarity appears to contradict the self-proclaimed individualism found elsewhere in Frank Chin's writings.[5] In relation to the present research question, therefore, one must ask: Does the art of one of the most vociferous Asian American writers reflect the mainstream view of American individualism?

Individualism European American style has had the connotation of "self-made" since the latter half of the nineteenth century.[6] The assumption is that, given enough ability, intelligence, and ambition, it is possible to make it on one's own in American society. If one does not succeed, it is one's "own damned fault." This myth—however unattainable for the majority of Americans—pervades popular thought. From Silas Lapham to Jay Gatsby to Citizen Kane, American letters is filled with self-made men. Mythically, all an enterprising individual has to do is to drop an ethnic name like Gatz for an Anglo-sounding Gatsby, and he is on his way to mansions and yachts. This version of the American Dream assumes that it is possible and desirable to turn one's back on one's cultural heritage and reinvent oneself. The art of Frank Chin indicates that this is not an easy proposition.

In the introduction to Chin's plays Dorothy McDonald quotes a reviewer who found the drama "gripping" and "so realistic that 'we are, oftentimes, tempted to watch with our faces averted'" (Introduction, xx). This is an apt description for the reading audience as well. The focus of the present discussion, *The Year of the Dragon*, is intense, bitter, comical, and obscene: it is not a polite play. The "aiiieeeee strategy" of shock and disorientation is evident throughout the two acts. Perhaps more uncomfortably than one would like, the general reader is startled into another culture and soon realizes that this is not the tightly knit, harmonious Chinese family of one's expectations. Critics disliked Chin's rawness and his self-proclaimed mission to "write theater like making war" (qtd. in McDonald, Introduction, xxviii). The playwright's own account of the play's reception bears quoting: "White reviewers like Julius Novick and Clive Barnes stuck in their Christian esthetic of one god, one good, one voice, one thing happening, one talk at a time get so dizzy in the atmosphere of Chinaman word strategy they gotta cancel out every white writer they know to make sense of my simple Chinaman backscratch" (qtd. in McDonald, Introduction, xxviii).

Creatively rendering the "Chinaman word strategy" is Frank Chin's self-appointed task as a writer. The editors of *Aiiieeeee!* emphasize the importance of language for Asian Americans: "Language is

the medium of culture and the people's sensibility. Language coheres
the people into a community. . . . The tyranny of language has been
used by white culture to suppress Asian-American culture" (35–36).
A recent book on the Chinese experience in America corroborates
this view: "Over and over, they [Chinese Americans] expressed the
pain of cultural estrangement and *alexia,* or the deprivation of a natural language of identity" (Tsai, *Chinese Experience,* 141).

Chin views his "Chinaman" as a "New Man"—one who is neither Chinese nor a clone of white America. In order to capture the
reality of the Chinaman he experiments with literary technique to
"duplicate the way people talk" (*Aiiieeeee!* xxxix). "People," in this
case, are ethnic Americans whose speech patterns reflect multicultural influences. Included in the paratactic structure of colloquial
speech is Chin's particular version of Chinaman language.[7] The
writer's vernacular inventiveness—what looks like a hodgepodge of
obscenities, street slang, Cantonese-English bilingualism, black English, mindless/racist songs, and comic wordplay—assaults our
senses and catapults us into the blood-and-gut reality of one ethnic
American household. As we shall see, the conflict between individualism and community emerges via Chin's strategy of using oral language to provide clues to character. An analysis of this "Chinaman
word strategy" requires a preliminary introduction to the play.

The Year of the Dragon portrays the disintegration of a Chinese
American family living in San Francisco's Chinatown. The central
conflict is between Pa, the authoritarian patriarch, and Fred, the eld-
est son, who has dutifully worked as tour guide for ten years to help
support the family. On the verge of death Pa rounds up the family
to make arrangements. He has brought over China Mama—his wife
from the Old Country and Fred's biological mother—so that he can
"die Chinese." This surprise, plus the return of Sis with her Cauca-
sian husband, Ross, throws the family into an uproar. Periodically,
the American-born mother, Ma, escapes the commotion by dodging
into the bathroom to sing to herself. There is also a juvenile delin-
quent son, Johnny, who aspires to fill his brother's shoes as top tour
guide. The noisy interaction of this confrontational ethnic family is
rendered through a variety of Chinese American vernacular speech
patterns.

Cantonese has at least nine tones, strong consonants, and short
vowels. To the untrained ear the language sounds choppy and harsh.

These qualities contribute to what Chin, in his play *The Chickencoop Chinaman*, calls "Chinatown Buck Buck Bagaw." Due to the different tones and an occasional exaggerated vowel, the language also has a singsong quality. Simply by inserting these linguistic elements into the general family discourse—which also consists of Chinese pidgin, Anglo, and black English—Chin generates a thick, folksy, cacophonous atmosphere. "Overlapping" and "having never stopped" are frequent stage directions for the simultaneity of two or more persons talking at once.

Juxtaposed to this sense of commotion is the WASP middle-class politeness of Ross. No matter how intense or vulgar the general discourse gets, Ross usually maintains his superficial refinement. His insensitivity and noncomprehension of ethnic family dynamics make him a comical character: there is a running vaudeville act between Ross and the intense and vulgar Fred. Ross periodically contributes assinine remarks to the general discourse. These platitudes (e.g., "I've always admired the superiority of Chinese culture" [128]) reflect his idealization of the Confucian stereotype and are irrelevant to the tensions within the actual Chinese American family. Chin uses this "outsider" character to show the miscommunication possible between European American and ethnic American cultures.

Since the dramatic genre precludes narrative descriptions and character analyses, individual speech patterns are used as clues to character. This strategy is not immediately apparent. In the opening scenes we encounter language shifts in Ma's speech. At times Ma expresses herself in formal English, as in " . . . before there didn't used to be. . . . " At others, especially when under stress, she reverts to pidgin, as in "Why dink you tell me and I'm make Fred give you two a honeymoon . . . " (74). These blatant shifts—as in *dink* versus *didn't*—are a mystery in Ma's speech pattern until Pa appears. We gradually realize that Chin has Ma switching codes for a specific purpose.

Ma's speech has several influences. Ma shares Pa's *donks*, for example, especially when Pa is on the scene. This unconscious identification corroborates other signs of her affection for and domination by her husband. Her singing of ditties like "Chinese Lullabye" reflects the missionary influence of a racist past. Ma's songs, like her visits to the bathroom, are safety valves for escape into a child's world. The adult voice makes pronouncements in standard English and is at times Chin's mouthpiece for conveying bits of Chinese American history (e.g., "You know, Rex, my Sissy is a very limited edition. Only twenty Chinese babies born in San Francisco in 1938" [73]). While this voice seems flat, it is in keeping with Ma's character and ethnic background (in which alternating between "standard" English and vernacular is the norm). Ma also picks up Fred's obscenities when she wishes to assert herself or rebel against Pa's domination. This secondhand cursing is inaccurate and comical ("Mugger fummer sobba nichie sandwich!" for "motherfucker sonofabitch"). Ma has trouble with gutter slang just as Pa has problems with formal English.

In contrast to Ma Pa speaks a unique blend of Cantonese English at all times. Contractions such as *donk* for *don't,* missing prepositions, misplaced gerunds, straight Cantonese, odd pluralization of words, etc., flow out of Pa's mouth as a language complete unto itself. The vernacular aspects of Pa's language are comically rendered through phonetic spellings of Pa's expressions for "don't interrupt" or "no interruptions." Chin varies the spelling as follows: "Donk inderup-son" (98), "No inda Russians!" and "No in-duh-rup-sons!" (99). These variations reflect the speech pattern of an immigrant with limited formal training in the adopted tongue. A language acquired orally often surfaces, when spontaneously uttered, as an approximation of the written version. Pa's language is consistently inconsistent and can easily become bilingual ("Dey got trees grow onna rote. Yut gaw retwoot tree ho die guh" [98]). It is important for the reader to voice the words rather than attempt to decipher them on the page.

The contrast between Ma's and Pa's speech patterns reveals opposite tendencies. Ma switches codes according to circumstances. She lacks a strong ego and sees herself only in relation to others. As an "American of Chinese descent," she is the female version of Chin's "chameleons looking for color" ("Confessions," 59). Pa, on the other hand, consistently speaks his hybrid brand of Cantonese English, except with China Mama. As authoritarian patriarch, Pa is the center of his ethnic household and feels no need to adjust his speech to accommodate others. In the above quote, "Yut gaw retwoot tree ho die guh" ("a redwood tree very big"), the English noun is framed by Cantonese modifiers. Pa's American-born children might not understand the Cantonese portion of the sentence, and China Mama does not know English. Thus, Pa's pidgin excludes parts of his audience. In the world outside Chinatown, however, Pa is an assimilationist. This becomes apparent when Pa is introduced to Ross. Stage directions describe Pa as "all smiles and giggling charm in front of a white man" (93). Pa's speech pattern shows hesitancy for the first time: "Oh how're you? Mattie husban? Huh?"

Pa asks Ross to help him write his speech while Fred, who was raised in America and majored in English, is ignored. This attitude reflects that of the dominant white culture: "What you know? No college graduation? Him Merican. Know da Engliss poofeck. You Chinese!" (104). Chin exposes the irony of this position when, through Ross's coaching, Pa prepares to play Charlie Chan as a "joke" in his speech. The effeminate, self-effacing invention of a white racist, Charlie Chan epitomizes the historical stereotyping of Chinese Americans. In his writings Chin uses this destructive image in American culture as an essential trope for ethnic self-contempt. The Chinese American son sees his father as the white man's pawn. "Pa's told his first joke without a word of Chinese in it!" observes Fred. "His first all-American joke! . . . Wonderful pa!" (131). Pa's accomplishment does not seem so wonderful when we consider the source of his success. "All-American" means racial suicide. The implications of Fred's comment are apparent within the historical context: the Chinese have become "American" at the expense of their cultural identity.

According to the editors of *Aiiieeeee!* "The perpetuation of self-contempt between father and son is an underlying current in virtually every Asian-American work" (xlvii). This negative literary theme, say the editors, reflects Asian American history. Rather than the result of generational differences, the clash between fathers and sons is the necessary product of racism. Several generations of Asian Americans have been deprived of an identifiable past and a language with which to express their American experience. Forced to be either "Asian" or "American," these ethnics have not been recognized for who they really are. The editors put it this way: "The concept of the dual personality deprives the Chinese-American and Japanese-American of the means to develop their own terms" (xlviii). "Dual personality" implies that the individual is split between two polar opposites: he or she is conflicted between East and West and has no center. "Their own terms," on the other hand, suggests an ethnic self and culture that is more than this either/or split. In addition to this destructive characterization of ethnic Americans, negative images of Asian

American manhood abound in American society. Charlie Chan figures are sources of shame and self-contempt within the Chinese American community: they create insurmountable barriers between fathers and sons. Chin pinpoints the problem in his play.

If we keep in mind that Pa thinks he is "Chinese," while his family members consider themselves "Chinese Americans," we gradually realize that the community-individual dichotomy is more complex in Chin's play than the simple equation of Chinese equals community and Chinese American equals individualism (as a reflection of dominant cultural values). While Pa is the product of a supposedly communal, family-oriented culture, he sees everyone only in relation to himself: it is the family's job to suit him. Hence, Fred has no identity outside his role as "number one son." This position is egocentric and reflective of patriarchal, capitalistic individualism. Since Pa is portrayed as a pawn for whites, the author is directly connecting "white" with "individualist." The Chinese American son, however, is not an automatic product of European American culture. In the final scene Fred tries to use his position as Pa's indispensable crutch to extract a concession. In order to "save" Ma and Johnny from a doomed future in Chinatown he wants Pa to tell the two to leave. He attempts to assert his separate identity: "You gotta do somethin for me. Not for your son, but for me." Pa retorts with, "Who you? You my son. Da's all. What else you ting you are. Huh?" (137). The son views himself as an individual in the communal context of family; the father views himself as an autonomous individual who has to answer to no one.

Fred's desire to save members of his family from his own fate undercuts our original impression of him as an individualist. As an aspiring writer, Fred takes the individualist position when he tells Sis, "I have to take care of myself now" (117). This sounds like the looking-out-for-number-one stance that social theorists have been attributing to contemporary American culture. In the play, however, the automatic response to such a statement is, "And what happens to the family, Fred?" An individualist might say, "To hell with the family—it's not my problem." Fred does not say this. Instead, he discusses Johnny's welfare.

Throughout the play all three siblings say to one another, "Let me help you out of here [Chinatown]." There is the sense of "we're all in this together," which reflects the communal bond among oppressed people. The discourse is unselfconsciously communal—almost at the level of Tocqueville's "habits of the heart," or cultural mores. While Fred is capable of giving but not receiving help, neither he nor his "assimilationist" sister, who had "married out white" (Chin's jargon), is able to forget the family. In other words, the brand of bourgeois individualism that is generally attributed to middle-class European Americans is inconceivable in this ethnic context.

As we have said, Fred is a community-based individual. The family, and by extension Chinatown, defines who he is. Although fear of the unknown—the hostile white world beyond Chinatown—does hold him back, it is ultimately the protagonist's own communal values that prevent him from fulfilling his dream of being a writer. Language, once again, provides clues to character. Especially noticeable is the way Fred talks to Ma. The combination of pidgin English ("Whassie la mallaw?" [132]), sexual allusions ("Last night I dreamed you were naked, ma" [100]), adult-to-child expressions ("Where's my girl?" [93]), and references to Ma's past ("You coulda been a singer, ma" [93]) indicates a very special relationship. In a complex and intentionally outrageous way Fred employs a private language of empathy and solidarity with his nonbiological mother.

To draw Ma out of herself and the pain she is feeling (the appearance of China Mama proves that Ma has lied about Fred being her son) Fred is capable of saying anything. The obscenities also serve as subterfuge against Pa. Basically, Pa does not understand Fred's pornographic language. His response to the most graphic gutter slang is "Too much noises" or "Get responsiboos" (101). Fred uses his ability to swear creatively to shock Sis, Ross, and Johnny; to get Ma's mind off her troubles; to vent his own frustrations; to express contempt and cynicism; and, finally, to use his verbal prowess and daring as a weapon against Pa and his Charlie Chan world. As long as Fred is able to swear, all is not lost. Chin ingeniously lets us know this through the tour guide spiels. Fred always ends his last tour with a string of curses, which indicates that he is not confusing his self with his persona. Contrary to middle-class values and expectations, cursing is a virtue in the play.

The five tour guide scenes encapsulate Chin's "Chinaman word strategy." Chin spotlights Fred's spiels as a powerful indictment against the white racism that "created a game preserve for Chinese and called it 'Chinatown'" ("Confessions," 60). These monologues are poetically rendered in vernacular diction to create an ambience of exoticism. Juxtaposed to the family drama, they serve as commentary on the action. The shallowness of Pa's "Mayor of Chinatown" role, for example, becomes apparent through this technique. In addition, act 2 opens and closes with variations on the following spiel ending:

> And now your eyes are inwards on your innards.
> You're hungry, folks.
> Hungry! And afraid to eat anything here.
> I know the feeling. . . . Bad feeling. . . .

                                                                        (113)

This passage is subversive in that it turns the tables on the oppressors by making them ill at ease. At the same time it connects the ethnic speaker to his white audience. The message of "I know what you're feeling because I've been there before" shifts the perspective from opposition to one of common humanity. This double entendre reflects the writer's ironic stance.

"Jussie like a lew kit!"—Pa's complaint about Fred is even more ironic. Once again Chin uses the technique of juxtaposition to make his point. Even as Pa is calling his forty-year-old son a "kid," he himself is playacting "father" with his Charlie Chan lines ("Hey, son! You got dah case solve yet?" [130]). Juxtaposed to this "Gee, Pop!" "Gosh, Pop!" surface action is the interaction between Fred and Johnny. By insisting that his brother leave in the morning, Fred is assuming the role of father. In fact, throughout the play Fred is portrayed as the real parent to his siblings as well as to Ma. While Pa's authority stems from his structural position as head of the family, Fred bears the responsibility for the family's survival and success.

Fred's compassion for Ma and contempt toward Pa are crystallized in a revealing outburst: "What'd ya do, pa? Just stick me onto the first fifteen-year-old girl you met off the boat? You know I really, really think ma coulda been a singer . . . " (137). With this background information Ma's childlike behavior and speech variations are now understandable. Fred identifies with Ma as another Chinese American victim who cares too much about people to get ahead in an exploitative environment. He does not blame Ma for not having been a proper mother to him; instead, he defends her against his biological mother. In contrast, while he cannot help loving his father, he also despises Pa for being an opportunistic egomaniac.

Through literary strategies such as vernacular speech and ironic juxtaposition, then, Chin communicates communal values in his art. The play conveys this position by siding with Fred and Ma while criticizing Pa and Ross. This critique of individualism, however, does not guarantee a happy ending. Given the play's sociohistorical context of a "colonized" culture as well as the individual character traits and specific circumstances of the Eng family, commitment can backfire. The play ends on an ominous note.

While slapping Fred, Pa drops dead from exertion. The son kicks the corpse and says, "You failure," thus repeating Pa's words to him. It is important to note that Fred is finally defeated by his inability to save Johnny; in other words, his communal values—without adequate support from those around him—could not withstand Pa's bourgeois individualism. Once more Chin calls on Charlie Chan to symbolize this defeat: "Dressed in solid white, [Fred] puts on a white slightly oversized jacket, and appears to be a shrunken Charlie Chan, an image of death. He becomes the tourist guide" (141). Fred adopts Pa's self-centered stance of viewing everything and everyone around him as his possessions ("This is my house now. . . . My ma. . . . My Chinatown. . . . If you're staying here man, you're mine!" [141]). The cursing goes out of control and becomes a symptom of hysteria rather than the previous sign of self-awareness. Fred's loss of identity is the family's ultimate tragedy.

In her assessment of a wide range of Asian American literatures, Elaine Kim concludes that Chin's protagonists are alienated characters and, therefore, "incomplete." According to Kim, Chin has not succeeded—his goals to the contrary—in forging a new Asian American male identity or a new language (189). The present examination of *The Year of the Dragon*, however, disagrees with this negative critique. D. H. Lawrence's dictum to trust the tale and not the teller is especially useful when applied to a writer like Chin. What the writers claim outside their art cannot be a fail-safe measure of their literary accomplishments (after all, some writers are better "critics" than others). Lawrence expresses this insight as: "An artist is usually a damned liar, but his art, if it be art, will tell you the truth of his day" (12).

In the present case the "tale" provides a moving example for Kim's statement that Asian American literature seeks balance between individualism and community.[8] Fred's aspirations toward autonomy are counterbalanced by his deep-rooted ties to community. We must realize, however, that this is a product of Chin's Asian American sensibility and not simply a function of "American" and "Asian" values. Chin successfully captures the tensions and complexities of this ethnic reality through his Chinaman word strategy. The protagonist, Fred, is a powerful depiction of an Asian American man's experience in contemporary American society. Within the contours of the play Chin has accomplished his goal. By associating *alienated* with *incomplete* and by looking for "protagonists who can overcome the devastating effects of racism on Chinese American men" (189), Kim is establishing standards that are unrealistic and inappropriate for literary works. Asian American literature should not be required to have integrated, optimistic protagonists to be considered seriously.

While Chin exhibits both brilliance and limitations as a literary/ cultural critic, it is clear that the writer of *The Year of the Dragon* has utilized language effectively to convey a specific worldview. Fred Eng is a failed writer, and Frank Chin is a successful playwright. If this assessment of Chin's sympathies as manifested in his art is correct— namely, that the writer and his protagonist ultimately champion community—then Fred's failure can be interpreted as the defeat of communal values in contemporary American society. Chin skillfully dramatizes this message through his art. His literary experimentation challenges our assumptions and forces us to read and listen differently. The intermixing of Chinese, Chinese American, and American speech patterns in pluralistic dialogue suggests the potential richness of ethnic literature. From the perspective of an ethnic American writer Chin offers a memorable if unsavory dramatization of the triumph of individualistic over communal values.

Literary Tricksterism: Maxine Hong Kingston's *Woman Warrior: Memoirs of a Girlhood among Ghosts*

> Most literary forms are not artificial. They reflect patterns of the human heart.
> —Maxine Hong Kingston, "Talk with Mrs. Kingston"

Since its 1976 publication and winning of the 1977 National Book Critics Circle Award *Woman Warrior* has received a significant amount of critical attention. Contrasted with postwar autobiographies published earlier by Asian American women, Kingston's first full-length work seemed a sophisticated "new" product. Here was definitely fresh talent on the literary scene—someone whom a growing body of ethnic and feminist theorists could support and use as a role model. That Kingston was attacked by a number of Asian American male writers and critics for distorting Chinese history only made others more adamant in the author's defense.[9] The controversy has engendered a rift in ethnic literary studies, which a discussion of Kingston's works cannot ignore. Consequently, the present analysis carries a double burden: it must address the broad issue of how *Woman Warrior* has been read or misread as well as what the work says about individualism and community. In other words, certain thorny theoretical issues regarding narrative must be dealt with before proceeding with this thematic study.

When an ethnic woman writer publishes an "autobiography" she is immediately confronted with a slew of inappropriate expectations. As readers, we must realize that neither the Ben Franklin paradigm nor the exotic world of Suzie Wong are valid points of reference for interpreting *Woman Warrior*. Ultimately, we must read the work on its own terms. In reading Kingston's "autobiography," we must recognize that the writer is a creative artist who consciously uses a strategy of narrative ambiguity to tell her story. In this case the ethnic woman writer assumes the role of a literary trickster.

When Kingston says in an interview that literary forms "reflect patterns of the human heart" ("Talk," 26), she is telling us how she views herself as a writer. By connecting form with heart rather than "life," she refers to the artist, not the sociologist. For Kingston artistic form is organic rather than artificial: it is part and parcel of the human spirit. This position directly contrasts with the stated premise of a major study on Asian American literature: "I have deliberately chosen to emphasize how the literature elucidates the social history of Asians in the United States" (Kim, *Asian American Literature*, xv). When applied to an artist who consciously manipulates form in order to be true to "patterns of the human heart," the belief that a literary text can and should be used as documentation of an ethnic culture seems misguided. Because many critics have made the same assumption, they tend to either blame or praise the *author* for the naive narrator's interpretation of Chinese American culture.

In *Woman Warrior* Kingston uses a narrator who has a child's passion for knowing. What is Chinese, and what is American? What is real, and what is make-believe? Do the Chinese despise women, or do they see them as potential warriors? Since we have an impressionable protagonist/narrator who feels bombarded by confusing stories in her childhood, this desire for definition is understandable and in character. Because the young protagonist single-mindedly pursues either/or options and because her voice dominates the book's first part, however, the unwary reader is easily lulled by her simplistic pronouncements. Due to her confusion, limited knowledge, desire for absolutes, and total subjectivity regarding people and events, this narrator is unreliable.

In an interview Kingston clearly distinguishes herself from this narrator: "Oh, that narrator girl. It's hard for me to call her me. . . . She is so coherent and intense always, throughout. There's an intensity of emotion that makes the book come together. And I'm not like that" ("This Is the Story," 6). The distinction between the "I" and "that narrator girl" is revealing. The reader must understand that the writer is, in her daily life, neither coherent nor intense, even though her narrative persona epitomizes these traits.

Had Kingston limited her narrative to the protagonist's naive point of view, she might not have departed significantly from Jade Snow Wong's *Fifth Chinese Daughter* (1945). In contrasting the literary forms of Wong and Kingston, Patricia Lin Blinde categorizes Wong's autobiography with the Horatio Alger paradigm of American success ("Icicle," 55). According to this critic, Wong simply "'repeat[s]' the white world's articulations and expectations as to what Chineseness is or is not." Consequently, autobiography becomes "a public concession as to her place (and by extension the place of Chinese-Americans) in the world and mind of Americans" (58–59). On the other hand, says Blinde, Kingston belongs to a generation with fewer illusions. The pre–World War II faith in a coherent world, "a world that still believed in the truths of its own imaginative constructs" (54), is no longer possible. To corroborate this distinction it is worth noting that the coherence of Kingston's "narrator girl" is drastically different from that presented in Wong's work. With Kingston we have an ambivalent narrator who compensates for her insecurities by reaching for absolutes, while the literary artist transcends her naive narrator's limitations through her use of technique. Before delving into these artistic strategies, however, we must first understand the author's definition of *autobiography*.

Blinde's perception that literary form separates Kingston from Wong is provocative. What does it mean to say that two autobiographies are worlds apart due to their forms? According to one scholar, autobiography is a literary form particularly suited to Americans' "individualistic and optimistic" self-image. Therefore, Ben Franklin's self-portrait as "an aggressive actor in a society of possibilities" is considered the prototype for "autobiographies in the American tradition" (Doherty, "American Autobiography," 95). Given this definition, ethnic women's stories are anything but "American" autobiographies. The self as confident actor selecting among various possibilities simply does not reflect the experiences of most women in America. In order to write a prototypical American autobiography, then, the ethnic woman must either conform to the Eurocentric male definition of the genre and produce a seemingly self-effacing, assimilationist work like *Fifth Chinese Daughter*, or she must subvert and redefine *autobiography* in some way. Kingston's own viewpoint on the subject is revealing. In an essay exposing her reviewers' racist assumptions she explains: "After all, I am not writing history or sociology but a 'memoir' like Proust. . . . " She quotes one reviewer who understood this and said that Kingston was "slyly writing a memoir, a form which . . . can neither [be] dismiss[ed] as fiction nor quarrel[ed] with as fact" ("Cultural Mis-readings," 64).

This distinction between *autobiography* and *memoir* is crucial to the Kingston controversy. By evoking Marcel Proust's massive *A la Recherche du temps perdu*, which one scholar calls "an autobiography of the mind" (Hornstein et al., *Reader's Companion*, 435), Kingston challenges the static notion of autobiography in the "American tradition." The Proustian memoirs emphasize fluidity and the presentness of psychological time. Memory is a private code of freely associated images triggered by seemingly insignificant details in one's environment. As such, the memoir is exploratory. Rather than positing a coherent, already constituted self, which only has to be "revealed" through the autobiographical act, it views identity as fluid and constantly evolving. This alternative understanding of the function of autobiography is particularly suited to women. Unlike their male counterparts' texts, as one critic points out, there is no "lost paradise" in *Woman Warrior* and other ethnic women's "semiautobiographical works" (Rabine, "No Lost Paradise," 477). In addition, since there is no "it" to return to, the absence of an Edenic past actually structures ethnic women's stories. But how can absence provide structure? In place of a linear, backtracking approach based on community decline and nostalgia, works like *Woman Warrior* depict continuity through change and creative adaptation.

In identifying her literary form with Proust's, Kingston not only refutes traditional definitions of *autobiography* and *nonfiction* but also legitimizes genres such as memoirs, diaries, and journals (all "female" forms, according to some feminist theorists) that have been considered—at least in America—less "literary" than *the* autobiography. Given the value judgments implicit in issues of literary genre, the publication of Kingston's first book as *autobiography* with *memoirs* in its subtitle suggests conscious manipulation. As we have seen, the two terms are not synonymous. If Kingston believes she has written an exploratory, quasifictive memoir, why did she allow her book to be published as autobiography without qualification? Given the general public's tendency to view autobiography as gospel truth, is the author somehow responsible for misleading the reader? After all, the absolutist position implicit in "American autobiography" and the dominant narrative voice in the text seem a perfect match. When the narrator tells us that her ethnic culture denigrates women— equating females with "slaves" and "maggots" and thus forcing her to "get out of hating range" (62)—should we not take her word for it? And, if we do, can we then conclude that Kingston defends the lone female against her oppressive ethnic community?

To address this question one might consult Ralph Ellison. "America is a land of masking jokers," he informs us. Franklin posed as Rousseau's Natural Man, Hemingway as a nonliterary sportsman, Faulkner as a farmer, and Lincoln as a simple country lawyer—"the 'darky' act makes brothers of us all" (*Shadow*, 70). Ellison is asserting that the smart-man-playing-dumb role is not the unique province of black culture. Rather, "it is a strategy common to the [American] culture" and "might be more 'Yankee' than anything else" (69). One historian corroborates this point when he identifies Ben Franklin as a social and literary trickster. In *Autobiography*, says John William Ward, when Franklin offers himself as Representative American, he acknowledges his awareness that this is a self-conscious pose ("Who Was Benjamin Franklin?" 93). This observation suggests that the prototypical American autobiography already has the markings of an "invented self" and does not provide the "straight goods" that the general public expects from the genre.

If we realize that masking is, in Ellison's sense, an American cultural phenomenon and that tricksterism is prevalent in American literature, we can then approach a writer like Kingston without misconceived notions of her "difference." Given that autobiography, like any other genre in literature, is an artistic construct, Kingston's ethnicity should not make her work "social history." If we can accept Franklin's pose in this supposedly nonfictional genre, we should be able to read autobiographies by ethnic women writers with the same understanding. Otherwise, our approach is both racist and sexist.[10] The parallel between scholarship on Frederick Douglass and Kingston illustrates this point.

In an enlightening analysis Henry Louis Gates demonstrates how virtually all of Douglass's biographers have misconstrued their subject by taking autobiography literally. The self that the famous abolitionist describes in his three autobiographies is, says Gates, a public image carefully crafted by the author to promote his cause (*Figures in Black*, 103). As such, it is "fictive" in the sense of "made by design." "Almost never," Gates points out, "does Douglass allow us to see him as a human individual in all of his complexity . . . " (109). In using an intentionally constructed persona as "fact," the biographers could only present an external view of their subject, a view that is the conscious manipulation of its trickster creator. In a way Douglass and Franklin are Representative Men today because we still believe in their autobiographical constructs. While the misreading of both Kingston's and Douglass's autobiographies stems from the same misunderstanding of the nature of literature, Kingston's situation is additionally complicated by the writer's non–Great Man status. If we cannot get quick facts about her ethnic culture from her autobiography, as we can from writers like Wong, then why should we even bother with Kingston?

From the wide readership that *Woman Warrior* enjoys it seems that many people find the work of value. This, I contend, has a great deal to do with artistry. In devising a narrative strategy of ambiguity that captures her multivariate ethnic reality, Kingston is a literary trickster in the best American tradition.

Critics accurately identify the various boundary-crossing strategies in *Woman Warrior* as ambiguous or ambivalent. Ambiguity plays a prominent role in the text. They miss the mark, however, when they attribute these strategies to the necessity of "bridging two cultures." If one understood that, as they say, "cultures are made, not born,"[11] he or she would know that Chinese America as an ethnic culture is not a "bicultural" dualism of either/or possibilities. Rather, it is a *new entity* that is neither Chinese nor European American. Because many people have difficulty with this concept (since we are so used to thinking in stereotypes and polarities), they sort between "Chinese" and "American" along with the naive narrator. As mentioned earlier, the narrator/protagonist's sorting does not reflect Kingston's worldview; rather, it is an artistic device used to create thematic tension between the female individual as protagonist and the ethnic community as antagonist.

A key element in Kingston's strategy of ambiguity is to offer alternative, often contradictory, versions of a story without value judgment. The narrator usually informs us when she is inventing; we are assigned the task, however, of sorting through her various "truths." Because we are on shifting sand, it is a convenient anchor for us to have a naive narrator who seeks absolutes with life-and-death urgency. The young protagonist's desire for easy answers when confronting her mother's "talk-stories" about China reflects the reader's need for firm ground on unfamiliar terrain. But, this is a literary "trick." Active participation in the text almost requires a level of confusion like the protagonist's. In an essay on fiction and interpretation Naomi Schor defines the relationship between "interpreter" (interpreting critic or reader) and "interpretant" (interpreting character in the text) as one of "narcissistic identification" ("Fiction as Interpretation," 168–69). When a literary work features an interpretant such identification makes distance difficult to maintain. In reading Kingston, however, distance is crucial.

In *Woman Warrior* the surface-level discourse is misleading, since the struggle between the protagonist and the immigrant community of Stockton is narrated from the protagonist's point of view. This view, as mentioned earlier, is naive due to the narrator's limitations. While antifemale attitudes and unusual practices of "the Chinese" are emphasized, limited space is devoted to cultural mores of European Americans. In addition, the protagonist's white male oppressors are never identified as such; instead, they are given the generic name "boss" and described as "business-suited in their modern American executive guise" (57). Since the narrator identifies her mother's vivid and grotesque stories as Chinese, the reader might conclude that the Chinese are truly barbaric. This unbalanced presentation of cultures should serve as a warning signal to the discerning reader. Why, one might ask, are white male oppressors bosses and ethnic male oppressors Chinese? In order to understand the seeming distortions of the work one must examine the text.

In *Woman Warrior* verbal articulation is necessary to survival. The protagonist shows how acutely she feels this when she tortures the quiet girl. "If you don't talk," she exclaims, "you can't have a personality" (210). People deprived of speech, as are the various crazy women cited in the text, do not survive. Here is the primary dilemma of the Chinese American experience. It is in *America* that survival is an issue for ethnic Americans, where deprivation of speech (a direct result of racist laws) leads to a lack of personality and even the lack of will to live.[12] Storytelling is thus an essential skill in a hostile environment, a skill that ensures the survival of the tribe as well as its individual members. To arrive at this interpretation the reader must piece together various elements in the text, or what might be identified as the subtext. What makes Kingston's memoirs so slippery is the implied author's refusal to spell out connections for the reader. Words such as *talk-story, personality,* and *survival* are linked by juxtaposition rather than cause-and-effect logic. The reader has to fill in the gaps.

Forcing active reader participation is, of course, a prevalent modernist technique. Nevertheless, a major problem for ethnic writers is the audience's lack of knowledge regarding ethnic American histories and cultures.[13] In *Woman Warrior* this is problematic, since historical information is scattered throughout the text and often is not attached to specific issues. When the narrator tells us that Chinese people are secretive in an earlier part of the book, for example, we might not understand why until much later, when the fear of deportation is mentioned. Thus, the reader is expected to suspend judgment and not jump to conclusions as the narrator does.[14] Kingston's technique of ambiguity, then, requires reconstructive reading skills. Although illuminating contexts for the story can be found in the text, only the alert reader can make the necessary connections.

Given the memoir's nonlinear form—that is, its achronological ordering—when Brave Orchid declares, "That's what Chinese say. We like to say the opposite," and the naive narrator inserts, "It seemed to hurt her to tell me that . . . " (237), readers need to step back and reconstruct an appropriate context for the exchange. We must realize that it is not a cultural clash we are witnessing: actually, *both* mother and daughter are Chinese Americans who share a common culture—though of two successive generations—in America. Brave Orchid calls herself Chinese when she wishes to rationalize her behavior. The evasiveness that both the narrator and her mother attribute to the Chinese as if it were a racial characteristic is easily explained within the context of Chinese American history. Even the protagonist's grudge against the "emigrant villagers" must be viewed in the appropriate context.

The misogynistic sayings that are repeated throughout the text must be understood in relation to the Chinese bachelor society in America. As a result of the Chinese Exclusion Act of 1882, Chinese women were extremely scarce for several generations in the States. Immigration laws toward the Chinese became somewhat more liberal only with the advent of World War II. This historical fact might have contributed to a brand of male defensiveness (a solidified posture against female encroachment) that is unique to the Chinese American experience. In other words, negative male attitudes toward women— at least as the protagonist experiences them—are partially American-made and, as such, cannot be blanketly attributed to the "Chinese" without locating them in their specific social and historical contexts.

Why is *Woman Warrior* so ambiguous in both its rhetoric and ideology? Some critics attribute the work's ambiguity to Kingston's bicultural background.[15] Not all ethnic texts, however, employ ambiguous narrative strategies. For Kingston ambiguity is a conscious choice that has little to do with bridging cultures. In various interviews she has commented on the need to play literary tricks in "nonfictional" works. On a pragmatic level she wanted to protect her subjects from immigration officers and police, "but what happened," she admits, "was that this need for secrecy affected my form and my style" ("This Is the Story," 10–11). In other words, ambiguity was necessary as a "cover." A second consideration has to do with the attempt to capture oral culture on the printed page.

As an ethnic woman writer, Kingston aligns herself with the Chinese oral tradition of storytelling, or talk-story.[16] "Oral stories

change from telling to telling," she points out. The written word, on
the other hand, is static and finite. "That really bothers me, because
what would be wonderful would be for the words to change on the
page every time, but they can't. The way I tried to solve this problem
was to keep ambiguity in the writing all the time" ("Talk," 18). This
structural ambiguity allows us to *experience* Brave Orchid's changing
the story with each telling.

Walter Ong has argued that there is no such thing as "oral literature" because "you can never divest the term 'literature' of its association with writing. This association inevitably deforms the study of
oral performance" ("Oral Culture," 146). Thus, he warns us against
the habit of viewing oral performance as literature *manqué*. Since
Kingston is, above all, a writer, can she be placed in Ong's category
of offenders? As she views it, however, the vitality of her ethnic
heritage resides in oral storytelling. The ability to talk-story is
equated in both *Woman Warrior* and *China Men* with communal survival and affirmation: it gives talkers like Brave Orchid "great power"
(*Woman Warrior*, 24). For Kingston, to claim her cultural status the
ethnic woman writer must make words "change on the page" in the
manner of oral performances. Thus, *Woman Warrior*, a work that is
literary in many respects, thematically privileges orality. Here ambiguity is the creative compromise of a literate mind conveying the
improvisational immediacy of oral culture.

By maintaining fluidity throughout the text Kingston assumes a
nonparadigmatic stance and challenges the frequently monolithic
Western tradition. In *Woman Warrior* fluidity between mature and
immature perceptions is maintained through two narrative voices:
one child, the other adult. "You lie with stories," the child screams
at her mother. "I can't tell what's real and what you make up" (235).
This accusation suggests that the young protagonist wants certainty
in her life. The conscious, forward thrust of the narrative seeks clarity—a release from confusing stories and nightmares. This seemingly
clear position is undercut, however, by an adult narrator who admits,
analyzes, and condones her own fabrications.

After describing in elaborate detail her aunt Moon Orchid's confrontation with her husband the narrator comments, "What my
brother actually said was . . . " (189). In other words, the story she
just told is her own creation. Her next concession is, "His version of
the story may be better than mine because of its bareness, not twisted

into designs." This implies that the reader has the right to choose among versions of the text. The adult narrator's own position, however, is clearly conveyed through a parable:

> Long ago in China, knot-makers tied string into buttons and frogs, and rope into bell pulls. There was one knot so complicated that it blinded the knot-maker. Finally an emperor outlawed this cruel knot, and the nobles could not order it anymore. If I had lived in China, I would have been an outlaw knot-maker. (190)

Why would she have been an "outlaw knot-maker"? For the mature narrator simplicity and clarity no longer seem important. Contrary to the "narrator girl's" anxiety about confusing ethnic stories, the unconscious penchant for telling stories "twisted into designs" like complicated knots is now a virtue. The adult protagonist has attained a "tolerance for ambiguity."

While presenting herself as an "outlaw," an exile from the Chinese American community in which she grew up, the adult narrator yet seeks a way to return to the fold *on her own terms*. She had to leave, she claims, because she thought that "the Chinese" despised females. Psychologically and spiritually, however, she has not given up her ethnic community. The cycle of departure and return is, as the narrative shows, a new and welcome possibility for ethnic females. Ultimately, women warriors do not ride off into the sunset.

Structurally, each story of the warrior woman—whether of the legendary Fa Mu Lan, the narrator's mother, Brave Orchid, or the narrator herself—tests the potential for reconciliation between the individual and her community. The narrator declares, for example, that both she and the legendary swordswoman have "the words at our backs" (63). That is, if she uses her verbal ability to avenge her oppressed ethnic community, might she not also be loved and admired by her people? The parallel between the two "warriors" seems perfect until we realize that Kingston's Fa Mu Lan story is a Chinese American myth and not Chinese history. In the classics Fa Mu Lan's parents do not carve words of vengeance on their daughter's back.[17] In traditional Chinese culture the legend serves as an example of a daughter's filiality toward her parents. Kingston's fantasy tale, on the other hand, emphasizes the hazards of crossing gender boundaries:

"Chinese executed women who disguised themselves as soldiers or students . . . " (46). Assertion of womanhood—by secretly having a lover and bearing a child in battle—is made a heroic act. These details do not correspond to legendary Chinese heroines who fulfilled the "neuter" role of warriors without strong sexual identification (Rankin, "Emergence of Women," 52). Hence, the narrator/author's "'chink' and 'gook' words" (*Woman Warrior*, 63) as well as Fa Mu Lan's tattoos and male/female assertions are creative constructs made in America.

Once we realize that the sense of Chinese historical truth conveyed in the "White Tigers" section is an illusion, then the narrator's next formulation in the same chapter can also be questioned. When the narrator declares, "My American life has been such a disappointment" (54), rather than falling into the bicultural trap of counterpointing Chinese heroism against an unheroic American life, we might ask: What other life does the narrator have? Since she has never had a Chinese life outside her imagination, the word *American* is meaningless and merely designates "reality." By the same token, when the narrator uses the term *Chinese*, the reader needs to substitute *illusion*. Because the swordswoman myth is mostly a child's wish fulfillment, it cannot serve as the catalyst for change. The "woman warrior" of the book's title is possibly the trickster's first joke.

Kingston herself has stated that Fa Mu Lan is *her* myth: "But I put [the "White Tigers" chapter] at the beginning to show that the childish myth is past, not the climax we reach for. Also, 'The White Tigers' is not a Chinese myth but one transformed by America, a sort of kung fu movie parody" ("Cultural Mis-readings," 57). Within the text the mature narrator exhibits the same awareness when she says, "Perhaps I made him up [the retarded man from her childhood], and what I once had was not Chinese-sight at all but child-sight that would have disappeared eventually without such struggle" (239). In a single stroke all of the naive narrator's insights are dismissed as "child-sight." The titanic struggle between Chinese and American is now seen as a made-up story. Given this interpretive turnaround, what is left?

Portrayals of women in *Woman Warrior* seem to alternate between positive and negative, depending on the narrative point of view. Both Fa Mu Lan and Brave Orchid are heroic when the naive narrator describes them, as evidenced in the "White Tigers" and

"Shaman" sections. These positive portrayals of privileged, exceptional individuals suggest that the warrior image is indeed promoted in the book. When we move to the omniscient narrative of the fourth chapter, however, we find a different view of strong women. Just as we gradually realize that Fa Mu Lan exists only as a fantasy, here we view the "real-life" warrior as less than perfect. While the episode between Brave Orchid and her sister Moon Orchid is humorous, it also exposes the destructive side of the rugged individualist. In this chapter Brave Orchid drives her sister insane. She is culpable, the implied author seems to say, because she cannot empathize with those weaker than herself. This negative judgment is periodically inserted into the text from the third-person viewpoint: "But Brave Orchid would not relent; her dainty sister would just have to toughen up." There is also intrusive commentary: "She looked at her younger sister whose very wrinkles were fine. 'Forget about a job,' she said, which was very lenient of her" (147).

Just as the negative aspects of heroic women such as Fa Mu Lan and Brave Orchid can be found embedded in the text, the reader also finds an alternative community of women with which the narrator is identified. In the Fa Mu Lan story "cowering, whimpering women" on "little bound feet" later form a mercenary army (called "witch amazons") of swordswomen (52–53). Although these women are described contemptuously from Fa Mu Lan's perspective ("They blinked weakly at me like pheasants that have been raised in the dark for soft meat" [52–53]), they also present a vivid image of the downtrodden who ultimately prevail. Throughout the text a string of oppressed, misunderstood women—including the no-name aunt, the witch amazons, Moon Orchid, the quiet girl, various crazy ladies, and the narrator herself, with her "bad, small-person's voice that makes no impact" (57)—counterbalances the superwomen. The protagonist waivers between the weak and the strong, as she does between her "outlaw" status and her ties to the ethnic community. Her fear of insanity causes her publicly to denounce the rejects, the "Crazy Marys" and "retards," of society. On the other hand, she is closely identified with them in the text (e.g., she asks her sister, "Do you talk to people that aren't real inside your mind?" [221]) and, in contrast to Brave Orchid, exhibits a deep understanding for this segment of society.

Halfway through *Woman Warrior* the adult narrator returns home for a visit. The familiar tug-of-war between mother and daughter resumes until the daughter confronts her overpowering mother with the confession "When I'm away from here, I don't get sick . . . ," and Brave Orchid responds with "It's better, then, for you to stay away. . . . You can come for visits" (127). Then the mother calls her daughter "Little Dog," a term of endearment. In this crucial scene not only does a mother learn to let go of her child, but the two women have established grounds for mutual respect as well. This hint of reconciliation is extended to the book's symbolic ending. The final story is a collaboration between her mother and herself, the adult narrator informs us. Rather than the usual vying over which version of a story is *truer*, we now have two storytellers enjoying equal time "without," as one critic puts it, "the privileging of one before the other" (S. Smith, *Poetics*, 172). This final juxtaposition suggests the recognition and acceptance of human diversity, mutual respect, and communal sharing.

The parable told by the two women moves reconciliation from the individual to the universal plane. Symbolically, a new community is formed. The poet Ts'ai Yen improvises lyrics to her barbarian captors' flute music. She joins her captors in a circle around the campfires in an image of camaraderie and human empathy. She later brings back her lyrics, which her people sing "to their own instruments" and they "translat[e] well" (243). Although this ending, with its metaphoric and tentative quality, does not offer a one-big-happy-family resolution, it does suggest the reintegration of the individual in society (one's ethnic culture and beyond) through the medium of language (including stories and songs). Ultimately, the individual—whether the protagonist, Brave Orchid, or Ts'ai Yen—must function in relation to others. This, however, does not mean the type of oppressive group control portrayed in the introductory chapter, "No Name Woman." Instead, it emphasizes the importance of the individual *within* the context of the cultural community.

As an artist and a Chinese American woman, Kingston finds the theme of individualism and community compelling. For various reasons she has played the trickster role in her first work. Even if misread to the extent it has been, however, the woman warrior as avenging angel or rugged individualist still comes through as problematic. This contrasts sharply with the individualist position of another woman autobiographer. Albert Stone cites the artist and psychoanalyst Anaïs Nin as an extreme case: "'There is not one big cosmic meaning for all,' she declares in *Diary I*, 'there is only the meaning we each give to our life, an individual meaning, an individual plot, like an individual novel, a book for each person. To seek a total unity is wrong'" (*American Autobiography*, 8). The other end of the autobiographical spectrum, says Stone, is where "the self is self-consciously submerged." In *Woman Warrior* Kingston seeks to reconcile the two ends of the spectrum without succumbing to either side.

In his 1988 Tony Award–winning play *M. Butterfly* David Henry Hwang offers the devastating critique that not only does "Western man" have a rapist mentality toward the East, viewing "the Orient" as Butterfly to his Pinkerton,[18] but the fantasy is so powerful that he himself is victimized by his own construct. Unlike much of contemporary ethnic American fiction, Hwang's play has a sensational plot line: a French diplomat, René Gallimard, is in prison for consorting with a Chinese spy, Song Liling. After a twenty-year love affair with Song, Gallimard is caught and tried. At this point he experiences a rude awakening: the beautiful Song, whom he has considered the ideal woman and equated with Puccini's Madame Butterfly, is actually a man. The question everyone asks about this plot is, of course: "How could Gallimard not have known for twenty years?" The plot of *M. Butterfly*, however, comes straight from a widely publicized news story that broke in 1986. As Hwang tells us in his afterword, the Frenchman said in a *New York Times* article that he never saw his lover totally nude: "I thought she was very modest. I thought it was a Chinese custom" (*M. Butterfly*, 94).

The ready-made irony of the true story proved irresistible. In the hands of an intelligent playwright the story became fertile ground for an exploration of racism, sexism, and other internalized and institutionalized forms of oppression. As will become apparent, the play is also a strong indictment of bourgeois individualism. The dramatic form makes it possible for the writer to attribute this critique to the main characters themselves. Thus, Gallimard's hindsight analysis of the affair forces him to voice the ironic truth: "We, who are not handsome, nor brave, nor powerful, yet somehow believe, like Pinkerton, that we deserve a Butterfly" (10). Now *where* does this faith in man's natural right come from? Indirectly, Gallimard gives us the answer: "Yes—love. . . . Love warped my judgment, blinded my eyes, rearranged the very lines on my face . . . until I could look in the mirror and see nothing but . . . a woman" (92). The question is: What kind of love is this, and from where does the image of this fantasy woman arise? In the statement, romantic love is exposed as narcissistic self-projection. Man sees what he wants to see; because Gallimard wants to see his version of the perfect woman in Song, this is what he sees. Within the framework of this study one might say that this phallic projection of Western man on the "seductive" East leaves no room for real connections. The individualist sees his own reflection in the mirror and needs this mirrored illusion in order to thrive.

In dealing with the theme of illusion versus reality, Hwang successfully explores the ambiguities of self-delusion. At the trial Song explains to the judge his lover's double bind. First, "The West thinks of itself as masculine—big guns, big industry, big money—so the East is feminine—weak, delicate, poor . . . the feminine mystique" (83). This colonizer mentality, which equates the Orient with female submission, is incapable of seeing Asian males as "complete men." Given this major handicap, Gallimard has no alternative framework in which to view Song. The irony is that, since Song is aware of the Frenchman's racist and sexist outlook, he is able to manipulate Gallimard into the role of Butterfly—a woman duped by love. Thus, Gallimard's comment regarding his mirror image is a double entendre: through the looking glass not only does he *see* the woman of his fantasy projection, but he *is* that woman. The play ends with Gallimard's imitating the same act as Puccini's Madame Butterfly: he commits seppuku (ritual suicide) on stage.

In the afterword the playwright declares the communal message of *M. Butterfly:* "I consider it a plea to all sides to cut through our respective layers of cultural and sexual misperception, to deal with one another truthfully for our mutual good, from the common and equal ground we share as human beings" (100). By writing this powerful indictment of Western individualism—in which the individual becomes the victim of his inability to cross cultures and connect with real human beings—David Henry Hwang performs a much needed demythicizing function through his art. According to the writer, "*M. Butterfly* has sometimes been regarded as an anti-American play, a diatribe against the stereotyping of the East by the West, of women

by men" (100). The critical response that Hwang is describing here
rests on both the explicit dualisms of East/West and men/women and
on an implicit equation of "American" with "West" and "men." Critics who think in these terms reflect the myth of the Western hero—as
enshrined in John Wayne—which it is so necessary to deconstruct.

In Hwang's play what gives Gallimard the confidence to pursue
his individualistic course is the discovery that either there is no God
or God is a man and "understands" man's need to oppress woman.
In other words, God is on the side of the individualist because "He"
is made in (Western) man's own image. The discovery comes through
an unexpected experience of being rewarded instead of punished for
wrongdoing. At one point in the drama, having successfully humiliated Song in a display of power, Gallimard anticipates retribution for
his cruelty. "There must be justice in the world," he thinks (36). That
evening, however, he finds that, instead of punishment, he is rewarded for his actions with a job promotion. His interpretation of
this experience is that there is no justice in the world, so he can do
unto others as he pleases. Gallimard's rationalization is apparent
here. Because God's justice does not take the form that he expects,
the implied author appears to be saying, the protagonist in effect
empowers himself to "play God"—meaning that he sets himself up
as the sole arbiter of values. With this self-serving construct the protagonist ensures that there will be no justice.

In another Asian American work the issue of justice is explored
in terms of an individual's rights versus one's obligation to one's
family. Milton Murayama's *All I Asking for Is My Body* ([1959] 1975) is
a Japanese American novel, which, like Kingston's *Woman Warrior*,
has been misread as evidence of intercultural conflict between the
Issei and Nisei[19] in Hawaii. Once again this misinterpretation is due
to the readers' equating a naive narrator's point of view with that of
the author. In an enlightening analysis the critic Stephen Sumida
shows, however, that, as the narrator/protagonist, Kiyo, matures in
this bildungsroman, his understanding of his family in the context
of Japanese American history also shifts and expands (*And the View*,
128–37). Thus, he is finally able to differentiate between superficial
and faulty constructs about the "Japanese" and the real, underlying
issues behind his family's major conflict: the matter of an accumulated six-thousand-dollar debt, which the Issei parents claim is their
Nisei offsprings' filial duty to repay. Trapped in the stoop labor plan-

tation existence with other ethnic groups, there is no way for Kiyo's older brother Tosh to repay the debt and begin a new life. "All I asking for is my body," Tosh tells his parents in his Hawai'in pidgin English. This demand appears to embody and assert the individualist position in the text.

Although Tosh *talks about* the right to his own life, however, he in fact does not take off to pursue his dreams. Like the first-born son Fred in Frank Chin's play, Tosh's internalized sense of duty to the family holds him back. So, while he rants and raves against his parents—accusing them of being *ko-fuko,* or undutiful to the children (42)—he also sacrifices himself for the family. When the mother says, "Don't worry, we won't depend on you. We'll depend on Kiyoshi," his communal values come through clearly; he tells his mother, "You don't think I'm going to leave Kiyo holding the bag" (42). Similar to that of Chin's angry and conflicted protagonist, Tosh's predicament—which might be viewed as being intellectually individualistic but psychologically and emotionally communal—looks like a dead-end street. In Murayama's work, however, the tension between the individual and the communal is resolved through the character Kiyo, thus making possible a happy resolution.

It is important to point out here that the parents' demands on their children are *not* indicative of Japanese Confucian culture, as the Japanese-versus-American surface structure of the text might lead one to believe. As Sumida points out, the Confucian ideal of filial piety, at least in its unadulterated form, requires reciprocity on the part of the parents. Thus, as Kiyo gradually learns, "It is his *issei* parents who have been untrue to the concept and value called 'filial piety,' not Tosh" (134). Like Fred Eng's self-centered father in Chin's play, the parents in this novel misrepresent Asian values of family and community in order to bail themselves out of their inherited obligations. Sumida explains this situation:

> With no elder to check them since Obaban's death, Mother and Father have been dictating their own misinterpretations of "filial piety." This is the advantage to being an immigrant: one can establish as "tradition" a practice only imperfectly remembered and understood, by one who left Japan while relatively young, with no elders around to make corrections. (*And the View,* 133–34)

In making up their own rules and attributing these to "Japanese custom," Tosh's and Kiyo's parents utilize an intended communal ethic in an individualistic way. Because Kiyo attains a larger picture of life, whereby he is able to understand, if not condone, his parents' actions within the context of their limited environment, his love for them remains intact. His more balanced perspective (thanks to role models like Tosh and the great-aunt Obaban) enables him to leave home (by joining the army) *as well as* look for a solution to his family's problem. By sending Tosh the six thousand dollars he wins at a crap game, Kiyo breaks the cycles of failure that have dogged the family for three generations. His scribbled note to Tosh confirms this: "Won this in crap game. Pay up all the debt. I manufactured some of the luck, but I think the Oyama luck has finally turned around. Take care the body. See you after the War" (103). This ending to the novel indicates that, through his ability to break free from the family, Kiyo not only succeeds in expressing communal values but, unlike the hotheaded Tosh, also manages to make this strategy work for rather than against him. Thus, Murayama 's novel does not sacrifice individual freedom to some rigid notion of family or community. Instead, it illustrates that communal values are only viable when the individual is a whole human being.

In her 1988 National Book Critics Circle award winner *Middleman and Other Stories* Bharati Mukherjee presents an array of recent ethnic Americans—"new" faces from Asia, Latin America, the Middle East, the Caribbean, etc.—and pits them against the myth of the American Dream. The writer's keen observations, expressed in acerbic, dagger-sharp prose, indicate a deep investment in her adopted country. Mukherjee's familiarity with American popular and street cultures shines a chilling light on those who would take this country for granted. While some stories are narrated from an immigrant female point of view, the majority are narrated by "middlemen": pimps, hustlers, hit men, and such. The disoriented Vietnam veteran is an especially poignant subject in this collection. Since many of the works in the present study stem from the Vietnam era, I will briefly examine two stories about Vietnam veterans in relation to the theme of individualism and community.

In "Loose Ends" a Vietnam vet hit man in Florida breaks up with his girlfriend, makes a commissioned "hit," is shaken down by crooked cops when he attempts to leave town, lands in a motel run by "aliens," and rapes the young clerk before taking off in another stolen car. While the plot sounds like a canned television script, the cultural-political analysis behind the story line catches us off guard with its insights. By narrating from the vet Jeb's perspective, the author shows us what an individualistic, dog-eat-dog ethic looks like close up. Jeb's story is a simple one. At seventeen he was trained for one career in life: to be an efficient killing machine. According to Doc Healy, the training officer, "If you want to stay alive . . . just keep consuming and moving like a locust" (45). Survival strategy quickly becomes a philosophy of life: "Job One is to secure your objective and after that it's unsupervised play till the next order comes down" (50). Given that Doc Healy's star pupil did his job so well in Vietnam as an all-American soldier, how was it that he became the outsider back in his own country? Jeb feels betrayed. "Where did America go?" he demands. "Back when me and my buddies were barricading the front door, who left the back door open?" (47–48).

Through the back door came the dark aliens: people wearing turbans, speaking in high, whiny voices, and traveling in packs. Kicking in a door marked Strictly Private at a motel, Jeb catches a family huddled around a feast on the floor. This confrontational moment is a classic racial encounter. Jeb resents these brown people not only for acting as if they had a right to America but, in his mind, because they mean to exclude him by virtue of their "un-American" difference. "They've forgotten me," he thinks. "I feel left out, left behind. . . . They got their money, their family networks, and their secretive languages." To break through this perceived barrier violence is his only recourse. He punches the wall and yells, "Don't any of you dummies speak American?" (53). The clincher in disclosing Jeb's racist, alienated mind is when he asks the "jailbait" where she was born and she says "New Jersey." Instead of recognizing this young woman as another American citizen, he rapes her for her audacity to look like one of *them* while feeling distaste for him. "I pounce on Alice [referring to Alice in Wonderland] before she can drop down below," he states, "and take America with her" (55).

Beneath the story's polarization of us-against-them, white-against-brown, English-against-gook words, etc., is the protagonist's major angst: his complete and total isolation. The implied author shows us that what irks Jeb the most as well as what he craves is the community of the aliens. Before he jumps "Alice" he thinks, "She's aiming to race back to the motel room not much different than this except that it's jammed with family" (55). This thought reveals the unacknowledged desire from a prewar, more human part of himself that would have liked to be in a motel room "jammed with family" rather than left alone waiting for "the next order to come down."

The extreme estrangement of Jeb the hit man transforms into a different story in "Fathering." This time the protagonist, Jason, is caught between his Vietnamese child, Eng, and his new Anglo wife, Sharon. Eng, a product of the war, expresses trauma in self-destructive ways. Sharon, who had actually encouraged Jason to send for his daughter from Vietnam, is no match for Eng and deteriorates into a sniveling child herself when Eng does not fit neatly into her "white girlish furniture" world (117). Unlike Jeb in the previous story, Jason cares about both women but is forced to choose. "I'm thirty-eight. I've let a lot of people down already," he tells us (120). Although Eng is an extremely difficult child, he feels a stronger affinity for her. The reasons for this are given in brief images of Vietnam; for example, "If I could, I'd suck the virus right out of her. In the jungle, VC [Vietcong] mamas used to do that" (115); "She bring me food from the forest. They shoot Grandma! Bastards!" (118). The snatched memories convey a communal ethos: they recall not only a desperate time but also a shared, caring way of life.

By comparing his Vietnam experience with his middle-class existence in America, Jason comes to a decision; his allegiance is no longer in doubt. "The doctor comes at us with his syringe," he observes. "He's sedated Sharon; now he wants to knock out my kid with his cures." On impulse Jason rescues Eng from the doctor's clutches: "My Saigon kid and me: we're a team" (122). Although the story concludes on a note of father/daughter solidarity, the resolution is certainly not a clear-cut happy ending. We know this because Jason describes the rescue in a fairy-tale context by calling his van a "chariot." In addition, his thoughts regarding Eng's skin color (e.g., "I can't help wondering if maybe Asian skin bruises differently from ours" [118]) and other qualities of "difference" reveal a slightly racist attitude toward Asians. His rescuing of his "Saigon kid," then, can be interpreted as two shell-shocked vets banding together. The ambiguous ending of this story suggests that cross-cultural fatherhood is no easy matter. For Jason to reach Eng he must move beyond exoticized, romanticized notions of Asia in his head. While "Fathering" warns us, however, that instant solidarity with the other is an illusion, Jason's deep, unnamed feelings for his foreign child give us hope. In neither of these two Vietnam stories, then, is isolation being advocated. In *Middleman* Mukherjee portrays individuals from disparate worlds whose cultural clashes in America mandate learning new ways of relating. The closeness of "brown peoples" in the stories seems to serve as a model for building communities in contemporary America.

In Amy Tan's *The Joy Luck Club* (1989) the deep, subtle connections between immigrant mothers and their American-born daughters are thoroughly explored. Structurally, the novel both fragments and interweaves the stories of four mother-daughter pairs, conveying the impression that the author is exploring one paradigmatic mother-daughter story from different angles. Amy Ling accurately points out that the generational split is more pronounced than "individual personalities" in the novel. "In fact," says the critic, "in existential fashion, actions and events define and identify the characters, who become who they are because of what they have chosen to do" (*Between Worlds*, 131). This narrative technique highlights the collective story of Chinese American women rather than privileging the unique characteristics of any one individual. Thus, one mother's desire that her children have "American circumstances and Chinese character" (Tan, *Joy Luck Club*, 289) is played out in the text as an ideal combination that mothers strive toward and daughters resist. Conflicts due to generational, cultural, social, economic, and linguistic barriers lead to misunderstandings, humor, and pain. As the daughters mature and the mothers age, the desperate confrontations eventually expose the underlying truth: that mother and daughter are one and the same. The case of the Woos makes this clear.

"My mother and I never really understood one another" Jing-Mei Woo states in the opening section of the book (27). In fact, she tells us, when she once mentioned to her mother that someone had said they were alike, the mother had been highly insulted (14–15). The tug-of-war between Jing-Mei and her deceased mother is a classic one. The mother, who immigrated to the United States believing that anything was possible in this country, worked on molding her daughter into a "genius" in order to fulfill the American Dream. The daughter, early developing a strong will of her own (in imitation of the mother?), determined to sabotage this and "put a stop to her [mother's] foolish pride" (149). In the novel, while each character is assigned two narrative sections apiece, Jing-Mei has four slots, since *her* mother is dead. Thus, it is through her that the mother has a voice. The novel opens with Jing-Mei's assuming her mother's role at the mah-jongg table of the Joy Luck Club. Her "substitute" role is recalled in the conclusion when she is in China and taking her mother's place once again. This literary frame alone suggests that, although the mother-daughter power struggle appears individualistic on the surface, there is a different message embedded in the text.

At the end of the book Jing-Mei tells us that her mother had been right; the minute she set foot on Chinese soil she was "becoming Chinese" (306). When she meets her two Chinese sisters the presence of their mother surfaces: " 'Mama, Mama,' we all murmur, as if she is among us." The sisters seem familiar, says Jing-Mei, although they do not *look like* mother. The sight of them triggers a realization: "And now I also see what part of me is Chinese. It is so obvious. It is my family. It is in our blood. After all these years, it can finally be let go" (331). The three sisters take a Polaroid picture and make a further discovery: "Together we look like our mother" (332). This composite image of three daughters who, together, make up one mother reflects the novel's communal subtext, which works as a counterpoint to the textual surface of individualistic strife between mothers and daughters.

Until an older Jing-Mei attains some level of understanding the narrator's interpretation of her conflict with her mother is one-sided and unreliable. Halfway through the text, for example, Jing-Mei tells us that, as a child, she had yelled at her mother: "Why don't you like me the way I am? I'm *not* a genius!" (146). Throughout the novel, however, we are told that (similar to the situation in *The Woman Warrior*) Chinese mothers never pay a direct compliment but, instead, express their support and love indirectly—through emblems such as food and meaningful gifts (227). If this is the case, then it is *because* Jing-Mei's mother "likes" her daughter that she wants her to be a genius. This means that the immature child sabotages her own talent because she is unable and/or is willfully refusing to decode the hidden message. Thus, the resolution of the novel quoted above— "After all these years, it can be let go"—suggests that Jing-Mei finally comprehends her mother's message: the message that, underneath the skin, we (mother/daughter, Chinese/American, etc.) are all one.

Chapter 3

African American Writers

Alice Walker's *The Color Purple* and John Edgar Wideman's *Sent for You Yesterday* were published within a year of each other and, according to one reviewer, "Both books are being hailed as highpoints in the Black renaissance in American literature" (Blue, "From the Ghetto," 34). The historical periods covered by each novel are roughly the same (Walker's from the 1920s through the 1950s, Wideman's from the 1920s through the 1960s). Each work represents a different region in America: Walker writes about rural Southern sharecroppers, and Wideman's Homewood is an Eastern urban ghetto. The two works are especially well matched for the present study in that each novel explores new possibilities for black people by drawing from traditional black American culture.[1] This approach reflects the shift toward cultural validation and celebration within contemporary African American literature.

In the 1980s W. E. B. DuBois's "double consciousness" no longer dominates black literature. The "sense of always looking at one's self through the eyes of others" (*Souls*, 45), while still hovering behind the scenes, is no longer featured among a whole crop of talented writers emerging from the late 1960s. From stories of racial oppression in which emphasis is placed on black versus white, African American fiction is now turning inward to explore the dynamics within the ethnic culture. This shift in focus offers opportunities for what Hoyt Fuller calls "exhortation and celebration" ("New Black Literature," 346). As various critics have noted, the new mood of affirmation is encouraged by the reexamination of black/slave culture by "historians, sociologists, folklorists, and black aestheticians" (Schultz, "Insistence upon Community," 171) since the early 1970s. A major "finding" is that, since the earliest days of slavery, resistance to their oppression had enabled Africans to not only retain aspects of their traditional cultures, but also to create an ethnic culture and community in America. This is manifested in revisionist history such as Eugene Genovese's *Roll, Jordan, Roll* (1972), which has as its subtitle "The World the Slaves Made."

That African Americans have had a viable culture in this country is a given for both Wideman and Walker. The damaging viewpoints offered by the noted black sociologist E. Franklin Frazier in the 1930s and Glazer and Moynihan in the 1960s to the contrary,[2] contemporary African American literature displays a heart warming array of creative attributes and traditional values drawn specifically from black culture. For a writer like Wideman tapping one's ethnic background artistically has required a process of reeducation, a going back to the people. This undertaking has taught the author that, by writing well about a specific black family and community, his writing has more "general resonance" (Wideman, "Going Home," 43). Interestingly, Barbara Christian has made the same point regarding contemporary black women authors. The first novels of Paule Marshall, Toni Morrison, and Alice Walker are all "insular," says Christian, in that they "seem to emphasize the major character's psychic connection to her natal community" (*Black Women Novelists*, 242). Nevertheless, this community immersion approach, though traditionally considered narrow and parochial by critics, is "more complex, perhaps even broader than many works in which the white world is prominent." When we do away with certain preconceived notions of literary legitimacy, then, the vitality of fiction built around a specific ethnic community begins to surface.

Writing from within a culture, however, does not mean naive glorification of that culture. In Walker's criticism of sexism and Wideman's advocacy of personal and communal responsibility one finds that the novels take a strong stand on pressing issues among black people. Fuller's idea of "exhortation" is definitely in these works, although neither writer is didactic in style or technique. Postmodernist ethnic literatures tend to be moral in that the survival of the ethnic culture within American society is of general concern. Both writers go beyond mere descriptions of black communities to advance alternative visions to the status quo. This is done through the effective use of black vernacular English.

The other side of exhortation is celebration. When we read words like "But they could sing. Yes, Lawd, those boys could sing. Ain't gon tell no lie" (*Homewood*, 389), we hear a language of support and affirmation. The words are direct, definite; they convey an exuberance that traditional "literary" language would be hard-pressed to duplicate. Wideman himself corroborates this point in an essay about the magic of black English: "One highly developed aspect of black speech and Afro-American oral tradition is the means by which its users can signify how they feel about what they're saying. Dual messages are transmitted in a single speech act" ("Black Writer," 28). As will be apparent in this analysis, Walker is especially adept at utilizing the double-duty aspect of black folk speech to convey strong emotions. By capturing folklore such as song (especially the blues), dance, lying (telling stories), signifying (talking about talking), and specifying (name-calling) in print, Walker and Wideman, in conjunction with other contemporary black writers, are inserting elements of black culture into traditional American literature—and rejuvenating the latter in the process.

"Sister's Choice": Alice Walker's *Color Purple*

> What the black Southern writer inherits as a natural right is a sense of *community*. Something simple but surprisingly hard, especially these days, to come by.
>
> . . . understanding among women is not a threat to anyone who intends to treat women fairly.
>
> —Alice Walker, *In Search of Our Mothers' Gardens*

"It's my happiest book. I had to do all the other writing to get to this point" (Walker, qtd. in Anello and Abramson, "Characters," 67). With these words Alice Walker identifies *The Color Purple* as the successful culmination of fifteen years of published writings. Although her literary voice has always been self-assured, its assessment of American society and the black people's place in it has not always been optimistic. As a former civil rights activist with a profound sense of justice, Walker has had to come to terms with violence and oppression in American culture. The writer attributes her former bouts of suicidal depression to feelings of inadequacy in the face of inhumanity: "I believe that part of my depression came out of anguish that I was not more violent than I was. For years I fantasized sneaking into various oppressors' houses. . . . The burden of a nonviolent, pacifist philosophy in a violent, nonpacifist society caused me to feel, almost always, as if I had not done enough" (*In Search*, 225).

This autobiographical insight helps to explain why *The Color Pur-*

ple is Walker's happiest book. In the novel the author confronts her own potential for violence (Celie standing behind Mr. _____ with an open razor in her hand) and successfully transcends it (with the help of another woman). Through art she succeeds in working out a viable alternative to violence, an alternative based on sisterhood and genuine human relationships. The quilt that Celie, Sofia, and Shug work on together, called "Sister's Choice," symbolizes this communal resolution. How the author develops communal values in what seems at first a desolate human landscape is the subject of the present inquiry. First, however, a brief discussion regarding the novel's critical reception will provide the context for this literary analysis.

The black-on-black oppression portrayed in Walker's third novel has enraged many people. Partly due to its phenomenal commercial success and its Pulitzer Prize,[3] *The Color Purple* has, according to Calvin Hernton, "driven some of its critics literally *crazy*" (*Sexual Mountain*, 33). Tony Brown, for example, did not feel it necessary to read the book or see the movie before launching a full-scale campaign against everyone connected with the novel (qtd. in Hernton, 33–34). Trudier Harris has written more than one article attacking Walker's portrayal of black men and women.[4] By exposing black men's abusive treatment of black women, declared a number of African American critics, Walker had betrayed her community and the gains of the 1960s Black Power movement. As Hernton puts it, these critics condemned the novel as the "most savage treatment of Black men since *Birth of a Nation*" (34). It appears that attacks on *The Color Purple* have rekindled the age-old debate of how black people should be portrayed by black writers. Whereas in the past, however, the debate always focused on literature by male writers—such as Richard Wright's *Native Son*—this time the writer is a woman.

In identifying *The Color Purple* as essentially a slave narrative in the African American literary tradition, Hernton sheds some light on the controversy (*Sexual Mountain*, 5–6). Historically, he says, the literary genre of the slave narrative has been devoted to exposing *white* oppression of *blacks*. In her controversial novel, however, Walker has appropriated this black-invented, male-dominated literary form and used it against black men. To add insult to injury she has taken the genre out of the male realm and "womanized" it. The parallel between racial and sexual slavery, implied by the novel's very form, cannot be overlooked. Hernton summarizes the situation:

Although we keep looking for the men in The Color Purple [*sic*—intentionally not italicized to designate both novel and movie] to be white, they are black men, *our* men, committing deeds we cannot help but associate with slavery. The analogy is unbearable, the irony is burning. . . . We barricade our minds. The Color Purple is "divisive" to black people, it portrays black men in a "totally unacceptable" light. (17)

This description of black male reaction to The Color Purple suggests a need for denial. It offers an insightful explanation for critics' fixation on the portrayal of black men in the novel. In a 1986 article, for example, Philip Royster seeks to discredit the artist by delving into the psychological motivation behind the art. As a result of the blinding of one eye at age eight, Royster claims, Walker has a deep need "to be both somebody's darling (that somebody is usually an older man) and an outcast (who uses her art as a means to rescue victims)" ("In Search," 349). According to Royster's reading of Walker and her novel, the distorted male characterizations in The Color Purple are a direct product of the author's childhood trauma: "Alice Walker's fictional characterizations include thinly disguised representations of perceptions of herself and her family that began in childhood. Unwittingly, she masquerades these perceptions, primarily the products of fantasies of sexuality and aggression, as the creations of a mature adult awareness" (368). By attributing Walker's fiction to "fantasies of sexuality and aggression," Royster is isolating one controversial writer as an aberration. His psychologizing backfires, however, when we consider that contemporary black women writers (including Toni Morrison, Toni Cade Bambara, and Gloria Naylor) as well as powerful voices of an earlier era (Ann Petry, for example) have come up with the same "aberrant" themes (wife battering, rape, incest, etc., within the black community) as can be found in The Color Purple. The practice of "bearing witness" in literature has been with black women for a long time.

While a tradition of African American literature has existed and flourished since before the Civil War, it was not until the 1970s that women gained recognition on the black literary scene. In fact, the time lag was so prolonged that we are now confronting a separate literary history for black women writers.[5] Women who worked and wrote alongside men in the civil rights and Black Arts movements of the 1960s were, in the eyes of male leaders, contributing to the "whole" race: namely, to black men in their struggle against white oppression. In other words, female literary artists were not considered legitimate in their own right. As Hernton puts it, "Traditionally, the World of Black Literature in the United States has been a world of black men's literature" (*Sexual Mountain*, 38). This blatant male domination is the tradition that contemporary black women writers are up against.

In exploring the themes of individualism and community in *The Color Purple*, one must face the issue of sexism—as black women writers are doing—squarely. While the African American literary tradition, as concretized by Richard Wright and Ralph Ellison, has focused on white racism in America, contemporary women writers tell us that racism and sexism go hand in hand. Within black communities sexism destroys human potential and, through socially sanctioned violence, can actually kill. So far, I have identified a major point of conflict within the black literary community: that, historically, the black literary tradition has been a male prerogative. Against this background Walker's and other women's labors in identifying a female literary tradition become an issue of artistic survival. Walker has been instrumental, for example, in resurrecting the hitherto neglected writings of Zora Neale Hurston.

As a role model, Hurston is essential to contemporary black women writers. In an interview published as an essay Walker points out how Nathan Huggins's influential *Harlem Renaissance* all but ignores Hurston, dismissing the anthropologist and writer with the judgment that "her greatest weakness was carelessness or indifference to her art." Walker disagrees. "Her work," she says, "far from being done carelessly, is done (especially in *Their Eyes Were Watching God*) almost too perfectly. She took the trouble to capture the beauty of rural black expression. She saw poetry where other writers merely saw failure to cope with English" (*In Search*, 261). Some of Walker's most effective literary techniques in *The Color Purple*, from the use of vernacular speech patterns to images of porch sitting and storytelling, are directly traceable to Hurston's major novel. What Huggins assumed to be stones were, from Walker's different angle of vision, diamonds in the rough.

By naming her literary foremothers (as well as important male writers like Jean Toomer and Langston Hughes), Walker places her-

self in a black literary community that is not dominated by the patriarchal tradition. The closing to *The Color Purple* is significant: "I thank
everybody in this book for coming," Walker writes. She then identifies herself as "A. W., author and medium." The sense of continuity
and connection that this simple gesture implies—that the author
serves as transmitter for all the nameless black women's stories—
reflects the folk spirit of the novel. The term *medium* suggests magic,
conjuring, elements drawn directly from rural black culture. In describing her writing of the novel, Walker conveys a real sense of
community between her and her fictional characters (*In Search*, 355–
60). She tells us how, after moving twice and finally finding an environment in which her characters were willing to visit, she spent
happy days chatting with what were to her real people: "They were
very obliging, engaging, and jolly. . . . Things that made me sad often
made them laugh. Oh, we got through that; don't pull such a long
face, they'd say" (359).

While the theme of enslavement makes *The Color Purple* a slave
narrative of sorts, Walker takes the literary genre beyond its protest
formula in innovative ways. By narrating the story entirely through
letters, she restricts herself to first Celie's then Nettie's point of view
and experience with language. This narrative strategy departs from
the anecdotal style of her previous writings,[6] in which she allowed
herself more structural flexibility. As a narrative form (one that harks
back to the earliest European novels), the epistolary style presents
new challenges in black literature. For one thing, the objective cannot
be separated from the subjective. The following discussion will show
that Walker uses the very structure and versatility of black English
to sustain the narrative.

The novel begins when Celie is fourteen years old and covers the
next thirty years of her life. Her brutal treatment by men, first by her
stepfather and then by her husband, Mr. _____, identifies her as a
generic black woman of the early twentieth-century rural South (what
folk culture calls "the mule of the world"). In an interview Walker
says that the character of Celie is based on a great-grandmother who
was raped and abused at age twelve (qtd. in Christian, "Alice
Walker," 270). The epistolary style, the form that feminist critics claim
is most reflective of women's daily lives, enables her to serve as a
transmitter of her "mothers'" collective story. By allowing a barely
literate and completely isolated black girl to tell her story in her own

words (at first Celie has no one to talk to but God), the author steps
in line with other American writers—from Dickinson and Twain to
Hurston and Hughes—who have struggled to create new literary
languages. *The Color Purple* successfully inserts black folk speech into
traditional American literature and supports the position that a functional, nonstandard English can carry the weight of "high" art.

While Walker's most vociferous critics seem to be fixated on the
"savage portrayal of black men" in *The Color Purple*, male violence
against women in the novel is only the starting point from which a
healthier way of relating must evolve. Walker takes pains to portray
sexism as the product of social conditioning. Black men are not inherently violent or evil; their attitudes toward women are acquired at
an early age. Walker conveys this point throughout the novel. Harpo,
Mr. _____'s firstborn, destroys a happy marriage by trying to force
Sofia to submit to his supposed male domination. In his unsuccessful
attempts to beat his wife Harpo is a failure by the standards of the
community. Walker does not restrict this false value to men, however. As a product of the same culture, Celie also buys into the norm.
Hence, she advises Harpo to beat Sofia just as Mr. _____ beats her.
Until such behavioral patterns are effectively challenged both men
and women are caught in a mutually destructive alliance.

The question posed by the novel is: Can an alternative way of
relating be envisioned through art? While Walker's answer points
toward family and community, it certainly does not promote the
status quo. It is the extant black community, especially those elements of the culture embedded in sexist and racist ideology, that
leaves a woman like Celie abused and friendless. Isolation in such
an environment does not lead to individual salvation. Had Walker let
the community define her protagonist's worth ("You black, you pore,
you ugly, you a woman. Goddam, he say, you nothing at all" [187]),
Celie would have been another helpless victim like Toni Morrison's
Pecola Breedlove—a black girl driven insane by her desire for blue
eyes. By empowering black vernacular speech, creating positive role
models, and providing specific illustrations of communal support,
Walker develops a different fate for Celie through her art. Moreover,
this alternative vision is drawn directly from African American culture.

In the sociological study *The Helping Tradition in the Black Family
and Community* Joanne and Elmer Martin offer a theoretical analysis

of the origin, development, and decline of communal values in the black community. Taking a historical approach, the study shows how the "helping tradition" stemmed from African laws and customs and, once transplanted to America through the institution of slavery, flourished in black communities until the Great Depression of the 1930s. The decline of the tradition can be attributed to black migration from rural to urban centers ("the increased urbanization of blacks brought the black helping tradition for the first time into general conflict with the dominant values of white society" [63]) and to the subsequent influence of bourgeois and street ideologies,[7] which tend to place tremendous emphasis on individualism (69). Patriarchy in the United States, the authors assert, is most destructive of the helping tradition. While traditional African society was patriarchal, it was also communal: "No matter how much wealth or power a man attained, he could not place his individual interests above those of the group" (13). Given the changes in modern society and the decline of the black helping tradition, however, the persistence of patriarchal values in American culture poses a real threat to the black family and community. The ongoing belief among many social scientists that a strong patriarchy will solve the "Negro Question" is, according to these researchers, a dangerous myth (6).

Traditional African American culture emphasized mutual aid, respect, and support. The male-female conflict being documented by contemporary black women writers reflects the shift toward patriarchal and individualistic values in modern society. From this perspective Walker's literary revisioning of transformed social relationships is also a return to black cultural values. The helping tradition is a central theme in Walker's earlier writings, from her first published story, "To Hell with Dying," to the novel *Meridian*. In the novel under discussion it operates as a palpable force in combating sexist and racist behavior in the rural South.

The Color Purple opens with an epigraph from a song by Stevie Wonder:

Show me how to do like you
Show me how to do it.

The novel shows us how to build genuine relationships through carefully constructed moments of connection. Initial alliances among the characters occur in twos and threes: individuals band together against a common enemy and, in the process, momentarily let their guards down with one another. For Celie these moments offer glimpses of an alternative, life-enhancing mode of existence. While literature in the Western tradition is used to thrusting an individual into a community in an adversarial relationship (Henrik Ibsen's *Enemy of the People* and Eugène Ionesco's *Rhinoceros* come to mind), it usually presents the individual as the Lone Ranger—the last holdout against the conforming masses. Walker turns around this one-against-many motif in the character of the blues and jazz singer Shug Avery.

The example that the free-spirited Shug provides is one of reciprocity. As Celie puts it, "Hard not to love Shug, I say. She know how to love somebody back" (247). As an existential outsider who has rejected destructive social norms, Shug serves as a catalyst for change in Celie's world. Rather than expound some self-righteous principle, Shug lives her philosophy and shows by example. The redeemed Mr. _____ says toward the end of the novel: "But Shug spoke right up for you, Celie. . . . She say Albert, you been mistreating somebody I love. So as far as you concern, I'm gone" (237). And she meant what she said, Mr. _____ tells us. It is rallying around an ornery, audacious, and unpretentious figure like Shug that triggers supportive communal behavior among individuals.

Celie and Mr. _____, whose relationship as wife and husband has been one of slave and master, find themselves on the same side after Shug appears on the scene. Celie's adulation of and Mr. _____'s love for Shug create a common bond. When Mr. _____'s father denigrates Shug, Celie and Mr. _____ band together against this common enemy ("Mr. _____ look up at me, our eyes meet. This the closest us ever felt" [59]). Although this first genuine connection is tenuous, it is nevertheless a first. Since Celie is the narrator, the connecting moments that she describes—even the fact that she mentions these moments—are significant. Gradually and at first imperceptibly within the confines of her alienated existence, Celie begins to express and value communal feelings. When Mr. _____'s brother Tobias shows up to make a play for Shug, Celie interprets the incident as one of group solidarity: "Us three together gainst Tobias and his fly speck box of chocolate. For the first time in my life, I feel just right" (61). As noted above, the epistolary structure of the novel leaves no room for authorial intrusion. Since the structure credits every observation to the letter writer, it is Celie's perceptions that confront us in two-thirds of the novel. This literary strategy makes the lessons that Celie learns appear internalized and not imposed from the outside.

In the first part of the novel Celie describes her personal dilemma more than once:

> Don't let them run over you, Nettie say. You got to let them know who got the upper hand.
> They got it, I say.
> But she keep on. You got to fight. You got to fight.
> But I don't know how to fight. All I know how to do is stay alive. (25–26)

Women—including Celie's sister Nettie, Mr. _____'s sister Kate, the strong Sofia, and the free-spirited Shug—all convey the same message: Celie must learn to stand up for herself. This does not mean, however, that the individual must be a solitary warrior. When circumstances permit other women lend a helping hand. Celie learns how to fight through the support of generous, self-respecting "sisters." Her interaction with the tough-minded Sofia is a case in point. Sofia as a role model not only serves as an example of a fighter but also elicits courage and honesty from her opponent. When Sofia confronts Celie about encouraging Harpo to beat her, a potential fight quickly turns into an empathetic exchange. Walker accomplishes this by tapping the capacity for compassion in black English:

> I'm *so* shame of myself, I say. And the Lord he done whip me little bit too.
> The Lord don't like ugly, she say.
> And he ain't stuck on pretty.
> This open the way for our talk to turn another way. (46)

By sharing a common language of suffering and the wisdom black people have gleaned from their group historical experience, the two contestants move beyond petty jealousies to form a sisterly bond. The scene ends in laughter, and, significantly, the two women plan to make a quilt.

Walker's use of black vernacular English not only makes her semiliterate narrator credible, but it also infuses written language with new vitality and flexibility. Consider, for example, Celie's description of Sofia's brother-in-law: "Jack is tall and kind and don't hardly say anything. Love children. Respect his wife, Odessa, and all Odessa amazon sisters. Anything she want to take on, he right there. Never talking much, though. That's the main thing" (191). Now consider Nettie's description of the missionary man she has grown to love:

> Samuel is a big man. He dresses in black almost all the time, except for his white clerical collar. And *he* is black. Until you see his eyes you think he's somber, even mean, but he has the most thoughtful and gentle brown eyes. When he says something it settles you, because he never says anything off the top of his head and he's never out to dampen your spirit or to hurt. (128)

While both portraits convey images of good men, Nettie's description requires a great deal more warming up than Celie's. A complete sentence is required for each point Nettie makes. Samuel's attractiveness is not immediately apparent until we get to the fourth sentence. Celie's description, on the other hand, throws out keywords so that, by the second or third word, we have progressed beyond Jack's physical appearance to his caring and supportive personality.

Celie's language is direct, economical, and unsentimental. The close correlation between signifier and signified—a relationship that Nettie's more "literary" English makes problematic—suggests a lack of guile, manipulation, and game playing. Thus, we trust Celie's perceptions because we believe she is "giving it to us straight." Her language moves us: it can make us laugh and cry. In contrast, Nettie's letters from Africa seem long-winded, flat, and blatantly pedagogical.[8] Juxtaposed with the emotive, "oral" narrative of Celie, Nettie's words are cognitive and literary. We get the sense that Nettie lost something—her connectedness to black folk culture and the spirit of the people—by living in Africa as an unwelcomed missionary. It is Walker's rendition of black folk speech, then, that so effectively carries the pathos, humor, and sense of celebration in *The Color Purple*.

In a scene as poignant as any slave narrative Celie describes how

Pa sold her to Mr. _____. Since Mr. _____ really wanted the prettier Nettie, Pa had to give an added incentive in order to unload the "ugly" daughter (and the one he had sexually abused). Without editorializing on the humiliation of being sold the narrative ends with:

> Mr. _____ say, That cow still coming?
> He say, Her cow. (20)

The deal is clinched with the bribe of a cow, which the seller has to provide the buyer. In this economic exchange Celie, who by the men's sexist and racist standards (racist because the black standard of female beauty reflects that of whites) is worth less than a cow, does not and is not expected to react. Walker conveys the pathos of the scene with a minimalist technique that black English makes possible. In the above quote the lack of the "to be" verb adds immediacy and finality to the exchange. A young woman's life is decided upon with the barest of words between men. "He say, Her cow"—the structure of language itself reinforces Celie's worthlessness and isolation.

Vernacular language also makes the sex scene between Celie and Shug seem natural and joyous:

> She say, I love you, Miss Celie. And then she haul off and kiss me on the mouth.
> *Um,* she say, like she surprise. I kiss her back, say, *um,* too.
> Us kiss and kiss till us can't hardly kiss no more.
> Then us touch each other. (109)

The use of the present tense; the directness of expression; the Southern formality of "Miss" Celie; the term *haul off,* which indicates spontaneous, "unladylike" behavior; the surprised "ums" following the sexual overture; and the homey "us" instead of "we"—all of these details together convey a sense of innocence and play. Love, as opposed to physical violence, is always positive in the novel. It is, like the color purple, for those brave souls who dare to be themselves. In Celie's mind both Shug and Sofia are associated with purple because they are, according to Walker's definition, "womanist" women. Walker defines *womanist* as "outrageous, audacious, courageous, or *willful* behavior," and a womanist is someone who is "committed to survival and wholeness of entire people [*sic*], male *and* female" (*In Search*, xi).

By being honest and open with one another despite destructive patriarchal influences, the women in *The Color Purple* create a vision of a new society. In Hurston's novel *Their Eyes Were Watching God* Janie shoots Tea Cake in self-defense. Walker interprets the incident as Janie's revenge for having been publicly humiliated by Tea Cake: "An astute reader would realize that this is the real reason TeaCake [*sic*] is killed by Janie in the end. Or, rather, this is the reason Hurston *permits* Janie to kill TeaCake in the end" (*In Search*, 305). In Walker's own novel not only is Harpo unsuccessful in his attempts to humiliate Sofia, but Celie's murderous rage against her oppressor is diverted toward constructive activities. In this way Walker builds upon her literary foremother to convey the sense of a new day. Shug gets Celie to make a pair of pants, an activity that eventually blossoms into a full-scale business. "And everyday we going to read Nettie's letters and sew," she tells Celie (137). The novel's response to violence is love, social networking, and creative production. The characters, male and female, help one another to combat society's sexist/ racist norms and be decent human beings.

The Color Purple teaches many lessons about social relationships. Mr. _____ changes from a despotic, abusive husband to one who learns to sew and befriend Celie. Walker gives Mr. _____ sufficient voice for the transformation to be convincing. From Nettie's letters Celie is able to tell Mr. _____ that African men sew. This detail presents a contrast between African patriarchy and male domination as practiced in American culture. Given this opening, Mr. _____ is able to confess: "When I was growing up . . . I use to try to sew along with mama cause that's what she was always doing. But everybody laughed at me. But you know, I liked it" (238). While working to destroy such myths as "men can't sew" and "women can't chop wood" on the one hand, the novel also provides models of selflessness and communal support on the other.

In the pivotal scene of female solidarity and the start of a new day two women, Celie and Squeak (Harpo's new partner), announce to the men around the dinner table that they are leaving for Memphis with Shug. Let the confrontation speak for itself:

Mr. _____ reach over to slap me. I jab my case knife in his hand.

You bitch, he say. What will people say, you running off to Memphis like you don't have a house to look after?

Shug say, Albert. Try to think like you got some sense. Why any woman give a shit what people think is a mystery to me.

Well, say Grady, trying to bring light. A woman can't git a man if peoples talk.

Shug look at me and us giggle. Then us laugh sure nuff. Then Squeak start to laugh. Then Sofia. All us laugh and laugh.

Shug say, Ain't they something? Us say um *hum*, and slap the table, wipe the water from our eyes. (182)

In this scene not only has Celie learned to stand up for herself, but she and the others are also able to laugh at the male supremacist myths that have subjugated women. Through laughter the pain of oppression is alleviated and violence avoided. Walker follows up this spirit of liberation with an act of selfless generosity drawn from the black helping tradition. When Squeak and Harpo's child shows an interest in Sofia (who has just returned home on parole), Sofia says to Squeak: "Go on sing . . . I'll look after this one till you come back" (185). This offer to take care of another woman's child reminds us of the black community's extended family network and communal child-rearing practices, which date back to slavery days if not before. In this instance the child belongs to Sofia's estranged husband's new lover. From stereotypes of catty women who fight over men this is certainly a radical vision of community.

In reference to her earlier writings Walker says, "I am trying to arrive at that place where black music already is; to arrive at that unself-conscious [sic] sense of collective oneness; that naturalness, that (even when anguished) grace" (*In Search*, 264). By capturing the poetry of black folk speech in *The Color Purple*, Walker is making headway toward her goal. The collective oneness, the naturalness, the grace—these are the qualities that we hear in Celie's language. And through this language of traditional black culture we are offered the renewal of genuine community between men and women.

"One More Time": John Edgar Wideman's
Sent for You Yesterday

> Now, I have returned to Homewood and have sort of settled in. I am trying to
> listen again. Fortunately, my people are being kind, compassionate, patient.
> They give me the benefit of the doubt. In spite of Thomas Wolfe, I can go home
> again.
>   —John Edgar Wideman, "Going Home"

> You stopped marching and started dancing because this was the edge, the very
> moment you knew you'd made it home one more time.
>   —John Edgar Wideman, *The Homewood Trilogy*

After publishing three highly acclaimed novels from 1967 to 1973
John Edgar Wideman remained silent for the next seven years. The
writer surfaced again in 1981 with a collection of stories, *Damballah*,
and a novel, *Hiding Place*. A third book, *Sent for You Yesterday*, appeared in 1983 and won the 1984 PEN/Faulkner Award. The three
books have been published both separately and together, as *The
Homewood Trilogy*.[9] By the author's own account all three were written simultaneously and do not progress chronologically from book
to book. The reader might look for stylistic progression instead: "By
the time I'd published the first two books in this sequence, I had
discovered and refined the narrative voice which creates the third
book" (*Homewood*, vii). Given the constraints of the present study,
my discussion will focus on this third book, which is, in some ways,
a synthesis of the first two as well as an independent entity. An
occasional connection between this novel and one of the other books
in the trilogy might be warranted, however, to assist us in making a
point. Such is the case when we explore the significance of the expression "one more time" in *Sent for You Yesterday*.

Toward the end of *Hiding Place* the "crazy and evil" matriarch of
Homewood, Mother Bess, says to herself: "Because once was
enough. Once was one time too many to watch people sing the blues
and die. Once was enough to listen and then have it all go away and
have nothing but silence. Once and then you got to say good-bye say
yes I'm hiding, yes I'm scared but what you know about it?" (341).
This passage captures the relationship between the blues and the
reality of black life. The blues *is* the black folk; as an integral part of
an oppressed culture, this musical form expresses and to some extent
alleviates the suffering endured by that culture. It was the blues, as

LeRoi Jones (Amiri Baraka) and others claim, that converted Africans into African Americans (*Blues People*, xii). From Bess's experience black Americans come into the world, sing the blues, and die. When one is deprived of the blues—since Bess had lost her blues-singing husband and her only child—one becomes defensive and afraid.

To counter her fears Bess lives alone in the dilapidated house on Bruston Hill, where her ancestor, the runaway slave Sybela Owens,[10] first planted her roots in the Pittsburgh community of Homewood. When "family" catches up with her in the form of a young man running from the law she refuses to help. Tommy confronts her with his own insight: "Thought you was cool at first. . . . Cold cool and even though I thought about busting your head and staying here anyway I was digging you. Digging the cool. Cause that's me. I been trying to stay cool all my life" (336). The admission of fear and the recognition of "cool" as a masking posture of nonengagement revive both young and old.

When Tommy is finally killed by the police, Bess finds the courage to leave her hiding place in order to tell Tommy's story to the townspeople. From the defensive "once was enough" she has found the strength to venture out "one more time" (a prevalent refrain in *Sent for You Yesterday*). The common bond is the blues. At one point Bess finds Tommy wrapped in a blanket, whistling the blues "like her man whistled" (341). This imaginative connection is enough for her to regain her humanity. The acceptance of her role as *griot*, or storyteller, affirms traditional African American culture and the tenacity of the black community. Thus, a gap of three generations is bridged with the African Americans' "native" language. Blues music also permeates *Sent for You Yesterday* in narrative form, style, and theme: it offers a narrative voice that pulls individuals into the larger community. Before investigating this point, however, it is important first to place the making of *Homewood Trilogy* in its proper context.

The resolution of *Hiding Place* mirrors the author's own position in relation to his hometown, the real-life Homewood. Wideman attributes his compassionate philosophy of life to his heritage: "My grandfather's favorite statement was 'give them the benefit of the doubt!' That argues for a kind of longer, slower look at people and situations. . . . That might be the most valuable inheritance I have" ("Going Home," 55). Wideman also credits the Homewood community of his childhood with giving him "the benefit of the doubt" (see first epigraph). This specifically refers to his "turnaround" as a writer. After a fast-paced, brilliant career as a Rhodes scholar at Oxford University, a basketball star, a university professor, and an accomplished novelist, Wideman paused to take stock. He realized that his success in the larger culture had moved him away from the values of his natal community. Being educated at elite institutions meant that "you get a value system imposed on you": "You don't just guess what the best is: people tell you what the best is" ("Going Home," 44).

Given this imposed value system, Wideman, in spite of his artistic talents, experienced the confusion of being a "black" writer in a white world:

> And my ambition still is to write as well as anybody has ever written. . . . I am sure now that for a long time I didn't know what really counted—what would really count as legitimate subject matter, legitimate language, for such an enterprise. To write the very best, didn't you have to cheat a little, didn't you have to "transcend Blackness"? Didn't you have to ground yourself in an experience that was outside . . . Homewood? (44)

This honest statement reflects a major concern of writers with ethnic backgrounds. When European American culture is the norm and other cultures are "substandard," wanting to write the best would imply turning one's back on one's ethnic culture. For literature to ring true, however, the writer cannot deny a large part of him- or herself or the community in which this self was nurtured. Wideman's experience as an upwardly mobile individual who became an unwitting assimilationist had direct bearing on his art.

Critics praised the earlier novels from a specific viewpoint. In contrast to the politically oriented Black Arts movement of the 1960s, Wideman was identified with the experimental literature of the American canon. According to Wilfred Samuels, "His intricate style . . . —coupled with the absence of a focus on racial or cultural experience—brought him immediate attention from critics who felt he had successfully established himself in a vein of contemporary American, rather than Afro-American, fiction." This identification contributed to Robert Bone's judgment that Wideman was "perhaps the most gifted black novelist of his generation" (qtd. in Samuels,

"John Edgar Wideman," 272). From the days when African American literature was used to show that black people were also human[11] to the early 1970s with Wideman's first literary productions, critical perspectives regarding ethnic writings have not evolved a great deal. It appears that, if an ethnic writer can imitate, duplicate, or even surpass the norms set by the Western Tradition, then he or she is to be embraced as an "American," which, in earlier days, was equivalent to being human.

The fast, competitive environment of superstardom was not conducive to taking a "longer, slower look." When the writer took stock, then, he realized he had missed something: "By 1973, I'd published three critically acclaimed novels. It was hard to admit to myself that I'd just begun learning how to write; that whole regions of my experience, the core of the language and culture that nurtured me had been barely touched by my writing up to that point" (*Homewood*, vi). Fortunately, though, Wideman had acquired an invaluable habit in his meteoric rise: "I didn't know what the hell was going on. It was best to keep quiet and sort of check it out before I exposed my game. The insider/outsider nature of my experience made me a listener" ("Going Home," 52). After reconnecting with his hometown he spent the next seven years reading black literature and *listening* to his people.

Homewood Trilogy is the product of a writer's return to his ethnic culture. The extent of Wideman's turnaround as a writer is especially noticeable in his use of language. Whereas the early works utilize the literary frame to legitimize black speech,[12] this is no longer the case since the publication of *Hiding Place* and *Damballah*. In a 1977 article, "Defining the Black Voice in Fiction," Wideman discusses the practice of framing black speech in American literature. "The frame implies a linguistic hierarchy," he notes, and this value judgment in language becomes the privileging of "one version of reality over others" (81). He goes on to argue that, while "pidgin" or "dialect" are accurate descriptions of black speech in earlier American literature, the terms are no longer accurate today. Contemporary African American literature has its own literary language, says Wideman, which is a creole forged out of the black oral tradition and American literary models. It is this language that makes the urban ghetto of Homewood real in our imaginations.

Just as Mother Bess comes down from her hill to tell Tommy's story, Wideman descends from his former intellectual heights to tell the story of Homewood.[13] *Sent for You Yesterday* is basically a fictionalized account of three generations of Homewood residents, covering the actual years 1934 to 1970. The narrative focuses on two families, the Frenches and the Tates. The "I" narrator, Doot, weaves in and out of the narrative as an omniscient eye. He can project backward in time (e.g., "I am not born yet") to tell the story of his grandparents, John and Freeda French, and their son, Carl. Then he can move forward up to and beyond his own birth within the family's history. While Doot's voice serves as a unifying device in a complex, multi-layered narrative, it is unobtrusive. Often, with its vivid characterization and its skillful handling of sophisticated literary techniques, the story seems to tell itself. More accurately, several generations of Homewood residents contribute to the narrative in a communal chorus (through barroom gossip, for example) while individuals mull over specific memories from various perspectives.

Sent for You Yesterday is a successful marriage of Eurocentric traditions—from the eighteenth-century English novel *Tristram Shandy* to Faulkner's Yoknapatawpha saga—and black oral and literary traditions. Fluid time, in the modernist style, is offset by a fixed setting: the one block of row houses on Cassina Way "teeming with life." Although the narrator might not have lived in the house on Cassina, he is connected to the past through the oral tradition of storytelling: "The stories of Cassina Way sit like that. Timeless, intimidating, fragile" (448). The narrator's feelings toward these stories are introduced by the book's epigraph, which begins with "Past lives live in us, through us." Through group memory and the creative imagination the narrator is able to bear witness to the joys and tragedies of his people. As the embodiment of a culture's collective unconscious, he serves as a connecting link that makes the past blend into the present. Wideman sustains this sense of continuity by patterning the narrative after the blues.

The narrator's very name, Doot, is a scat sound uttered by Carl's albino friend, Brother Tate. Having abandoned speech altogether after the death of his son Junebug, Brother expresses himself through motion, gesture, and nonverbal sounds such as scat singing. By naming Carl's nephew Doot, Brother is in effect identifying the boy's role as "blues singer," or storyteller, for his people. Viewing the narrative structure of the novel from a blues/jazz music perspective helps us better understand its difference from traditional European American narratives.

Houston Baker provides an eloquent description of the blues: "Rather than a rigidly personalized form, the blues offer a phylo-genetic recapitulation—a nonlinear, freely associative, nonsequential meditation—of species experience. What emerges is not a filled subject, but an anonymous (nameless) voice issuing from the black (w)hole" (*Blues, Ideology, and Afro-American Literature*, 5). The qualities emphasized here are freedom ("freely associative") and collectivity ("phylogenetic," which refers to the historical development of a racial group, and "the black [w]hole"). When applied to Wideman's novel Baker's description suggests a starting point for interpretation. The narrator in the novel is "not a filled subject," meaning that his individual personality is not what counts in the blues tradition. We do not really know Doot as we know the other characters. Rather, he is "an anonymous (nameless) voice" telling the black people's collective story. Thus, the name Doot is "anonymous" in that it claims the individual for the oral tradition. This treatment of narrative voice—in which the individual serves the community—is very different from having an Ishmael or a Huck as narrator.

The literary frame disappears in *Sent for You Yesterday*, then, as a result of the blues vernacular running through the narrative. "Standard" and "nonstandard" English are so intertwined that there is no clear demarcation between one and the other. Wideman accomplishes this by attributing a type of empathetic identification to his characters.[14] Shadows (Brother is Carl's "shadow"), projective dreams (one character dreams he is someone else), mirror images, shared rhythms of song and dance—these and other elements in the novel suggest the elimination of boundaries between the self and other. As one critic puts it: "The linking goes beyond the need of the author for artistic unity to the emotional need of the characters for each other. . . . The result is that the reader apprehends the characters as an interlinked group, which is the way in which Doot views them in his own memory" (Bennion, "Shape of Memory," 144). These highly subjective connections create the ambience of an interdependent community. Since Doot is a member of the community, albeit a community that has disintegrated by his generation, his narrative language easily changes registers as he transforms himself from one character into the next.

In the first pages of the text a paragraph begins with "I hear the door slam behind Carl . . . " (362–63). The word *hear* indicates that Doot has made an imaginative leap back to his uncle's childhood. The next sentence—"My grandmother cringes because she's told him a thousand times not to run outdoors like a wild Indian, not to bust through doors like a hog out its pen . . . "—switches the narrative to Freeda French's folksy register. At this point there is still Doot the narrator and "she," the character he is telling about. By the third sentence, however, Doot has disappeared: "Miss Pollard hears it." Now the hearer, who offers a new narrative point of view, is a neighbor of the Frenches. Having transcended time by projecting himself into a scene from the past, Doot is no longer needed. Instead, we get a firsthand account of the Frenches's activities from a habitual window watcher. This narrative strategy enables Wideman to retain the immediacy and directness of oral speech patterns. When Miss Pollard reflects on the albino ("He's a peculiar one. Looking and acting"), we get thought fragmentation—a typical modernist technique—*and* the appropriate linguistic register of an oldtime resident of Homewood.

Finding creative ways to utilize vernacular in literary form is an objective that Wideman shares with other ethnic writers. Even so, that the novel under discussion is "Afrocentric" rather than "Eurocentric" in its mode of discourse does not automatically mean that Wideman is advocating communal values.[15] To determine where Wideman stands on the issue of individualism and community we must examine what he says in addition to how he says it.

"Sent for you yesterday, and here you come today" is the blues refrain of an old Jimmy Rushing tune. Is the title of the novel suggesting that it is too late for the black community as a viable culture? In a somewhat nostalgic tirade the now aged Lucy Tate tells Carl, "I love you more than any man, but the old Homewood people taught me you don't have to give up" (522). Carl and his generation, says the feisty Lucy, allowed the community to disintegrate. "We got scared and gave up too easy and now it's gone." In fiction, of course, what a character proclaims is often offset by other elements to generate alternative meanings. While the surface reality—that Homewood is now an urban ghetto—seems bleak, the writer's artistic vision reaches beneath the surface to challenge this reality. In various ways throughout the text Wideman inserts alternatives to the message of doom in the expression "sent for you yesterday."

Fear immobilizes and causes one to retreat from life, as in *Hiding Place*. It takes a conscious act of will to transcend one's fears and, in spite of them, relate to others. From his own experience as a writer, Wideman has learned that "Afro-American culture is conservative; and it gives you a chance to go back" ("Black Writer," 28). In the third volume of the trilogy the author explores this conviction in varying degrees of complexity. In his treatment of the piano player Albert Wilkes, for example, the theme of return is double-edged: it all depends on how one perceives oneself in relation to the group. On a communal level the memory of Albert's music is an integral part of Homewood. The music is timeless, mystical ("A moody correspondence between what his fingers shape and what happens to the sky, the stars, the moon" [397]). Through it Homewood residents are united into one entity ("The good old days when Albert be playing and Homewood hanging on every note" [404]).

From the perspective of the community, then, Albert belongs. This point is narrated through interior monologue. After a seven-year absence running from the law Albert returns to Homewood and his piano playing. His best friend, John French, thinks: "Like he never left. Like he got a brother . . . and that brother could hang around in Homewood and save Albert's place till Albert gets back" (406). While the community and John French view the piano player one way, however, Albert has different ideas about himself. Basically, he has a chip on his shoulder. "Your black head ain't made for no satin pillow," his father used to say as he hit him "upside the head" (407). Albert's reaction to a background of deprivation and violence is to sleep with a rich white woman in "acres of satin." The consequence of his rash behavior is, of course, death.

According to John French, Albert does what he wants and listens to no one. Simply returning to one's community, then, does not guarantee survival: a man must take responsibility for himself and others. Albert returns to Homewood, but he behaves like the isolated individualist he had always been. Wideman conveys Albert's alienation through an analogy with his music. While people in the community hear affirmation in Albert's notes, Albert himself is fixated on the silence in between the notes:

> One more time. Somebody had named the notes, but nobody had named the silence between the notes. The emptiness, the space waiting for him that night seven years ago. Nobody ever would name it because it was emptiness and silence and the notes they named, the notes he played were just a way of tipping across it, of pretending you knew where you were, where you were going. (392)

Wideman's treatment of the blues theme is a combination of opposites: both joy and pathos, group participation and individual isolation. After all, one could relate to a heritage of suffering singly or in a collective sense. Although Albert understands and expresses the blues through his music, as an isolated individual he is unable to transcend his self-destructive course of "acting a fool"—"Running wild. Come and go like you please" (400). He is, in Freeda French's idiom, "trouble."

In contrast, despite the humiliating work conditions and excessive drinking, John French is sustained by the love of his family and, by extension, his community. By pairing John and Albert, the author presents two alternative ways of being a black man. In thinking over Albert's question "How come you a family man?" John flashes on an image of his little girl "when he caught her planted like a flower in his boots, in that polka-dot dress Freeda had made" (400). The tender memory, which Wideman develops into some of the most touching writing in the novel, leads John to conclude "what else you gon do but . . . be a family man" (401). The repetition of these words in various forms through John's reverie staunchly affirms familial and communal values. From this character's point of view just thinking about his wife and child conjures so many positive memories that he has no choice but to be a "family man." By ending part 1 ("The Return of Albert Wilkes") of the three-part novel on a note of family solidarity and the profound love between husband and wife, the implied author is making a statement about traditional values and the soul of Homewood.

In the novel's three-generation alignment of the artist-as-outsider characters, from Albert to Brother to Doot, there is also an indirect message of salvation through community. After Albert is shot down by the police his piano-playing skills are reincarnated in Brother. The progression from Albert to Brother is from a filled subject who is lost to a colorless, transparent, unfilled subject who knows himself. Using color as a metaphor for *barrier*, Wideman gives his albino character almost supernatural powers of empathy and compassion. The colorless, wordless Brother is a free spirit with the soul of an artist. According to Lucy Tate, "Brother picked the way he wanted to live. And how he wanted to die" (523). Since individuals in Homewood as well as in the larger racist, appearance-conscious American society are not ready for him, Brother performs an ultimate act of courage by committing suicide. Metaphorically, he "plays chicken" with trains, just as he and Carl used to do: "He wanted to play the game one more time. He wanted to teach it to Junebug. The scare game on the tracks. He needed to teach his son to play so Junebug never be afraid of anything again. Because they [the community] were all afraid. All of them and him too" (505).

Brother's suicide is an individual choice made in the spirit of sharing. The implied author suggests this interpretation by having those close to Brother, namely Carl and Lucy, view the death as an act of love. In the novel Brother's legacy is symbolically passed on to the next generation through Doot. As Brother's surrogate son (Doot reminds Brother of the son he had lost), Doot learns the lesson of courage, love, and continuity. This is manifested in two ways. First, Doot has absorbed the story of Homewood and is assuming the role of *griot* for his people. Second, Doot is helping to revitalize the community's black culture by learning to dance. The novel ends on a tentative note of communal rejuvenation: "I'm on my feet and Lucy says, *Go boy* and Carl says, *Get it on, Doot*. Everybody joining in now. All the voices. I'm reaching for them and letting them go. Lucy waves. I'm on my own feet. Learning to stand, to walk, learning to dance" (531).

The phrase *one more time* attains its full significance with Doot. Although Albert Wilkes was not able to relate to the naming of his music, through the example of Brother, Doot recognizes the affirmation in the idea of doing something "one more time." Right before Doot gets up to dance in the finale Lucy remembers the tune that Doot had danced to as a child. It was "Sent for you yesterday, and

here you come today." From the title of the novel to this ending the
story has come full circle. A blues complaint of "too late" can now
be interpreted as "better late than never." Doot's understanding and
appreciation of black culture make his "com[ing] today" a positive
act. As the artist of the new generation, Doot embodies the promise
that Homewood will rise again.

For the master's tools will never dismantle the master's house.
                                             —Audre Lorde, *Sister Outsider*

Audre Lorde's gift to all oppressed peoples is the insight that not
only is community necessary, but it must also be forged by those
outside the "master's" structure *without* buying into the master's construct. This requires "learning how to stand alone, unpopular and
sometimes reviled, and how to make common cause with those others identified as outside the structures in order to define and seek a
world in which we can all flourish" (*Sister Outsider*, 112). Lorde's use
of *alone* and *common* in the same breath, along with an earlier statement that "without community there is no liberation," corroborates
what Walker, Wideman, and others mean by *community building*. To
attain freedom from oppression one must be strong enough to reject
the crutches offered by the master that keep one down. The master's tools, however, are seductive. As Trinh Minh-ha points out in
her essay on "difference," even as formidable a thinker as Virginia
Woolf fell into the trap of explaining why there was no female
Shakespeare in Shakespeare's day (*Woman, Native, Other*, 85). Thus,
Woolf used up valuable time embroiled in the "master's concerns"
(Lorde, *Sister Outsider*, 113). The literary career of one contemporary
African American writer, Ernest Gaines, exemplifies Lorde's pre-
cepts. Given space limitations, the present discussion will focus on
the trope of "the master's house" as it is explored in one story in the
collection *Bloodline* (1968) and in the 1983 novel *A Gathering of Old
Men*.

    To reviewers and critics alike Ernest Gaines's sense of commu-
nity—his affinity with the Louisiana plantation locale near Baton
Rouge—is unmistakable in his works. As one reviewer puts it, "The
lives of Gaines's men and women are shaped by fields, dirt roads,

plantation quarters, and the natural elements of dust, heat, and rain" (Forkner, "Ernest J. Gaines," 1430). Gaines himself has said that he needs to return to his former stomping grounds periodically "not only [to be] with the people, but to be with the land" ("This Louisiana Thing," 39). Alice Walker, whose own Southern black background enables her to relate to Gaines, states, "The community he feels with them [Southern black people] . . . goes deeper than pride" (qtd. in "Gaines," 200). The five stories in *Bloodline* reflect the writer's sense of place in terms of scene, characterization, language, and point of view. The first-person narratives, with their particular blend of vernacular speech (coming at the crossroads of, as Gaines says, "English, Creole, Cajun, and Black" [qtd. in Rowell, "Quarters," 148]), capture the oral richness of the "quarters" community in the deep South, which, according to Charles Rowell, "continued into the 1970s" (149). The stories should be read aloud in the oral storytelling tradition of sitting around the campfire after the day's work is done. Gaines—himself a descendant of slaves—demonstrates, through his characterization and narrative technique, cultural assumptions that stand fully outside the master('s) narrative.

"Bloodline," the longest story in the collection, plays out the master-slave relationship to its logical absurdity. In both theme and plot line the work offers an insider look at the remnants of the "peculiar institution." As the story opens, the narrator, Felix, and his female counterpart, 'Malia—two septuagenarians who have spent a lifetime on the plantation working for the Laurents—are indirectly running the show. The master, Frank Laurent, is an ailing man whose paternalistic notions of "the white man's burden" force him to hang on to the plantation, where generations of "freed" slaves still reside. The delicate balance between Frank and his "niggers" is threatened when Copper, a mulatto son of Frank's deceased brother, shows up after many years to "demand his birthright." The tragicomedy revolves around unsuccessful efforts to make Copper enter through the back door at Master Frank's summons. An additional complicating factor is that Copper is the nephew of *both* Frank and 'Malia. The Laurent side of his blood is credited with cruelty and violence, traits inherited from his father. As 'Malia confesses to Felix, "Copper scares me" (191).

Thus, as the symbol of a new day, Copper's "contaminated" bloodline, his self-proclaimed "army of one," and his threat to "bathe this whole plantation in blood" (217) when he returns all fall short of the ideal. By utilizing a character like Copper as the harbinger of change, Gaines seems to have little confidence in shirking off the master's tools. Frank's favorite line, "I didn't make the rules," indicates that both whites and blacks on the plantation are trapped by the former slavery system. "You the authority" is Felix's tongue-in-cheek response whenever Frank childishly asserts his power. Part of the stagnation implied in the text is that both master and slave play their respective roles too well. The technique used to convey this impression also contributes to the story's humor. As the narrator, Felix explains to us, the audience, the nuances of the master's words and actions as well as his own responses to them. These dramatic "asides" give the black man the upper hand; they also show, however, that the game has been going on from the beginning of slavery and is likely to continue, since, as Frank says, *he* is not about to change the rules.

"Do you know how old these rules are? They're older than me, than you, than this entire place. . . . And I—an invalid—am I supposed to change them all?" (188). By arguing that "the system is bigger than all of us," people like Frank manage to retain their privilege and maintain the status quo. The implied author in the text critiques this position, even as he would agree with what Frank states more than once—that no single individual can effect radical change. How Frank, as a white man, exhibits his racism and bad faith, however, is in not advancing to the next step: the fact that, collectively, they, black and white, *can* overthrow the system of oppression in the South.

As a critique of individualistic thinking, "Bloodline" illustrates *why* the master—as Frank tends to think of himself—is trapped in the master's role. His own race has power and wealth but maintains only a superficial community, while, with his *real* family, 'Malia and Felix, he must play an interminable role to avoid crossing the color line. In the story the potential for a new community is lodged in the love and respect that people like 'Malia and Felix demonstrate toward others. When, for example, someone tells Felix that Copper had beaten up two blacks, Felix thinks to himself: "Only it hadn't darted my mind that one human being would do that to two more of his own kind" (178). 'Malia's values are also intact. When Frank calls Felix a "traitor," 'Malia intercedes: "Is that any way to talk to Felix? Who you got beside me and Felix, Mr. Frank? Who?" (184). Caught offguard for a moment, Frank says, "Nobody."

In the novel *A Gathering of Old Men* Gaines manages to conjure an army to stand up to the white man. This "army," however, is not comprised of Copper's bloodthirsty lynch mob. Instead, it is an army of old folks from the quarters—decent people like Felix and 'Malia—who come together to "stand up" for the first time in their lives by each claiming that he murdered the white man. Once again Gaines's flair for high (melo)drama and his sense of humor jointly couch the serious message in the text. The shootout at the end of the novel, in cowboy-and-Indian style, serves as comic relief for the hidden tensions in the story. From "Bloodline" to *A Gathering of Old Men,* one might say that Gaines has found an imaginative way to dismantle the master's house without the master's tools. He does this by making the master a headstrong young white woman who, unlike the ailing Frank, is willing to do anything to "protect" her surrogate black parent (the courageous Mathu)—even confessing to a murder she did not commit. Just when Candy's altruism begins to stir the reader's disbelief, Gaines pulls us back to the realities of human character. While Candy's love for Mathu and protective feelings toward the black people on her land seem genuine, she is not above using power and money to make people mind her; that is, she still wields the tools of the master.

To deconstruct the power relationship between Candy and Mathu the text reverses the master-slave roles by exposing the willful child in Candy. Toward the end of the novel, when the old men call a meeting without their "protector," Candy threatens to disown them. At this point the interaction between Mathu and her reveals that, despite her self-identified "noblesse oblige" role toward her tenants, she is actually the child and Mathu the adult (173–77). This point is important since the infantilization of slaves has been one of the master's tools. That the young woman has had considerable power is evident when one character, Clatoo, says, "But we don't want you there this time," and the narrator continues: "That stopped her. Nobody talked to Candy like that—black or white—and specially not black" (173). The fact that now *all* the black men symbolically "talk to Candy like that," including Mathu, indicates that the slaves have finally thrown off their shackles. Removing Candy from the scene here makes an especially strong statement. While the men's treatment of Candy can be called sexist (her fiancé picks her up and tosses her in her own car), it is not without provocation on her part. More important, the significance of this scene is not simply in the humiliation of a strong-willed woman but, rather, the necessary giving up of the master's tools by the black men.

The community initiated by these newly liberated old men—a connection based on their common history of oppression and the desire to fight back—is not perfect, to be sure. For one thing none of these men even considers inviting the women along. There seems to be a clear demarcation of gender roles in the text; this could be attributed to traditional Southern socialization as well as to Gaines's specific objective of writing about black male liberation. The use of a young white woman to embody the master's power suggests a stereotyping of the inconsequential female with a large ego—a laughable stock character (her loyalty to Mathu might redeem her, though). That the black men are all old and, therefore, have nothing more to lose makes their stand seem a "feeble" revolution. It is spiritual strength, however, that the novel is portraying. The sense of solidarity in "a gathering of old men" conveys the message that it is never too late to take a stand. Moreover, it offers an alternative to the assumption that one has to stand alone. Mathu acknowledges that the support he received from the men changed him. He is no longer a bitter, "hardhearted old man" (182) who hated the others for their cowardice and who saw himself as a loner. The men's banding together also encourages Charlie, the real killer, to return for his punishment. "A nigger boy run and run and run," he says, "But a man come back. I'm a man" (187). Ernest Gaines's fiction reclaims the positive meaning of *manhood* in valuing courage, self-respect, and community.

On the issue of coming together in a common cause one of the most effective writers, Toni Morrison, states in an interview: "The gap between Africa and America . . . the living and the dead . . . the past and the present does not exist. It's bridged for us by our assuming responsibility for people no one's ever assumed responsibility for" ("In the Realm," 5). With these words Morrison articulates the communal ethic that makes her 1988 Pulitzer Prize winner, *Beloved*, a bridge connecting the "sixty million and more" Africans who "never even made it into slavery" (Clemons, "Gravestone," 75) with our sense of humanity.

Although critics have studied the work from a variety of angles, the textual tension between individualism and community raises many interesting issues, which the present study will only briefly consider here. In a 1988 interview entitled "In the Realm of Responsibility" Morrison shares her fascination with a moral dilemma that seems especially compelling for women:

> The story [Beloved] seemed to me to yield up a persistent struggle by women, Black women, in negotiating something very difficult. The whole problem was trying to do two things: to love something bigger than yourself, to nurture something; and also not to sabotage yourself, not to murder yourself. (6)

In this statement Morrison seems to be saying that the ability to bear children, and the all-consuming emotional commitment that motherhood implies, renders women especially vulnerable to the conflicting claims of the communal (as the nurturer of others) and the individual (as the nurturer of oneself).

In *Beloved* the story of a runaway slave's killing of her child is tested against large moral issues. The sociohistorical context of slavery might enable us to view Sethe's act as affirmative in that, in the face of dehumanization, a slave woman claims her humanity by assuming the right to "protect" her child from evil. Through Sethe's conversation with Paul D—her lover and the spiritual healer in the novel—we derive a different interpretation. Sethe's description of her feelings for her children is a curious mixture of self-assertion and broad humanity: "It was a kind of selfishness I never knew nothing about before. It felt good. Good and right. I was big, Paul D, and deep and wide and when I stretched out my arm all my children could get in between. I was *that* wide" (162). What Morrison explores here is double-edged: first, there is the danger of turning a communal instinct (maternal love) into a self-serving one due to the lack of opportunities for (slave) women to experience the self in other ways; second, in merging the self with her children and believing that she and they are one and the same so that she has the *right* to kill her child, Sethe can be viewed as no longer human. According to Morrison, "She almost steps over into what she was terrified of being regarded as, which is an animal" ("In the Realm," 6). This is what Paul D implies when he says, "You got two feet, Sethe, not four" (*Beloved*, 165). In other words Sethe's "thick love," which causes her to lose perspective and to assume the power of determining another human being's life (Paul D describes this as "This here new Sethe didn't know where the world stopped and she began" [164]), dehumanizes her even as she is asserting her humanity. While Paul D understands that being able to love "deep and wide" means that one is truly free, he is not willing to cross the line and have this freedom encroach on the freedom of another human being.

From the perspective of the Cincinnati black community Sethe's transgression is her "arrogance" ("Was her head a bit too high? Her back a little too straight? Probably" [152]) in believing that she is an individual who has to answer to no one. To her neighbors Sethe's newfound individualistic attitude means that she cannot be trusted in the community. Since she has upset the delicate balance between her sense of self and her communal responsibilities, she is left to her own devices without the community's help or support. The "re-memory" that she undergoes after the appearance of Paul D as well as the battles in (house) 124 among Sethe, Beloved, and Denver are all necessary confrontations for Sethe to regain her humanity, to understand that she is part of a larger whole dating back to the first Africans abducted into slavery. Hence, the murdered child must return and hold her accountable,[16] and the collective memory of slavery and the Middle Passage must be passed on.

When Sethe's daughter Denver finally decides to leave 124 and go to the neighbors for help, this is described in the text as "She would have to leave the yard; step off the edge of the world, leave the two [Sethe and Beloved] behind and go ask somebody for help" (243). Referring back to Paul D's comment about Sethe's not knowing where the world stopped and she began, this allusion serves a bridging function between the real world, which the women had shut out, and the isolated, self-absorbed world of 124. At this point the all-consuming "love" between Beloved and Sethe, in which the insatiable Beloved is now the parent and Sethe is the devoted child, is extremely self-destructive. Sethe's "deep and wide" love for her children has become a trap, which, as Morrison states in an earlier quote, is acting to "sabotage" and "murder" the self. Excessive maternal love, then, can be harmful to one's health. An excessive sense of self, however, also leads to trouble.

The recognition of one's humanity in common with others seems to be the resolution offered in the text. Not only do the women in the community turn out to save Sethe at the end, but Paul D reinforces Sethe's self-worth by saying, "You your best thing, Sethe" (273). The type of community that *Beloved* advocates is having faith in oneself, without arrogance or pride, and being willing to share this strength with others. The simple statement regarding Paul D, that "he wants to put his story next to hers" (273), suggests a communal way of being based on equality and the passing on of a story that the oppressors do not want passed on.

Chapter 4

Native American Writers

In discussing Indian ritual time and mythic space,[1] the Native American writer and critic Paula Gunn Allen concludes that T. S. Eliot's *Four Quartets* (1944) tries to enter a state of timelessness but accomplishes this only intellectually. She says, "This [poem] makes you contemplate, or makes you reflect, but it does not make you dance. And what an Indian knows is that when you are in that mythic space, you *dance*" ("MELUS Interview," 23). This original observation suggests a specific worldview, a mode of being to which a non-Indian writer like Eliot is an outsider.[2] The Native American novels *House Made of Dawn* by N. Scott Momaday and *Ceremony* by Leslie Marmon Silko, on the other hand, attain a sense of mythic space through their ritual structures. When we ask, "What is an Indian novel?" what comes to mind is a narrative structure drawn not only from the Eurocentric written culture but also from the Indian oral tradition of storytelling.

The writers discussed in this chapter are vital to the cultural renewal and unification of Native American peoples since the 1960s. According to Vine Deloria, Jr., there are "some 315 distinct tribal communities" left in the United States (*Custer Died*, 20). From this perspective, Silko (Laguna Pueblo "mixed blood") and Momaday (Kiowa who has lived among the Navajo and the Jemez) present but two versions of "Indianness." As more writers are gaining recognition (Kenneth Lincoln notes "the 'new' field of teaching American Indian literature" [*Native American Renaissance*, 9]), however, some basic affinities can be identified among various Indian nations. Allen is especially helpful in expressing Indian beliefs that are non-Eurocentric in values and orientation. In a sense contemporary Native American writers are transmitting a communal voice through a variety of literature, which includes poetry, poetic prose, and critical essays.

Perhaps due to their historical position as the indigenous population in this country with an identifiable set of traditions and an inherited place and language, Native Americans are often strong advocates of communal values. Through their literature one gets the sense that these values are crucial to their survival as a people. No matter how isolated protagonists like Momaday's Abel or Silko's Tayo might be, there is always a sense of collectivity—like an ongoing chant—in the narratives. In the minds of contemporary Indian writers, at least, the "social rather than individualistic" nature of oral culture must be retained in print (Ong, "Oral Culture," 145). The spirit of continuity and community is expressed even in critical studies, as witnessed in Arnold Krupat's 1985 book title, *For Those Who Come After*.

In Deloria's "Indian manifesto," *Custer Died for Your Sins* (1969), there is the message that it is *our* turn to tell the story. In response to the call Silko not only rewrites Momaday's novel in some ways (after all, it is all part of the same story—and the story belongs to everyone),[3] but she also "updates" traditional myths with one of her own. Halfway through *Ceremony* we learn from Betonie the medicine man that it was Indian witchery that invented the white people. A magician tells a story, and, as he talks, the story begins to happen. The white people, says the witch,

> *see no life*
> *When they look*
> *they see only objects.*
>
> . . .
>
> *They fear*
> *They fear the world.*
> *They destroy what they fear.*
> *They fear themselves.*

(142)

With this tour de force of artistic invention Silko incorporates the "enemy" into Indian mythology as part of the larger whole. Even though the witch's creation counters the Indians' traditional worldview, it is still an Indian product. Not only does this turn the tables on those who persist in talking about what whites do *to* Indians, but it also neutralizes the Indians' fear of whites ("They want us to believe all evil resides with white people"). This particularly ethnic literary strategy of countering oppression is cathartic. Of course, Silko's witchery story has had some critics up in arms.

During a panel discussion on *Ceremony* (Sands, *Special Symposium Issue*, 63–70) an academic from the audience complained that "all American Indian novels seem to condemn the white race in their curing ceremonies, incorporating us into Indian sickness" (69). A panelist (Larry Evers) responded that the scholar was reading Silko literally (expecting a "blueprint for social change") and missing the humor (Silko had said that the witchery story was "one of the most outrageous things she thought up"). When we read Silko's and Momaday's novels we must realize once again that we are dealing with artistic constructs. The ethnicity of the writer or the work does not transform creative fiction into prescriptive blueprints. When asked about the Indianness of contemporary Indian fiction, for example, Momaday replies:

> The reflection of the Indian world in *House Made of Dawn* is of course a matter of literary considerations, and it is important on that level. But there is a distinction to be made between the Indian world and the Indian world reflected in literature. As a writer, it is the reflection, the appearance that matters to me . . . as an Indian it is the reality that matters. The one thing is negotiable by definition; the other is indeed exclusive. ("MELUS Interview," 72)

Despite our desire to read Native American literature as ethnography, we must remember that Silko and Momaday are, above all, creative artists.

"Running after Evil": N. Scott Momaday's *House Made of Dawn*

> He was running, and under his breath he began to sing. There was no sound, and he had no voice; he had only the words of a song. And he went running on the rise of the song. *House made of pollen, house made of dawn. Qtsedaba.*
> —N. Scott Momaday, *House Made of Dawn*

N. Scott Momaday's first novel was published in 1968 and awarded the Pulitzer Prize in 1969. This unexpected event marks a "renais-

sance" in Native American literature,[4] which, as one user of the term
defines it, "is a written renewal of oral traditions translated into
Western literary forms" (Lincoln, *Native American Renaissance*, 8). A
major phenomenon of the 1960s was the banding together of native
peoples in a new pan-Indian consciousness. According to Kenneth
Lincoln, "These days, the center of a country or city powwow may
be one Indian drum of 'All Nations'" (9). In this spirit of ethnic pride
Momaday serves as a unifying force and role model for younger
writers. As Joseph Bruchac, an Abenaki Indian writer and editor,
points out:

> it opened the eyes of a new generation of Native American writ-
> ers. They read the novel and heard the deeper message of its
> powerful writing: a person caught between cultures can, despite
> the deepest of problems, find a way to survive, a road which
> circles out of the past, "The House Made of Dawn," and ends in
> understanding. (Qtd. in M. Harris and Aguero, *Gift of Tongues*,
> 200)

Pulitzer Prizes, however, do not ensure favorable critical reception or accurate readings. Apparently, the author's cultural background presented formidable obstacles. The Jemez Pueblo, Navajo,
and Kiowa cultures portrayed in the novel—all parts of Momaday's
background—had some critics stumped at the outset (Schubnell, *N.
Scott Momaday*, 96–99). The book's own publisher came up with a
description of the novel that sounded like a grade-B movie script.
According to Matthias Schubnell, Momaday's biographer, while
some reviewers did their homework and wrote informed critiques,
others exhibited a complete lack of comprehension: "Some of the less
favorable reviews were marred by their writers' lack of understanding, racial bias, or inability to see the novel as something more than
a social statement" (98). Inevitably, at least one reviewer suggested
that the prize was a token, that Momaday's novel was "a pet instead
of a work of art" (99). Complaining that the novel's structure was
complex, abstract, obscure, and ambiguous and its mood nostalgic,
sentimental, bleak, and pessimistic, patronizing critics dismissed the
work out of hand.

Given that *House Made of Dawn* combines the oral tradition of
Indian cultures with modernist literary techniques, the novel's new-

ness was bound to confuse critics at first. After all, a Eurocentric tradition provided the only framework for critics trained in the American school system. Furthermore, in the past two decades several scholars have persisted in misreading and, consequently, undervaluing the novel. One major offender is the novelist and critic Charles Larson. In the first and one of the few book-length studies of Indian literatures to date, *American Indian Fiction* (1978), Larson exhibits severe cultural limitations in his analysis of Momaday's novel. The critic's misinterpretations, from the significance of the albino to Abel's supposed suicide, reflect an inability to transcend Eurocentric cultural assumptions and meet the ethnic writer halfway. As a result, Larson indicts Momaday as well as other Native American writers through this myopic lens:

> I would speculate, too, that some of these novelists have written themselves into a quasi no-man's-land from which there is no escape. This appears to be true of N. Scott Momaday, whose publications since *House Made of Dawn* have been marred by a kind of repetitive preciousness and pretentiousness, indicating that Momaday has become trapped in a literary holding pattern (or a kind of circle, to use an image from his novel) from which it is impossible to move forward or backward. With a vision as bleak as his, one wonders whether Momaday can write another novel about the Native American without making a complete reversal and thereby undermining the validity of his earlier work. (167–68)

Other insults aside, from Larson's point of view Momaday's primary offense is his "bleak vision." Apparently, pessimism is unbecoming for Native American writers, and Momaday is the most pessimistic of the lot. How does the critic come up with this conclusion? The eighteen pages he devotes to *House Made of Dawn* seek to prove, beyond the shadow of a doubt, that Abel commits suicide by ritually running to his death. By periodically reminding us of the novel's "overriding images of death and destruction" (87) and the "ubiquitous images of death, sickness, and pain" (90), Larson believes he has clinched the "bleak vision" argument. This evidence enables him to portray Momaday as a man fixated on his past—a disaffected Indian preoccupied with his "dying race" (93). The prose works published after the novel, the memoirs *The Way to Rainy Mountain* (1969) and *The Names* (1976), are thus "repetitive," "precious," and "pretentious," since they display the same self-indulgence. Larson continues: "Reading any one of these volumes is a frightening experience since in each one of them Momaday has created a painful image of his self: a man in search of his roots. I would further suggest that Momaday has yet to solve the dilemma of his own identity" (94). In this strange quote Larson's negative judgment of Momaday reveals a strong bias. It is a matter of shame, Larson seems to be saying— even a "frightening experience"—for an adult to seek his roots. Obviously, the critic implies, this is regressive and weak. What is more, the seeker has not succeeded, which is doubly unforgivable. Embedded in this criticism are the assumptions that the rest of us are sure of our identities and that issues of identity are an individual responsibility that should not be exposed to public view—especially when they are "painful" to see. Larson's position, or pose, is that of the rugged individualist: tough, callous, self-sufficient.

In direct response to Larson, the present discussion will focus on the significance of the "running after evil" image in *House Made of Dawn*. Does the mysterious running image framing the novel encourage an interpretation of nihilism and despair? As the central image in the text, what does Abel's ritual run convey in terms of individualism and community? Do answers to either of these questions reveal the author as a self-indulgent and ineffective writer? Before we can address specific points in the text we must first understand the broader context of the issues involved. This requires a few words about "tribalism," the alienated hero, the power of language, and "achronological" time as these issues relate to Momaday's art.

As a "renaissance" novel, *House Made of Dawn* crosses the old with the new, the oral tradition of the author's Native American background with the Eurocentric literary tradition in America.[5] While the writer's literary training is stylistically apparent in the novel, the narrative point of view is primarily Indian. In terms of the present thesis this means that, as individuals from the Native American community have been saying for years, the individualist ideology of contemporary Eurocentric culture is problematic for Indians. The concept of tribalism is above all communal. Writers who identify with Indian cultures, as Momaday does, seem to have a built-in sense of tribalism. Lincoln describes this phenomenon:

Grounded Indian literature is tribal; its fulcrum is a sense of relatedness. To Indians tribe means family, not just bloodlines but extended family, clan, community, ceremonial exchanges with nature, and an animate regard for all creation as sensible and powerful. . . . Tribe means the basics of human community shared, lean to fat, a catalyst to the creation of common bonds against suffering. (*Native American Renaissance*, 8)

When Momaday says in an interview that "Abel reflects his ethnic experience in virtually everything he does. . . . He is recognizably Indian" ("MELUS Interview," 68), he is referring to Abel's embedded tribalism. The discrepancy between "white" and "Indian" beliefs revolves around the issue of individualism versus community. As one scholar states the case, "If these novels [the six Indian ones in his study] assert a trans-individual tribal identity, it is not surprising that whites should overlook the phenomenon. Whites have long overlooked tribalism, preferring to project onto Indians their own individualistic fantasies" (Bevis, "Native American Novels," 594). It is this self-projection that prevents scholars like Larson from seeing the pattern of individual and communal healing in Momaday's fiction.

Numerous scholars have noted that there seems to be an abundance of alienated individuals in the American literary canon.[6] Usually, these characters have no viable alternatives to their isolated state. As a composite of young men the author had known in postwar Jemez Pueblo ("An appalling number of them are dead; they died young, and they died violent deaths" Momaday wrote in a letter [qtd. in Schubnell, *N. Scott Momaday*, 102]), Abel seems another alienated hero bent on self-destruction. By incorporating the Navajo Night Chant ceremonial structure into the novel, however, and by presenting Indian culture as a viable alternative for the protagonist, Momaday manages to break the pattern in his art. The American Adam motif is reversed. Rather than lighting out for the territories to (re)invent oneself, the hero triumphs through reconnecting with elements of life that are, in Black Elk's lovely phrase, "old like hills, like stars" (qtd. in Lincoln, *Native American Renaissance*, 21).

Reconnection, however, does not mean nostalgia or sentimentality; neither does it mean denial of the present. As this examination of Momaday's novel will show, from the Indian point of view the past *is* the present: time is fluid and eternal. Due to the Indians' all-encompassing vision of the world, the escape motif of the American romance novel cannot be applied to a work like *House Made of Dawn*.[7] When everything is viewed as a part of the whole there is no possibility of, and no need to, escape from the past. An individual's identity is equated with the totality of experience—past, present, and future. The severing of human ties at any level results in disharmony and illness. As one scholar puts it: "A culture believing that power corrupts, naturally encourages dissent. A culture believing that power is benign, naturally respects its elders" (Bevis, "Native American Novels," 589). Critics who attribute nostalgia or "running from the self" to Momaday's protagonist are missing this point.

Oral cultures place primary importance on the ability to articulate experience. If an event—something we first perceive with our senses—can be put into words, it can be incorporated into our lives. Momaday is fond of narrating one aspect of Kiowa history ("Man," 104–5). On 13 November 1833 there occurred an explosion of meteors. This cosmic event was entered into Kiowa calendars as "the year the stars fell." By giving the historical event meaning in the imagination—by naming it and making it into a story—the Kiowa were able to endure everything that happened to them thereafter. Language makes meaning possible, and finding symbolic meaning in things seemingly beyond one's control ensures human survival. Through language the mythic mind finds a reason for being. The philosopher Ernst Cassirer explains the primacy of language for indigenous cultures as follows:

> Indeed, it is the Word, it is language, that really reveals to man that world which is closer to him than any world of natural objects and touches his weal and woe more directly than physical nature. For it is language that makes his existence in a *community* possible; and only in society, in relation to a "Thee," can his subjectivity assert itself as a "Me." (*Language and Myth*, 61)

When Momaday says, in a convocation address published in 1975 as "The Man Made of Words," that "an Indian is an idea which a given man has of himself" (97) and "we are what we imagine" (103), he is making a connection between the imagination and language. Basically, language creates reality in our imagination. Without the verbal dimension we have no access to the world; in fact, the world does not exist, since we cannot imagine or visualize it. Momaday puts it this way: "Generally speaking, man has consummate being in language, and there only. The state of human *being* is an idea, an idea which man has of himself. Only when he is embodied in an idea, and the idea is realized in language, can man take possession of himself" (104). Because our very being is dependent on language, Indians believe that, when used properly, words have the power to heal.

As a verbal construct, *House Made of Dawn* is both a novel and a vehicle for healing. Knowledge of the Navajo Chantway practice enables Momaday to structure the narrative according to the ceremony of the Night Chant. When critics say that the novel is "complex" or "obscure" they are referring to this unfamiliar narrative structure as well as to style and content. At least two articles by Native American writers (based on published anthropological studies) describe the Chantway structure of Momaday's novel. Linda Hogan emphasizes the healing purpose of the Night Chant—"its oral use of poetic language as a healing power." Specifically, "The author, like the oral poet/singer, is 'he who puts together' a disconnected life through a step-by-step process of visualization" ("Who Puts Together," 172). In other words, the Navajos, like other Indian tribes, use language as medicine—as a powerful force that, when utilized ritualistically, can heal physical as well as psychological and spiritual ailments. The belief is that, as Hogan puts it, "those who understand the potential of words as accumulated energy, as visualization of the physical, can find balance and wholeness" (172). When we understand the novel in this context Abel's ritual run becomes the most life-affirming symbol in *House Made of Dawn*.

Paula Gunn Allen identifies specific rituals (there are approximately a dozen standard rituals in a Chantway) that are incorporated into the novel ("Bringing Home," 572). She emphasizes the experimental nature of healing by Chantway ceremonies. If one does not work, something else is tried. Thus, Abel undergoes seven years of trial and error before he finds the appropriate ceremony to heal him. In addition to the specific use of Navajo ceremonial structure in the text, Momaday also incorporates other elements from oral culture to narrate the story.

According to Allen, a major difference between the tribal novel and novels written *about* Indians is the attitude toward time. *Achro-*

nology is a word that Allen coined in reference to Momaday's writing. In pointing out that there are four narrative lines in *House Made of Dawn* that do not fit neatly together, she describes the Native American disregard for linear progression in time: "These people can actually think four stories at the same time. And they can do it simultaneously in their brain" ("MELUS Interview," 19). Allen calls the meandering form of this achronicity "wilderness structure." Applied to literature, this potentially new structural mode offers Native American writers the opportunity to affirm life through art. The conventional chronological narrative, on the other hand, can only prove negative for Indians: "And what you're going to have, when an Indian writes a chronological tale, is a tale of colonization and death. That's what's going to happen. Nothing else *can* happen to an Indian in a chronological time frame" (19). And nothing else *does* happen when the reader imposes a chronological reading on an achronological text. Hence, believing his own chronological construct, Larson is able to turn a story of ritual renewal into "a run toward death" (*American Indian Fiction*, 91). In using words such as *goal* and *toward*—linear concepts that are not part of the Indian ritual framework—the critic condemns Momaday's protagonist to oblivion.

When Momaday says in an interview, "I suspect that the Indian, even the contemporary Indian novelist or poet, has a different concept of history than has the non-Indian, and the so-called 'historical novel' is not congenial to that understanding" ("MELUS Interview," 67–68), he is corroborating Allen's point. "In a way," he goes on to say, "history for the Indian is an account in shorthand; it is an image, a pictograph." Like the Kiowa's "the year the stars fell," Indian history is event- and image-oriented rather than chronological. The term *historical progression* would be meaningless from such a point of view. The difference between Indian and white attitudes toward human history is blatantly apparent in the case of *Black Elk Speaks* (1932). Arnold Krupat makes the significant point that John Neihardt, who collaborated with Black Elk on the writing of the book, actually distorted the shaman's vision with his own agenda. The argument is that, while Black Elk told his story as an ongoing process with a view "to make the tree flower once more" for his people, Neihardt imposed his own white man's views of "civilization" and "progress" (history means the inevitable demise of Lakota lifeways) on the "autobiography" (*For Those Who Come After*, 128–34). Thus, what was

meant to be open-ended and hopeful became despairing and romanticized through Neihardt's collaboration. The lyrical conclusion of the
book is Neihardt's, not Black Elk's: " . . . for the nation's hoop is broken and scattered. There is no center any longer, and the sacred tree
is dead."

Stylistically, then, Momaday had to break out of Eurocentric literary conventions in order to tell an Indian story that did not end in
death. He had to author this story without "collaboration," since this
would leave the tale open to distortion. His experimentations in narrative structure and literary form have opened doors for Native
Americans who are now writing their own stories. To people who
have identified with oral cultures for so long writing can be intimidating. An assimilationist approach would be to digest Eurocentric literary techniques and insert a plot *about* Indians. For a *tribal* story to
become literature, however, the teller/writer must draw from the
Indian's traditional connection to the Word. Momaday's achronological narrative—the blending of Indian ritual structure with modern
fictional techniques such as stream of consciousness, flashbacks,
multiple points of view, time shifts, and interior monologue—demonstrates the potential power and versatility of language. As the
following discussion will show, *House Made of Dawn* offers, in form
as well as meaning, an alternative to the limitations of bourgeois
individualism.

The primary symbol in Indian mythology is the circle. The sacred
hoop used in Indian ceremonial rites represents wholeness and com-
pletion. Lincoln puts this succinctly:

> The circle remains a balanced form in motion, evincing unity
> among the people. It runs continuously, fusing endings and be-
> ginnings in history, so that time is projected as spatial curvature,
> rather than linear sequence. The circle lies equidistant from a still
> center, imaging equality among all things. It is unsegmented,
> symbolizing the shared necessities in tribal life. (*Native American
> Renaissance*, 89)

The circular structure in *House Made of Dawn* suggests unity and continuity. By showing Abel running at dawn in both the prologue and
the ending, Momaday creates the illusion of circularity. The novel
begins with the word *Dypaloh* and ends with *Qtsedaba*. This Jemez

Pueblo convention of beginning and ending a story conveys the impression that we are participating in an oral performance or a ceremonial ritual. The two words are needed artificially to signal cutoff points on a continuous circle. Simply by repeating an action—Abel running alone at dawn—Momaday succeeds in bypassing chronological time.

While the prologue and ending depict the same action, they are not identical. The opening paragraph of the prologue paints a primordial vision of the land: everything is visually described. We see Abel running, and we are told what Abel sees. This freeze-frame technique places the vision outside time by stopping the clock, rendering it eternal and universal. Abel is part of the landscape: "He seemed almost to be standing still, very little and alone" (7). Contrasting with this vision is the final run. This scene is described with physical sensations (pain, cold sweat, exhaustion), a break in action (he falls and gets up), and an additional act (he sings). If we keep in mind Linda Hogan's point about visualization in healing rituals, the meaning of the two parallel but not identical descriptions of Abel's run becomes apparent. The prologue presents, in capsule form, the visualization process necessary for healing. It equates Abel's story with the Navajo Night Chant. In other words, Abel is not only the protagonist in the contemporary story line but also a "patient" undergoing a healing ceremony. The mythic dimension that this implies warns against viewing him as a loser caught between two cultures. That Abel is running at the opening of the novel, that he is performing a ritual act, already contradicts such an interpretation.

At the end of the novel Abel's run is envisioned differently. Visualization is now conflated with willful action. Abel is no longer just a speck in the landscape. His broken body in tremendous pain, he pushes on until he is beyond physical sensations, until "he could see at last without having to think." There is no reason to run, the narrator tells us—meaning no goal to achieve, no trophy to win. Abel simply runs, sees, sings: he simply *is*. In this scene he has shifted from being a symbol to being a real-life individual who has chosen to rejoin the human race. The ritual chant he sings, "House made of pollen, house made of dawn," indicates that he now accepts the oneness of the universe and his part in it. Being cured means understanding the ritual run and participating in it as his grandfather had before him. Being cured means regaining his tribal identity.

Halfway through the novel, in "The Priest of the Sun" chapter, Abel is on the verge of death. Having received a severe beating from a sadistic policeman, he finds himself on a beach in Los Angeles at night, unable to move. While delirious, he has a vision:

> Men were running toward him. . . . The runners after evil ran as water runs, deep in the channel, in the way of least resistance, no resistance. His skin crawled with excitement; he was overcome with longing and loneliness, for suddenly he saw the crucial sense in their going, of old men in white leggings running after evil in the night. . . . They ran with great dignity and calm, not in the hope of anything, but hopelessly; neither in fear nor hatred nor despair of evil, but simply in recognition and with respect. Evil was. (96)

For the first time since his return from the war Abel connects with his people. This imaginative connection occurs when his defenses are down. Having hit bottom and in complete isolation, the meaning of one ritual—the symbolic run to clear the irrigation ditches and protect the harvest by warding off evil—penetrates his consciousness and signals his salvation. Like his final run for "no reason," the old men in his vision run "hopelessly." In Eurocentric tradition these terms suggest futility and failure. The same words from a tribal, ritualistic point of view, however, indicate success. Coming to terms with what *is*—without resistance, manipulation, or resentment—is the ultimate accomplishment. With this realization Abel is able to name his problem: "He had lost his place. He had been long ago at the center, had known where he was, had lost his way, had wandered to the end of the earth, was even now reeling on the edge of the void" (96). The "place" he had lost is his tribal identity. The loss, as Momaday suggests throughout the novel, is a loss of language.

Since his return to the Pueblo after the war, Abel has been "inarticulate." While everyone speaks English, the words that he has are no longer adequate—they are no longer "tribal" and therefore no longer connected to the land or the people. His sojourn in the white man's world has unvoiced him. He now suffers the frustration, the anguish, of not being able to sing or pray, or to verbalize his sensory impressions. Without language Abel is truly, in Tocqueville's phrase, "shut up in the solitude of his own heart" (*Democracy*, 508). Throughout the text the words *alone, loneliness,* and *longing* crop up periodically. The narrator carefully distinguishes between being alone or silent, which is a positive condition, and being lonely or inarticulate, which is extremely negative. In the epiphany passage quoted above Abel is "overcome with longing and loneliness" because he finds himself removed from the vitality of the community. He longs for connection, even if he does not realize this consciously, since he has lost the language to express communal values. The narrative conveys this point through emotive description and symbolic gesture: "Then suddenly he was overcome with a desperate loneliness, and he wanted to cry out. He looked toward the fields, but a low rise of the land lay before them. The town had settled away into the earth" (97).

In a scene of fewer than two pages, the author manages to name the problem and offer a solution. The images—the men running and Abel looking toward the fields—register their impact almost subliminally. Momaday's art has to be comprehended at the gut level as well as the cognitive one. In an astute observation Lincoln finds that James Welch and Momaday "countervoice each other": "Whereas Welch selects particular words in end-stopped, declarative sentences, Momaday gathers rhythms of phonemes and phrases to build a sense of the movements beneath exact renderings of things" (*Native American Renaissance*, 268 n.55). This point is significant when we realize how literal-minded and static some critics have been in reading Momaday. Regarding the short scene mentioned above, Larson, wholly insensitive to the rhythm and accumulative power of Momaday's prose, focuses on a sentence like "He wanted to die" (*House*, 92) out of its context, and thus concludes that Abel commits suicide.

Distorting language and losing the truth-value in words is a habit that Momaday attacks in the novel as a white culture phenomenon. In "The Priest of the Sun" chapter Tosamah gives a sermon contrasting white versus Indian attitudes toward the Word. "Old John was a white man," he preaches, "and the white man has his ways. . . . He talks about the Word. He talks through it and around it. . . . He adds and divides and multiplies the Word. And in all of this he subtracts the Truth" (87). Tosamah's grandmother, on the other hand, is a storyteller who respects and takes delight in language: "She had learned that in words and in language, and there only, she could have whole and consummate being" (88). This sentence resembles the one cited earlier from Momaday's nonfictional discourse ("Generally speaking, man has consummate being in language, and there only" ["Man," 104]) and thus suggests that Tosamah speaks for the author. The use of juxtaposition in this chapter, in which a splicing technique utilizes Tosamah's sermon on the Word to articulate Abel's inchoate state, effectively communicates the novel's theme on language. Basically, it is in white society that Abel loses his connection to the Word.

Momaday follows up this treatment of Abel's problem with a commentary by Abel's Navajo friend Ben Benally. From living and working in urban Los Angeles Ben has made the same observation about white versus Indian English: "And they can't help you because you don't know how to talk to them. They have a lot of *words*, and you know they mean something, but you don't know what, and your own words are no good because they're not the same; they're different, and they're the only words you've got" (144). In an interview Paula Gunn Allen says that she did not understand her own problem with language until she read Momaday's novel: "They [non-Laguna, non-Indian] speak a kind of English that is different from the one I learned as far as what certain phrases or words mean" ("MELUS Interview," 8). For a people who view the Word as sacred and whose very existence depends on the ability to express themselves through language, being denied verbal expression or not having the right words is equivalent to self- and communal annihilation. Momaday makes this point in his novel by having Abel finally realize the value of healing rituals and thereby regain his voice.

While Abel is inarticulate, he reacts violently to what he perceives as evil. Hence, he kills the albino, the "white" man (who is actually an Indian) as the personification of evil. Momaday has had to explain to readers that the albino represents an evil force, like the whiteness of the whale in *Moby-Dick* (Schubnell, *N. Scott Momaday*, 97). It is interesting that literary allusions are lost on critics when it comes to a novel by a Native American writer. Abel's resemblance to Melville's Billy Budd[8]—who is also inarticulate and kills the evil Claggart, just as Abel kills the albino—is often overlooked due to false cultural assumptions.

In an important essay Momaday indirectly makes the connection between the ritual killing and Abel's loss of language. Being able to imagine oneself through language is what keeps a human being moral: "An Indian is an idea which a given man has of himself. And it is a moral idea, for it accounts for the way in which he reacts to other men and to the world in general. And that idea, in order to be realized completely, has to be expressed" ("Man," 97).

Tribal rituals, as some scholars have pointed out, are cathartic (Schubnell, *N. Scott Momaday*, 115). Had Abel been able to participate in Pueblo ceremonials effectively, especially the mock violent ones like the Pecos Bull Dance and the Chicken Pull, he might not have killed the albino. The killing is the act of an individual who has lost contact with the tribal community. Hence, Abel reacts to the albino's advances in fear and violence. It is only after Ben teaches him the Navajo chants and prayers, thus helping him to regain his voice, that he learns to utilize his body in affirmation rather than destruction. By running after evil, then, Abel has shed his isolated individualism and reintegrated into the tribe. It is significant that Momaday does not show him running with the pack. In both the prologue and ending Abel is alone. As mentioned earlier, being alone is not the same as being isolated or lonely. Alone, in touch with the land, performing a tribal ritual—these clues point to the Indian concept of community, which is the totality of life. Abel has not "regressed" into the past of the Pueblo community; rather, he has incorporated positive tribal values into his individual consciousness. He is an individual who belongs to a community.

Abel is alone and alienated throughout much of the story, and the wasteland imagery and "bleakness" of the narrative reflect his isolation. Through his vague and inarticulate longing, however, the reader senses a better alternative beyond the knoll—in the fields or town that symbolize a sense of belonging. The full context of the novel suggests the communal values that Abel has lost the words to express. Furthermore, he has reached this condition because of his exposure to an alien, noncommunal culture in which individualism reigns. Even in this condition, however, he is not able to assert individualistic values and act accordingly. For an Indian man the loss of communal language leaves him with nothing: Abel is simply inarticulate.

Momaday once said in an interview, "You have heard the expression, 'white man speaks with forked tongue' . . . it seems to me to reach farther into basic perceptions than most of us would understand at first. It is, unwittingly or not, a sensitive commentary upon the way in which the Indian and the non-Indian look at language" ("MELUS Interview," 69). This observation stands as a much-needed admonition to those (like Larson) who insist on projecting a non-Indian frame of reference on Momaday's work.

Storytelling as Communal Survival: Leslie Marmon Silko's *Ceremony*

> They are all we have, you see,
> all we have to fight off
> illness and death.
>   . . .
> You don't have anything
> if you don't have the stories.
> —Leslie Marmon Silko, *Ceremony*

The publication of *Ceremony* in 1977 can be considered a milestone for Native American literature. After all, Leslie Silko's first novel had not been "midwived" or "mediated" by a white editor/coauthor—a practice, according to Mary Dearborn, that was common among ethnic women's works.[9] From what Dearborn terms a "slightly schizophrenic book" (*Pocahontas's Daughters*, 20)—Mourning Dove's mediated *Co-ge-we-a* (1927)—to Silko's *Ceremony* the Indian woman writer has come a long way. Scholars were so enthusiastic about the novel that the *American Indian Quarterly* promptly devoted a special symposium issue (February 1979) to its study. A key question for the panelists was: What is American Indian literature, and how do we go about critiquing it? Six essays covered specific aspects of the novel, including landscape, animals, memory, ritual, event structure, and circular design. Their composite picture presents a worldview in direct contrast to the assumptions of European American culture. It seems as if the unmediated Native American novel, from *House Made of Dawn* to *Ceremony*, is forcing us to redefine American culture and its modes of literary expression.

Even though *Ceremony* was written by Silko in her own voice, bibliographers and critics (Native Americans included) still question its authenticity on grounds of ethnicity (Silko is only a half-blood Indian and an academic to boot) and authorship (e.g., Is a person who writes down tribal stories an author?). Regarding Silko, Dear-

born states her position on the problematics of ethnic female authorship as follows: "In studying ethnic women's fiction, we need at
times to accept a collectivity of authorship seemingly antithetical to
literary study, to be alert to evidence of compromised authorship,
and to relax our standards and expectations of genre itself" (15). In
her grudging acceptance of Silko the author of this statement betrays
her elitist position. While a full critique of Dearborn's work is not
appropriate here, a brief examination of the above quote will illustrate how even a sympathetic critic can miss the mark when discussing ethnic literature.

By saying that collective authorship is "seemingly antithetical to
literary study,"[10] Dearborn equates literary study with individual
authorship. This reveals a specifically Eurocentric bias (since *ethnic
women's fiction* is considered the antithesis). Further, she ignores the
phenomenon of collectively authored texts from at least the *Iliad* on.
Given that her sole-authorship definition of *literary study* is the norm,
she seems to say, an occasional concession is necessary to incorporate
the quirks of ethnic women's fiction. To do this *we*, the "mainstream"
literary critics, might have to "relax our standards." In a full-length
study on gender and ethnicity the scholar manages to devalue ethnic
literature at the outset. Even if Dearborn's comments are valid for the
manipulated texts of "compromised authorship," they are certainly
misdirected when applied to Silko's novel. As we shall see, the "collectivity of authorship" in Silko's case cannot be equated with the
questionable authorship of mediated works. The sense of communal
authoring evident in *Ceremony* is a product of Silko's Indian worldview as realized through art.

The general attitude of Native American writers toward the concept of "authorship" differs sharply from that of European Americans. The word *author* stems from the Latin *augere*, which has the
double meaning of "to originate, create" and "to augment, increase."
According to Arnold Krupat, while Native Americans have retained
the idea of "augmentation" in their definition of authorship, the rise
of individualism in European American culture has caused this meaning to disappear from usage in white society (*For Those Who Come
After*, 10). Whether an author is viewed as an originator or an augmenter says a great deal about a culture's values. Eurocentric American society tends to remove the author from the cultural context:

In European and Euramerican culture, the rise of the author parallels the rise of the individual. Homologous with the bourgeois conceptualization of an opposition between the individual and society appears the corollary opposition between individual (private) and collective (public) production and composition. (Krupat, *For Those Who Come After*, 10)[11]

Native American cultures, on the other hand, view the individual as inseparable from the community. This perspective is apparent when we listen to their stories.

In examining six contemporary Native American novels and contrasting these with traditional American literature, William Bevis finds that, while leaving home is the basic premise for success in white literature, "homing in" represents success by Indian standards. Home means a society, a past, and a place: "In all six novels, the free individual without context is utterly lost. . . . Individuality is not even the scene of success or failure; it is nothing" ("Native American Novels," 591). Bevis contrasts this attitude to that in literature with "leaving" plots such as in Melville's *Moby-Dick* and Dreiser's *Sister Carrie*: "The individual advances, sometimes at all cost, with little or no regard for family, society, past, or place. The individual is the ultimate reality, hence individual consciousness is the medium, repository, and arbiter of knowledge" (582). When dealing with Native American literature, therefore, the reader must keep in mind the specific orientation of indigenous cultures. This different outlook is evidenced in the Indians' attitude toward the telling of stories.

Leslie Silko once stated in an interview, "Storytelling for Indians is like a natural resource. . . . I think it has to do with community, with growing up in certain kinds of communities as opposed to others" ("Stories," 18). The sharing of stories is, above all, a communal act: among other things it helps alleviate suffering by guarding against individual isolation. "I realize now how the telling at Laguna was meant to prevent the withdrawal and isolation at times like this," Silko says in a letter (qtd. in A. Wright, *Delicacy and Strength*, 69). From the rich diversity of her Laguna Pueblo culture she has learned to respect storytelling as an integral and necessary part of life. Her faith in the power of stories to heal and bind in a collective sense offers an alternative to Tocqueville's judgment of Americans as isolated individuals who "form the habit of thinking of themselves in isolation and imagine that their whole destiny is in their own hands" (*Democracy*, 508). The present analysis focuses on some specific ways in which *Ceremony* offers an American identity that sharply contrasts with the nineteenth-century Frenchman's image of the isolated, self-sufficient American.

By attributing the novel to the thoughts of the mythic creator Thought-Woman ("I'm telling you the story she is thinking," says the narrator), Silko identifies her authorial role as augmenter and transmitter, rather than originator. In the style of oral performances the teller of *Ceremony* is conveying a story that is traditional and, through her act of telling, also new and unique.[12] As Thought- or Spider Woman is creating the story by thinking and naming, Silko the teller is conveying, interpreting, and augmenting. This collaboration suggests both continuity and change—continuity, because stories coming from a mythical deity are part of the people's heritage, and change, since stories are contextualized and recreated with each telling (while the feeling of the story is retained). It also suggests collective as well as individual input: Thought-Woman creates on behalf of the community, and the teller adds his or her input to the narrative. The arrangement forgoes individual ownership of the text in the Eurocentric sense. At the outset of the novel, then, the author places herself within a communal context of shared authorship. The story belongs to everyone. This strategy not only makes a statement about communal values but also sets the stage for the prevalent use of myth in the narrative.

In *Ceremony* myths in the form of poems are scattered throughout the text, paralleling and augmenting the story line. These "time immemorial" stories from the Pueblo cultures serve as contextual backdrop for the contemporary prose narrative. This splicing technique simulates the atmosphere of storytelling—as if the reader were actually listening to and watching an oral performance. It effectively disabuses us of arbitrary separations such as past versus present, dream versus reality, and the animate versus the inanimate. In other words, with one un-novel-like stroke the author places us in a different reality, a view of the world that is cosmic and holistic rather than compartmentalized. What is more, the sense of cosmic order and need for balance is gradually elicited from the reader through the process of reading. As Silko once said of the participatory nature of oral performance: "The storytelling always includes the audience and the listeners, and, in fact, a great deal of the story is believed to be inside the listener, and the storyteller's role is to draw the story out of the listeners" ("Language," 57). This special teller-listener relationship, when translated into a literary framework, expands the parameters of fiction beyond the European American construct.

According to one critic, the beauty of Silko's art is that it gets us to "go along with the story" (Evers, "Response," 72). The author manages this through her deep understanding and successful application of the art of storytelling. The Pulitzer Prize poet James Wright makes the same point in a letter to Silko: "I don't think it's mere flattery to tell you that no living writer known to me so deeply grasps that truth [that the story must be told], and its significance, as you do" (qtd. in A. Wright, *Delicacy and Strength,* 22). While any narrative can be considered a story, in Silko's case the term *story* reaches beyond general usage to encompass an entire way of life. Thus, a people's stories are regarded as rituals that help the individual maintain balanced relationships with the environment. As such, stories are sacred and must be tended with infinite care. Silko's first novel effectively recruits the reader in the ceremonial process of storytelling.

The title of the novel encapsulates the spirit of the book. According to Paula Gunn Allen, "The purpose of a ceremony is integration: the individual is integrated, fused, with his fellows, the community of people is fused with that of the other kingdoms, and this larger communal group with the worlds beyond this one" ("Sacred Hoop," 119). In Indian cultures the term *community* extends beyond human society to include other life forms and other worlds. When one or more elements in the ecological system is out of balance a ceremony is necessary for reintegration. As a novel grounded in the Laguna Pueblo culture, *Ceremony* is itself a curing ceremony for anyone who works through it. Silko is not only telling the story but, shamanlike, she also facilitates healing through language and ritual. When the novel is viewed as a process rather than as a finite product it incorporates the reader into the text. The work becomes "accessible"—a quality that, according to the author, is the foremost criterion for good literature ("to make accessible perceptions that the people need," Silko says in an interview ["Stories," 22]). While Silko's idea of accessibility might seem farfetched to the uninitiated reader, cultural barriers are less intimidating when we understand the circular pattern of the narrative. Repetition, which is central to oral presentations, plays a significant role in structuring the text.

According to one critic, "It would be possible to begin reading the novel at almost any page and continue from there since the images are circular, related to one another by imaginative association" (Larson, *American Indian Fiction*, 152). This observation overstates the case, since *Ceremony* does have a chronological component: Tayo's cure advances by degrees and via specific spiritual and interpersonal encounters. That is, chronology enables Silko to convey a sense of change and reconnection over time. The use of recurrent imagery is, nevertheless, an important unifying technique. Adopting the seemingly random strategy of oral narrative, Silko structures the novel according to how the mind works through memory and associative chains. The erratic presentation of events reflects the hero's consciousness. Thus, the first part of the novel is fragmented with disjointed images of the Philippine jungles, Tayo's childhood with his "brother" Rocky and uncle Josiah, the hospital in Los Angeles, etc.—because Tayo can no longer make connections. He is at the mercy of memories that haunt him: "He could get no rest as long as the memories were tangled with the present" (6). His regret and guilt over the loss of loved ones impair his vision. Gradually, as Tayo undergoes healing rituals with the aid of medicine men Ku'oosh and Betonie, recurrent images become interwoven into a larger pattern and are no longer disconnected fragments. As we shall see, this narrative device almost imperceptibly moves the reader from an individualist to a communal frame of mind.

In support of Bevis's homing-in idea for Native American novels, *Ceremony* does present individuality as "nothing," as meaningless alone. Thematically, this is apparent in the parallel drawn between Tayo's illness, the six-year drought over Laguna Pueblo land, and the individualist outlook on life. The teller/critic shows how Tayo's suffering—the nausea, hallucinations, and nightmares—is a result of misinterpreting the nature of the world. Tayo believes that, because he had cursed the rain in the Philippine jungles, the Laguna land is drying up: "So he had prayed the rain away, and for the sixth year it was dry. . . . Wherever he looked, Tayo could see the consequences of his praying" (13). This simplistic cause-effect formulation, which is a major source of guilt, misses the larger context. He makes the mistake of translating the natural cycles of life and death to an indi-

vidual plane. In this state of mind he has grown to fear the interconnectedness of things in life. When he spots a little Japanese boy who
reminds him of Rocky, he "crie[s] at how the world ha[s] come un-
done, how thousands of miles, high ocean waves and green jungles
[can]not hold people in their place" (18). His efforts to keep everything separate and manageable only result in further entanglements.
By losing sight of the Indian belief that land, animals, and people are
all parts of the whole and have meaning only in relation to one
another, Tayo suffers from the pain of viewing himself in isolation.
The fragmented narrative structure reflects this breach in his Native
American psyche.

Basically, the world seems out of whack to Tayo and the other
war veterans because exposure to white culture has taught them to
erect artificial barriers. The range of reactions to this sense of alienation is represented by Tayo and Emo. While Tayo internalizes his
disorientation by taking it out on his own body, Emo externalizes his
loss of self through violence and hatred. Emo's bag of human teeth,
a war trophy, symbolizes the level of degradation possible among
younger generations of Indians. For the reader to understand how
bad things have become Silko juxtaposes Tayo's memory of deer
hunting with a contemporary bar scene. Both are presented as rituals.
In accordance with Indian beliefs the hunter must perform a series
of tasks to show love, respect, and appreciation for the deer's sacrifice. Tayo initiates the ritual by covering the dead animal's head with
his jacket. While Rocky scoffs at the gesture, Tayo's two uncles carry
on the ritual. The memory is sacred because Tayo had experienced
communion with the deer in its natural environment. There is no
indication that animals are inferior to humans and no false barrier
between two forms of life.

Within the text the deer hunt episode appears in the middle of
drunken reminiscences of the war. The barroom scene is also presented as a ritual. This narrative treatment establishes ironic contrast
between sacred Indian tradition and the profanity of alcohol, sex, and
violence: "They repeated the stories about good times in Oakland and
San Diego; they repeated them like long medicine chants, the beer
bottles pounding on the counter tops like drums" (44). The drunken
stories start with how well Indian soldiers were treated during the
war ("trying to bring back that old feeling, that feeling they belonged
to America") and ritually progress to hating the enemy ("they are to

that part of the ritual where they damn those yellow Jap bastards"). The narrative becomes short, choppy, relentless as a discharging semiautomatic: " 'We were the best. U.S. Army. We butchered every Jap we found' " (63). On the next page the third-person narrator reiterates Emo's words: "But he was the best; he was one of them. The best. United States Army" (64). The narrative point of view is clear. Through repetition and the switching of pronouns the implied author conveys her values. Emo's use of *we*, like the comraderie of drinking buddies, suggests a community in which bravado and self-contempt substitute for genuine sharing. The narrator ironically undercuts this false sense of community by reducing Emo's accomplishments to an individual status with the pronoun *he*.

In addition to the bar and hunting scenes in this part of the narrative, a myth is also introduced here that runs through the rest of the novel. Basically, it is a story about duty. Because the people subscribed to a Ck'o'yo medicine man's magic and neglected the mother corn altar, Corn Mother got angry and withdrew her beneficence. Hence, the plants and animals died, and the people starved. The myth reminds us that life is based on mutual respect and communal responsibility. By subscribing to false magic and neglecting their duties, the people ultimately hurt themselves. As a parallel story line to the story of Tayo, this myth presents in capsule form the theme of *Ceremony*. Traditional wisdom is used to enlighten the present in a continuously vital relationship. Josiah's words, a reminder from Tayo's past, make the point even more succinct: "The old people used to say that droughts happen when people forget, when people misbehave" (47). The world is out of whack, then, because humans are abusing their privileges in the natural order of things. A curing ceremony is thus necessary to purge this abuse and make the world whole again. In Tayo's troubled mind killing Emo—a personification of the evil that "witchery" has set loose upon the world—is the catharsis needed. It takes another two hundred pages of storytelling before Tayo is able to make the right connections and recognize killing as a part of the witchery.

The narrative structure of *Ceremony* is thus multilayered, with one "story" informing a second, and so on. If we pull together all the stories, we get a composite picture of *the* ceremony that is underway as we progress through the novel. When the ceremony that the

Navajo medicine man Betonie prescribes for Tayo is completed the protagonist's realization is also our own:

> He cried the relief he felt at finally seeing the pattern, the way all the stories fit together . . . to become the story that was still being told. He was not crazy; he had never been crazy. He had only seen and heard the world as it always was: no boundaries, only transitions through all distances and time. (258)

In attributing Tayo's sickness to a loss of perspective and its concomitant self-imposed isolation, Silko never resorts to absolutism. Tayo is both an individual *and* a part of the community in the larger sense of the word. His Native American sensibility hovers beneath the surface of his distorted psyche. The affinity with animals, insects, land, and sky suggests mythic qualities in his character. Tayo has retained a great deal of his communal memory through the teachings of his surrogate parent, Josiah. One way in which Silko inserts Laguna views into the narrative at the outset is by having memories of Josiah invade Tayo's confused consciousness:

> Tayo thought about animals then, horses and mules, and the way they drifted with the wind. Josiah said that only humans had to endure anything, because only humans resisted what they saw outside themselves. Animals did not resist. But they persisted, because they became part of the wind. (27)

Josiah's words reflect the collective wisdom of the people. Through them Tayo remains connected to Indian beliefs—even if tenuously at times.

According to Josiah, everything in nature is sacred. As Paula Gunn Allen explains, "We [Laguna Pueblo Indians] see all things as of equal value in the scheme of things, denying the qualities of opposition, dualism, and isolationism (separatism) that characterize non-Indian thought in the world" ("Sacred Hoop," 114). Tayo's cure and reintegration into Indian culture depends on the recognition of this fundamental viewpoint. Silko allows her protagonist to reconnect with the source of his Indianness through Betonie's cryptic prescription for a curing ceremony. Look for stars, spotted cattle, a mountain, and a woman, Betonie says. Appearing halfway through the novel, the shaman's ingredients for a successful cure also function as clues to a mystery story. This narrative strategy accomplishes several things: it captures our interest, makes us really work through the ceremony, and sets the stage for holistic imagery in contrast to the fragmented structure earlier in the novel.

As Tayo puts together the pieces of the puzzle, he begins to understand how things are interconnected. After he meets Betonie and the real ceremony begins certain relational words are repeated throughout the rest of the novel. Whereas the contemporary action in the first part of the novel, such as the barroom scene, is narrated in predominantly negative language (e.g., *nausea, crying, damning, entanglement*), the latter half repeatedly uses words like *balance, pattern, totality,* and *convergence*. A brief glance at the vocabulary in each part of the text would suggest that, for Tayo to get well, relationships must be seen as positive again. The entanglement imagery prevalent in descriptions of Tayo's sickness converts to visions of clarity and unity by the end of the ceremony: "He had arrived at a convergence of patterns; he could see them clearly now" (266).

When Tayo first encounters Betonie he resists the responsibility placed on his shoulders to help the people:

> There was something large and terrifying in the old man's words. He wanted to yell at the medicine man, to yell the things the white doctors had yelled at him—that he had to think only of himself, and not about the others, that he would never get well as long as he used words like "we" and "us." (132)

This individualistic point of view is identified with Tayo's distraught state. In the same paragraph, however, the narrator also says that Tayo knew better: "But he had known the answer all along. . . . His sickness was only part of something larger, and his cure would be found only in something great and inclusive of everything" (132). Tayo's communal side knows that, as Silko says, "one does not recover or get well by one's self, but it is together that we look after each other and take care of each other" ("Language," 59). Even this distinction between the communal and individual sides is a dualism uncharacteristic of Betonie's view but indicative of Tayo's malady.

In *Ceremony* telling the story is the individual's responsibility to the community. Ku'oosh, the first medicine man Tayo encounters, wants Tayo to tell his war story. The world is "fragile," says Ku'oosh, and to keep it intact one must guard the stories, for "that [is] the responsibility that went with being human." While this medicine man does not have the power to make Tayo well, he initiates the healing ceremony by reminding Tayo of his people's values: namely, that no one should or has to operate in isolation. An individual who acts on his own without considering others is not a model of success but has lost his way. When Ku'oosh says, "It is important to all of us. Not only for your sake, but for this fragile world" (37), and later, "I'm afraid of what will happen to all of us if you and the others don't get well" (39), he is expressing this fundamental value. When, at the end of the novel, Tayo shares his story with the people we know that he is cured and the community will survive.

As if in direct response to Josiah's statement that only humans resist what is outside themselves, Tayo finally comes to terms with the interconnectedness of life and no longer fears or resists personal loss. As one critic puts it, "He now acts, aware of his own spaciousness and unworried by the finitude of individuality. He moves into a world he knows is whole" (García, "Sense of Place," 42). This new understanding suggests that nothing is lost when the individual sees him- or herself as part of the whole, because memory lives on.

Ceremony can be viewed as an American writer's challenge to the cult of individualism in contemporary society. As an ethnic work, it offers a nonassimilationist perspective of American cultural diversity. It challenges the belief in "assujetissement," which is, according to Bevis, in citing Krupat's reference to Indian as-told-to autobiographies, "the adjustment of Indians as well as whites to the ruling mythology: individual advancement" ("Native American Novels," 617). What good are ceremonies against wars, bombs, and lies? Tayo demands at one point in the novel. Silko would say, they remind us that we are all in this together.

Tracks, the third of a series of novels by Louise Erdrich (a mixed-blood Chippewa from North Dakota), utilizes a dual narrative structure, which exemplifies well the communal versus individual theme of the present study. Before examining this aspect of the text some preliminary remarks are in order. That Erdrich and her husband, Michael Dorris, collaborate on virtually everything they publish is common knowledge from interviews, which they always seem to give jointly. To discuss any one of the three novels published under Erdrich's name to date, *Love Medicine* (1984), *The Beet Queen* (1986), and *Tracks* (1988), seems somewhat inadequate since the novels are interrelated and, according to Dorris, form parts of a quartet (Erdrich and Dorris, "An Interview," 89). Once again, Paula Gunn Allen's comment about tribal people's ability to think four stories simultaneously comes to mind. Writing four instead of three interconnected works seems especially appropriate from an Indian point of view, given that elements of nature generally come in fours. Dorris mentions that each novel has a central elemental symbol. In their publication order the first novel is water; the second, air; the third, earth; and the last, fire (92). The *form* attributed to these works—that they are "novels," parts of a quartet, etc.—is somewhat arbitrary, however, in that *Love Medicine*, at least, started as "disjointed little bits" with no master plan (89). As a storyteller and writer, Erdrich has a simple definition for her art: "Storytelling is having an audience waiting for the next word" (98). Thus, the artistic collaboration, the idea of four interrelated books, and the general expectation of telling a story to an audience (rather than putting words on a blank page) indicate that the identified author of *Tracks* operates in a communal mode.

The novel has two alternating narrators, Pauline Puyat and Gerry Nanapush, who tell the stories of several interrelated families in a twelve-year span from 1912 to 1924. It opens with Nanapush telling his granddaughter, Lulu, her family history, and throughout the work he is talking to Lulu. In this way Nanapush, the trickster figure from *Love Medicine*, doubles as community historian/storyteller. Pauline, on the other hand, speaks only for herself and speaks *to* no one. Instead, she is an eyewitness, in that her unattractiveness makes her unnoticed by those around her—giving her the power of invisibility. This enables her to spread gossip and cause harm to others.

In her first narration Pauline tells us that right before the plague, which wiped out entire tribes, she had left her family in order to assimilate into white society: "I saw through the eyes of the world outside of us. I would not speak our language" (14). Thus, the symbolic contrast between the two narrators is established early in the book. Nanapush, having saved Fleur Pillager's life and adopted her and her daughter, Lulu, as his "family," represents the communal voice in the story. Pauline, having abandoned her people before they died from the plague, represents the isolated individual voice. It is important to note that although each narrator can be considered an outsider in his or her way, only Nanapush's trickster/outsider role is sanctioned within the community. In contrast, Pauline's individualistic behavior—her materialistic values, her *not* helping Fleur during the rape, her malicious gossiping, etc.—has no legitimate place. Nanapush even warns us that Pauline tells lies to gain attention: "For while I was careful with my known facts, she was given to improving truth" (38). What we have here, then, is a traditionally "unreliable narrator" (after all, this is the job of the trickster) telling us that the *other* narrator is unreliable. If it were not for the clearly communal ethic found everywhere in the text, this narrative strategy might have backfired.

As trickster, Nanapush is privy to people's lives, and his pranks and sexual jokes are entertaining examples of tribal humor. In fact, the ribald banter between him and Margaret offers some of the liveliest dialogue in the novel (see, e.g., 48). While the one-upsmanship between these two old friends can get out of hand at times, the spirited way in which each opponent comes up with the next biting line indicates that both are enjoying the exchange. The game is not to exceed the other's level of endurance. Once Nanapush *does* go too far, and Margaret disappears for weeks. He tells us, "Without her presence, there was little to remind me what life was good for" (127). We are to understand, then, that the banter is one manifestation of love and support between two old people.

The trickster Nanapush is also used to expose Pauline's hypocrisy. From Pauline's own testimony we learn how she manipulates people. Having harmed Fleur in several ways, for example, Pauline shows up one day with a humble demeanor. When Fleur again gives her the benefit of the doubt she brags, "Fleur forgave me, left an unguarded spot to attack" (143). Thus, when Pauline "gets religion" and goes around doing penance to get close to God, Nanapush the trickster strikes. Knowing that the devout Pauline is practicing an especially difficult abstinence—that of relieving herself only twice a day—Nanapush gives her several cups of tea and then begins telling a story filled with water imagery. The narrator Pauline states: "In the old language there are a hundred ways to describe water and he used them all—its direction, color, source and volume" (149). With such torture Pauline is eventually forced to run for the outhouse and give up her opportunity for eternal life. Her prolonged narrative regarding her approaching saintliness is thus discredited in the text.

Nanapush is good for laughs, and he is also wise. Toward the end of the novel he offers an astute analysis of Fleur's downfall. Throughout the narrative Fleur's treatment of others, including Pauline, suggests that she holds communal values. After Margaret's "scalping" by attackers, for example, Fleur shaves her own head in solidarity with her mother-in-law. Her constant show of strength, however, takes its toll. Because Fleur had extraordinary powers (as the lone survivor of a bear clan), Nanapush explains, when her powers started to fail her she lost faith: "But in her bearing, as she rose and walked away from me, I saw the barrier of her obstinate pride had kept my words safely beyond belief. In her mind she was huge, she was endless. There was no room for the failures of anyone else" (178). The responsibility of being the last surviving Pillager, "the funnel of [the community's] history" (178), proves too great for one person to bear. The wisdom of the text may very well be found in Nanapush's assessment: "Power dies. . . . As soon as you rely on the possession it is gone. . . . I never made the mistake of thinking that I owned my own strength. . . . And so I never was alone in my failures" (177). As the community-oriented narrator/protagonist in *Tracks*, Nanapush teaches us a valuable lesson.

Many of the insights offered in Erdrich's novel regarding the dangers of possessiveness, greed, and self-aggrandizement can also be found in the popular 1972 book *Lame Deer: Seeker of Visions*. While the work is the Lakota Sioux medicine man John Lame Deer's story "as told to" the writer Richard Erdoes and has been categorized as "sociology," it seems more appropriate to consider it a collaborative artistic "memoir." In the 1991 edition of his anthology, *American Indian Literature*, Alan Velie includes this title under the heading "Memoirs." He warns us, though, to distinguish between such collaborative texts and memoirs written by Indians without collaboration (154). The example of John Neihardt's tampering with Black Elk's meaning has already been mentioned in this chapter, but it is important to note that *Lame Deer* came out forty years after *Black Elk Speaks*. In the time between the two texts, writers have become more sensitized to issues of distortion and misrepresentation. From Erdoes's epilogue it is also apparent that the two had an ongoing relationship over several years during which Erdoes was adopted by the Indians. This is a very different relationship from that between Black Elk and Neihardt. The idea of two like-minded individuals working on a joint text, with one utilizing the oral form and the other the written, should be easily accepted in our contemporary setting. The Erdrich/ Dorris collaboration, while "new" from a Eurocentric perspective, is certainly fitting to Native American practices. Given these considerations, I propose to examine *Lame Deer* as a literary production.

Above all, it is the narrative voice in the text that makes a strong case for viewing the Lame Deer/Erdoes collaboration as a carefully crafted, creative construct. The narrative persona is humorous, insistent, and earnest; he is also sarcastic and outrageous. In short, he resembles Nanapush the trickster in his attitude toward life. Such a memoir from a medicine man who had lived a full life ("A medicine man shouldn't be a saint. He should experience all the ups and downs . . . of his people" [79]) holds up a mirror to European American culture. The book specializes in making ironic observations that force readers to laugh at themselves even as they feel the sting of truth. The narrator, for example, shares a reservation joke: "What is cultural deprivation?" Answer: "Being an upper-middle-class white kid living in a split-level suburban home with a color TV" (121). When we read *Lame Deer* often those who laugh the loudest are these very same kids.[13]

The insights in the text are profound—far beyond the factual information one normally obtains from a sociological monograph. What makes *Lame Deer* appropriate for this study is that it is a concerted creative effort to promote community by drawing from the ongoing "religious" healing practices of a specific American Indian tribe. The selection of details, the repetition of leitmotifs, and the conscious construction of language makes this text not only a social document but also a work of art with a social message. In other words, it is oral literature written down and serves the function, as many tribal stories do, of teaching the audience a lesson through the art of storytelling.[14] The lesson is about modern European American society's desperate need for community—the need for taking a responsible attitude toward all living beings. "Let's roll up the world.

It needs it," says the wise narrator, who calls all of us an "endangered species" because we are destroying the earth.

While the text's message regarding communal responsibility is hardly new, it is filtered through a particular angle of vision that is at once unique to the narrative persona Lame Deer—in the *way* this persona expresses himself—and organic to the Lakota worldview. Thus, it carries an aura of conviction that is hard to resist. In its assumption that developing communal values is essential to all of our survival the text offers us a powerful expression with which to experience community. Lame Deer/Erdoes tell us that, when people are taking a sweat bath and someone is about to faint from the heat, he says, "All my relatives!" and the person nearest the entrance to the lodge will open the flap to let in cool air (14). These three simple words for summoning assistance from spiritual ancestors convey the extent to which community is a practiced way of life rather than an intellectual concept. The fact that a holy man from South Dakota and an ex-Viennese man born into the former Austro-Hungarian Empire can come together to write this book demonstrates that, indeed, we *are* all related (268).

In a collection of stories, *The Sun Is Not Merciful* (1985), by the Pawnee/Otoe Anna Lee Walters, key Native American practices are graphically illustrated in contemporary settings. The much anthologized opening story, "The Warriors," is an adult narrator's recollection of a very special man in her childhood, Uncle Ralph, who was already an anachronism in his day. As an "ancient Pawnee warrior" who lived for beauty and who still played his drum at powwows, Uncle Ralph was a tremendous influence on the narrator and her feisty younger sister. Communal values in the story are both overtly expressed through anecdotes and subtly alluded to through character interaction. The narrator tells us that she was more timid than her sister; therefore, she was more often a witness than a doer. This narrative posture enables simultaneous description and analysis. She says, for example, that one day she and Sister ventured out to the railroad tracks where hoboes lived. "Who's your people?" Sister asked a ragged man who crawled out of the weeds. The man, we are informed, was "about Uncle Ralph's age." When the man insisted that he did not have anyone, meaning any relatives, the little sister was bold enough to scream, "Oh yeah? You Indian ain't you? Ain't you? . . . We your people!" (16–17).

Apparently, the hobo Indian forgot that he had "people," so he was lost. We are left with an image of this lost soul, who was obviously floored by the little girl's conviction and vehemence, staring after them with "his topcoat and pink scarf flap[ping] in the wind" (17). The story then continues with how Uncle Ralph reprimanded the girls for going where they should not have gone. He took them by the hand, sat them on the steps, and, after a long silence, said, "I want to tell you all a story" (17). He then began a story about two rats who ran around everywhere and never did what they were told. "Sister, do I need to go on with this story?" he asked each child in turn. The answers were "No." In a couple of pages the implied author manages to convey central concepts about community and responsibility from within the Pawnee culture. In addition, she also manages to foreshadow Uncle Ralph's downfall by drawing a parallel between the uncle and the hobo through their approximate ages. When we learn that later Uncle Ralph himself had succumbed to alcohol and was living as a hobo, Sister's words echo in our minds: "We your people!"

The story is saved from the nostalgic stereotype of the "vanishing Indian" by showing the vitality of traditional Indian practices, such as childrearing, through the example of Uncle Ralph. Even though Uncle Ralph eventually lost the battle for beauty, the next generation—the children he influenced—will carry on the values he fought for. Like the lesson of *Lame Deer*, the purpose is to "pass it on."

In the story "The Laws" Native American laws are contrasted with European American ones. Two uncomprehending "laws," or white policemen, peripherally move in and out of the main story line and, right through to the end, never understand a thing about the "damn Indians." The reader is thus privy to an insider's view of how tribal law operates. When Sonny, a young man who, having been spoiled by a doting mother, gets completely out of hand and resorts to robbery and beating up the elderly, the tribal elders are called upon to punish and attempt to reform him. The mutual hostility between Indians and whites serves as the backdrop against which Sonny's punishment is measured. From the Indian side we have the grandmother's remark: "Those white laws can't smoke bunny rabbits out of the hills if they try" (100). According to the orange-haired cop, however, Indians "don't have no kind of rule, brought up lyin and cheatin all the time" (96). The stage is thus set for the dramatic confrontation.

The omniscient narrator explains that excessive individualism is punished within the tribe: "The tribe had been known to whip a man when he got too big for his britches, when he acted as if he alone lived in this world" (100). Where does the implied author stand in relation to this fact? There are several details in the text to indicate that she supports the tribal ways when they are not practiced irresponsibly. The seriousness of the people and High Water, the tribal leader, for example, shows that the community does not mete out justice frivolously: "The mood of the people was pensive as they remembered something they had witnessed thirty years earlier" (101). In addition, the hundreds of people on hand for the public beating are "all related to Sonny and each other in complex relationships" (102). After the whipping, in which Sonny is reduced to a bloody mess on the ground, "the people's eye glistened; tears streamed down their faces" (104). While this type of tribal law can also be found in works by other ethnic writers, such as in the "No Name Woman" chapter of Kingston's memoirs, it is not always depicted with such care and understanding. In Walters's hands tribal punishment seems a "gift" that hurts the people as much as it hurts the evildoer.

A public beating and three weeks in the hospital still do not do the trick. Sonny goes to High Water's house, thirsting for revenge. What finally breaks down Sonny's bravado is the care in High Water's voice. Once Sonny starts sobbing he loses all control. Not only that—"High Water cried with Sonny, too, as did High Water's old woman, hidden behind the door" (107). This empathetic crying is one of the best illustrations of a communal ethos. Lest the reader misinterprets such spontaneous feeling, Walters offers the clincher. "What are *you* crying for?" asks Sonny. "It's one of the laws, boy," High Water tells him. "We can't let none of our people cry alone" (107). The two patrolmen, who witness this scene from a distance, can only ask, "What in hell just went on?" We the readers know *exactly* what went on. If the "law" says that no one should be allowed to cry alone, then it is saying that the individual *is* the community and vice versa. In this respect, according to Anna Lee Walters's short stories, the law is a just one.

Chapter 5

Chicano/a Writers

An introduction to this section requires a clarification of terms. In the preface to *Occupied America* (1988), his major study on the history of Chicanos, Rodolfo Acuña points out that the word *Chicano* had been associated with working-class Mexicans (used by themselves as well as pejoratively by the middle class against them) until, in the radical movements of the 1960s, the term became politicized to reflect a new consciousness and group solidarity. The label *Hispanic*, on the other hand, was used in the early 1970s by the U.S. government to refer to Chicanos and Latin Americans. This is a misnomer, says Acuña, since Mexicans are not Spanish: "The choice of the designation 'Hispanic' represents a 180-degree about-face from use of the term 'Chicano.' It almost seems as if we learned nothing from the late 1960s and early 1970s" (ix–x). Acuña's distinction is crucial to the present study of literature by Americans of Mexican descent. Writers who call themselves Chicanos or Chicanas do so with some degree of historical and political awareness. Contemporary Chicano literature has a specific identity, which stems from and aligns itself with events of the 1960s.

The year 1965 has been used by scholars as the beginning of the "Chicano Movement" (J. Chávez, *Lost Land*, 134; Bruce-Novoa, *Chicano Authors*, vii). This is not quite accurate, since there had been a history of Mexican resistance against colonization of the present-day Southwest since at least the Mexican-American War of 1848. César Chávez's United Farm Workers' strike in 1965, however, with its accompanying Teatro Campesino started by Luis Váldez, initiated a series of events that corresponded with the protest mood of the 1960s. In 1969, for example, "over three thousand Chicanos met in Denver to draft *El Plan Espiritual de Aztlan* [sic], a series of resolutions leading to freedom from economic, social, and political oppression" (Fisher, *Third Woman*, 307). Thus, here I use *Movement* with the capital *M* to refer to this new phase of Chicano protest. A key literary text during this period, and one that reflects the Chicano-Mexicano oral tradition, is Rodolfo ("Corky") Gonzales's 1967 epic poem, *I Am Joaquín*. The first verse captures the mood of the times:

> I am Joaquín,
> lost in a world of confusion,
> caught up in the whirl of a gringo society,
> confused by the rules,
> scorned by attitudes,
> suppressed by manipulation,
> and destroyed by modern society.
> My fathers
>   have lost the economic battle
> and won
>   the struggle for cultural survival.
>   (Qtd. in Bassnett, "Bilingual Poetry," 139)

Using Gonzales's poem as a jumping-off place, we might think of both Tomás Rivera and Sandra Cisneros in relation to "the struggle for cultural survival."

Born into the Chicano migrant community of Crystal City, Texas, Rivera was twenty-eight when the Chicanos took control of the local government in 1963. According to a friend and colleague, "Today after years of turmoil, Chicanos and Anglos in Crystal City see each other as equals and there is a remarkable degree of social harmony" (A. Rodríguez, "Tomás Rivera," 78). Rivera's novel, . . . *y no se lo tragó la tierra* (1971; hereafter referred to as *tierra*), creatively documents the state of the workers prior to this turning point in history. Thus, as the friend proclaims, "*Tierra* is the radiography of a people" (81).

The migrant trail brought many Chicanos to the Midwest through the 1960s and into the early 1970s. The census count of 1970 reported that "eighty-three percent of the U.S.-born Chicano population had lived in Chicago for five years or more" (Acuña, *Occupied America*, 316). As part of the next generation after Rivera's migrant experience, Sandra Cisneros's background reflects this geographical relocation. Though not spelled out in her novel, *The House on Mango Street* (1985) takes place in an urban barrio of Chicago. Even with the differences in time and place between the two works, the Chicano heritage and identity—in terms of the mestizo combination of Indian and Spanish as well as present-day Mexican and Anglo-American cultures—are still assumed in both. This is not surprising since, historically, according to Acuña, "Neither distance nor the lack of sun diminished the Mexicans' nationalism and their ties to Texas or Mexico. The differences between Chicanos in the Midwest and Southwest were obvious. . . . The similarities were stronger" (315).

In examining Chicano/a texts in relation to the theme of community and individualism it is important to keep in mind the sociohistorical context from which the works stem. Time and geography, for example, help to account for the choice of language in each novel. While *tierra* is written in vernacular Chicano Spanish, reflecting the border reality of Rivera's childhood, *Mango Street* is written in vernacular English, reflecting the proximity of the barrio to Anglo society in the urban Midwest (although Cisneros herself observes that "Spanish syntax and word choice" tend to crop up in her English ["Writer's Notebook," 72]). Another major issue is the degree of awareness regarding gender oppression within each work. Rivera's novel certainly does not feature this topic, although critics have argued both ways on the subject.[1] Cisneros's text, on the other hand, deals specifically with female oppression and the need for liberation. This means that, while the communal ethos found in each work is grounded in the ethnic cultural experience, at this point in Chicano literary history it has been gender-identified to a greater or lesser extent. As more Chicano/as continue to produce quality works, however, critiques of patriarchal oppression will eventually result in literary models of community based on gender equality.

"A Ritual of Cleansing and a Prophecy": Tomás Rivera's *. . . y no se lo tragó la tierra/. . . and the earth did not devour him*

We are not alone
if we remember and
recollect our passions
through the years
the giving of hands and backs
"dale los hombros a tus hijos"
We are not alone
Our eyes still meet with the passion
of continuity and prophecy

—Tomás Rivera, "The Searchers"

His hands knew about the harvest,
tasted the laborer's sweat in the sweet
cantaloupes he sliced, knew how to use
laughter to remove stubborn roots
of bitter weeds: prejudice, indifference,
the boy from Crystal City, Texas
not a legend to be shelved
but a man whose *abrazos* still warm
us yet say, "Now you."

—Pat Mora, "Tomás Rivera"

In 1970 Tomás Rivera's novel *. . . y no se lo tragó la tierra* was awarded the first Quinto Sol Prize. This event inaugurated what has been known in the past twenty-odd years as a self-consciously "Chicano" literature. The 1971 publication of the work (published bilingually with Herminio Ríos-C.'s translation) identifies it as "a continuation of the past, a landmark in the present, and a point of departure into the future of [the Mexican American] literary tradition" (xv).[2] What makes the work a literary "landmark" is its correlation with the Chicano Movement of the 1960s: the novel is both a reflection of and a response to the culmination of a long history of resistance in the Mexican American Southwest. As one scholar puts it: "*tierra* registers and apprehends a new political consciousness which came into being during the late 1960s and early 1970s in the United States" (J. Saldívar, "Ideological," 103). That a mere seventy-odd pages of prose written in vernacular Spanish helped launch a new political, social, and economic movement in this country says a great deal about the conscious positioning of the Movement's leadership. If nothing else, the Quinto Sol publishers and readers were staking a claim for Chicano Spanish in the "American" literary canon. This position was radical indeed.

While Rivera's literary output (before his untimely death in 1984) is limited to a novel, essays, stories, and two books of poetry, the writer and educator has had a tremendous impact on the Chicano community.[3] A key factor in Rivera's renown is his formulation of and dedication to what he termed Chicano literature's "basic hunger for community." In the essay "Chicano Literature: The Establishment of Community" (1982) Rivera attributes key concepts of community to the majority of Chicano works published in the 1970s. According to the article, *community* means "place, values, personal relationships, and conversation" (12). In locating the literature among "folk wisdom," through which writers were able to give form to "a very disparate and amorphous nation or kindred group" (17), Rivera explains and defends the ideological and "utopian" projection of a Chicano communal ethos.[4] Within the scope of the present study this stated ideological position can serve as a guide to the artistic assumptions behind Rivera's seminal work. Before examining the text, however, it is important to examine two opposing critical views regarding Rivera's work that have a direct bearing on the present discussion.

A 1990 study on Chicano literature states in a footnote: "Rivera's work has had the good fortune of having been treated by exceptionally fine critics" (R. Saldívar, *Chicano Narrative*, 80). While I generally agree with this statement—especially since the novel *has* been amply analyzed by cultural "insiders"—I also find that a few questionable literary assessments by well-respected critics have gone unchallenged. This situation is noteworthy as it directly relates to my study of community in ethnic literatures. When a writer like Rivera is criticized for being *both* "too community-identified" (implying that he benefits from his communal stance) *and* "too individualistic" (implying that he has "sold out" the ethnic community),[5] the criteria by which we judge the ethnic literary text once again have to be called into question.

In his discussion of the canonization of Chicano literature since the early 1970s Juan Bruce-Novoa claims that texts that "end in positive affirmations of the Chicano community and its creative process" were instantly canonized (*Retrospace*, 136). Thus, the writers who fit the description in the early 1970s—Rivera, Rudolfo Anaya, and Rolando Hinojosa—became the "Chicano Big Three" (135) and enjoy a privileged status to the present day. It is this rigged system, says Bruce-Novoa, that caused Chicano critics to ignore writers like John Rechy "in favor of aesthetically inferior texts" (135). While the critic's assumption of a monolithic aesthetic standard for a fledgling literature might be questioned, his viewpoint on the issue of literary "universality" is even more problematic: "I wanted to go beyond the reductionist vision of our literature as political statement and find its human elements. . . . I wanted to demonstrate its universality" (168). By connecting the Big Three, however peripherally, to terms such as *aesthetically inferior* and *reductionist*, the critic's assessment of Rivera's novel seems to be based solely on the work's ethnic cultural ties. Thus, *tierra* is "too communal" to be considered "universal."

The opposite logic, that *tierra* is not communal enough, is reflected in a second critic's assessment of the work. The "problematic"
in Rivera's novel, says Juan Rodríguez, is its "false, nonprogressive
interpretation of Chicanos and Chicano reality" ("Problematic," 132).
Based on his reading of *tierra* as well as biographical details about the
author (namely, that he was a university chancellor), the critic concludes that Rivera was an assimilating, elitist intellectual who deni-
grated his people.

The two critiques taken together—one that attributes Rivera's
literary success to his fitting the mold of Chicano group solidarity and
the other faulting the writer for his individualistic assimilation into
the academic mainstream—seem to cancel each other out. If Rivera
was "canonized" for the communal ethic in his novel, as Bruce-
Novoa claims, then how could Rodríguez find a totally individualistic
ethic in the same novel? It seems odd to attribute two completely
opposite, mutually exclusive tendencies to a single work, especially
when these opposing qualities are simplistically formulated and tend
to move out of the realm of literature altogether.

When a work of art is inextricably connected with a cultural-
political movement, it is extremely difficult to separate the literary
text from the political agenda or the author from the text. To do the
work justice, however, critics must find valid ways of practicing literary criticism—despite or because of the unavoidable confusion.
Given the numerous positive statements (in both fictional and nonfictional writings) that Rivera made over the years about himself in
relation to his ethnic community, to conclude that the writer looked
down on his people once he became an educator or that he took a
self-serving stance in his fiction would seem to require substantial
proof. Within the parameters of informed literary criticism I believe
that critics should give writers the benefit of the doubt. This requires a critical approach that consults a variety of evidence before
drawing conclusions about the work of art and, by extension, about
the artist.

A point of departure for my analysis of Rivera's novel is the
question: What is Chicano literature? For many scholars the fact of
Chicanismo is embedded in its specific historical experience. Ramón
Saldívar's aforementioned study, for example, includes the following
statement: "For Chicano narrative, *history* is the subtext that we must
recover because history itself is the subject of its discourse. History

cannot be conceived as the mere 'background' or 'context' for this literature; rather, history turns out to be the decisive determinant of the form and content of the literature" (*Chicano Narrative*, 5). By equating Chicano literature with the history of the people, Saldívar is requiring a specific self-awareness and group identification on the part of the writer. In this sense a writer of Mexican American background who makes no connection with his or her ethnic history in the United States would not be producing "Chicano narratives."[6] This selective definition reflects a self-consciously forged literary identity, one that parallels the efforts of the Movement.

In line with this position was Rivera's personal experience. According to the writer, at age twelve he experienced an awakening when he met Bartolo, his hometown's itinerant poet: "I was filled with *alegría*. It was an exaltation brought on by the sudden sensation that my own life had relationships, that my own family had relationships, that the people I lived with had connections beyond those at the conscious level" ("Chicano Literature," 20). In the novel Bartolo is strategically placed in the Chicano oral tradition: "Recuerdo que una vez le dijo a la raza que leyeran los poemas en voz alta porque la voz era la semilla del amor en la oscuridad" (I recall that one time he told the people to read the poems out loud because the spoken word was the seed of love in the darkness) (95, 199). By giving voice to their people's history through the written word, says Rivera, poets experience a common bond. He identifies this as being "part of the same ritual," or, as he explains, "a bond that comes from a feeling of uniqueness, from a common set of beliefs, from a sense of destiny" ("Chicano Literature," 21).

In utilizing terms such as *ritual* and *prophecy*, Rivera identifies his own expectations for a specifically Chicano literature: he and other Chicano writers are engaged in a unique enterprise, that of recording "a fast-disappearing past—the conserving of past experiences, real or imagined, through articulation." By locating this group effort in the ritual act, he emphasizes the progressive and communal aspects of the enterprise. In this sense Chicano literature becomes "a ritual from which to derive and maintain a sense of humanity—a ritual of cleansing and a prophecy" ("Chicano Literature," 22). Rather than wallowing in nostalgia for an Edenic past, the ritual enhances life by projecting an optimistic future *through* communal memory. It is this definition of *ritual* that makes Chicano literature, in Rivera's words, a "fiesta of the living." Rivera's concept of group ritual provides the key to understanding the novel.

At this point in my study it is helpful to reiterate my primary assumption regarding the literary text. To avoid confusing a creative work that must be read as "fiction" with a nonfictional social document,[7] it is important to keep in mind that the "implied author" of *tierra* cannot be equated with Rivera, the man outside the text. The fictionalized implied author is an entity framed within the literary text and should be distinguished from the "historical author," who is responsible for the existence of the literary text. My view is that what the ethnic writer says outside the work of art can be used as a clue to the cultural assumptions embedded within the work. Nevertheless, although the present analysis consults these statements, I mean to use them only as a guide to Rivera's self-identified intention as a writer and/or as a cultural voice—not as the primary or sole evidence on how to interpret the text.

Consistently, the major concern in my study has been that which is revealed through the textual strategies of ethnic American fiction. My position in the Rivera debate is that *tierra*, as a self-consciously "Chicano" literary text situated within a specific ethnic culture, offers significant insights that present an alternative vision of North American society. As such, the novel has value over and beyond its origin as a founding document of the Chicano Movement and the subsequent tendency to canonize such works. To support this contention it is useful to take a closer look at the text itself. The following analysis focuses on critical elements that directly impact a communal-versus-individual reading of the novel.

The first thing one notices about . . . *y no se lo tragó la tierra* is its unconventional narrative structure. While modernist techniques come to mind for the European American reader, it is important *not* to equate Rivera's culturally-specific accomplishment with Faulkner's or Hemingway's literary innovations. Because of the Chicanos' specific social/historical/political experience in the United States, a person writing out of this cultural background would operate on assumptions quite different from those of Anglo-Americans. By examining the work's narrative structure, use of point of view, thematic treatment, characterization, and linguistic tensions, I will seek to locate as well as articulate the author's assumptions within the text.

Structurally, *tierra* is made up of a prologue, twelve main narratives (ranging from two to seven pages each), and an epilogue. Spaced in between these narratives are individual vignettes that serve as commentary on the preceding and/or following story. The twelve episodes loosely represent a year of labor in the migrant stream,[8] a year that in several ways reinforces the theme of being "lost." In this way the form of *tierra* is dictated by the migratory existence of Chicano farmworkers in south Texas during the 1940s and 1950s.

What makes the work a novel, albeit an unconventional one, is the cohesion built into a seemingly fragmented text. Perhaps part of the genius of Rivera's technique is to loosely narrate individual and collective experiences that coexist *without* an overbearing central consciousness. This is accomplished by varying the points of view among the fourteen narrative units as well as within each individual unit. The use of a first-person, close third-person, or omniscient narrator to introduce a unit, followed by dramatic dialogue, interior monologue, or stream-of-consciousness fragments within the unit itself, creates what Rivera identifies in an essay as a "labyrinth" in which the Chicano can "invent himself" and "vicariously live his total human condition" ("Into the Labyrinth," 91).

It is significant that Rivera's labyrinthine literary form does not pit the individual *against* the community. Instead, it juxtaposes a range of narrative perspectives that documents a people's singular and collective struggle for a better life. The use of both first *and* third person is one way in which this is accomplished. In the novel the boy protagonist gets only four first-person narrations, which are scattered throughout the novel. While his sense of alienation, fear, and anger impacts us, we do not identify with him exclusively because we are always reminded that there is a larger story in which the boy's story plays only one part. In fact, the fourth of these I-narratives, "El retrato" (The Portrait), is not about him at all. Instead, he is strategically placed as an eyewitness to recall an incident in the neighborhood in which several families are cheated by ruthless con artists. In this way he doubles as a chronicler for the community. By the same token the first I-narration in the novel, which precedes the boy's first-person accounts, is that of a mother praying to God for the safe return of her son. This strategy simultaneously decenters the individual consciousness and establishes the mother-son theme in the text.

In conjunction with this restricted use of a first-person narrator the third-person narratives gain significance. The key units that concern the boy's development—from his initial lost state to his two confrontations (one with the Devil, the other with God) to the moment of enlightenment under the house—are all narrated in the third person. This strategic control of narrative distance, in which the reader observes rather than identifies with the protagonist, lends the episodes a universal quality. The boy's acts of protest in response to his confusion and rage are thus mythicized into "the human condition": the inconsequential individual who dares to defy God and Satan acquires universal proportions with the generic *he*.

Out of the twelve-month narrative cycle only half are filtered through the boy's consciousness. Of these six three I-narrations are directly related to the boy's concerns (school, crime, communion), while the other three express the boy's sense of outrage on behalf of his family and community. The prologue and epilogue, which frame the body of the text, are also narrated through the boy's consciousness. Again, however, the dreamlike aspects of the narratives neutralize any sense of a single entity. The boy's mind serves as a sieve through which the migrant workers' thoughts and experiences are sifted. As this narrative technique implies, the story is not *about* a specific Chicano boy.

Even the typography offers supporting evidence for this interpretation. In the final unit, in which events of the lost year coalesce in the boy's consciousness, for example, the narrative point of view moves from third person (normal type) to first person (italics) to third person (normal type), followed by four pages of narrative fragments (italics), which are continuations of what we learned earlier from individually narrated episodes about the community. This heteroglossic dream sequence is then followed by another first-person narrative (italics) before the unit ends in third person. The fact that the communal fragments and the boy's first-person narrations are both in italics is significant. Visually, this places the boy *among* his people and subliminally suggests that there is no I-they dichotomization in the novel's resolution.

Even while stating that *tierra* is not *about* an individual Chicano boy, if one were asked what the novel *is* about, he or she would be hard-pressed to offer an exciting plot line. We might say that the story is about Chicano farmworkers at a specific place and time. We watch, overhear, and think about the migrant workers' reality: the brutal sun, the cruel boss, the human casualties. Reading the work superficially, we might find only the "simplicity" of the "little people," as some critics contend. "The passive, humble peasant who endures" would be a deadly message to convey in the literature of a colonized people—and even more so on the eve of social change. If the author of *tierra* were promoting a point of view toward the migrant workers that suggests that they alone were responsible for their miserable lives, he would have been siding with the oppressors and blaming the victims. To draw this conclusion from the novel, however, requires a critical approach that views the literary text as a one-dimensional artifact. Joseph Sommers makes this important point in "From the Critical Premise to the Product," (1977), a seminal essay that uses *tierra* as a case study for his theoretical argument.

If we applied a "static descriptive analysis" to the novel, says Sommers, then we would review the list of characters who are associated with oppression and find a "relatively passive acceptance of oppression" (73). Or, if we focused on the child protagonist as an individual, with his "personal psychological profile" as *the* text, then we would conclude that the novel's ending indicates a triumph of the self away from the migrant community. Neither of these readings interprets the text within its appropriate historical and cultural contexts. A dynamic or dialectical reading, however, yields an entirely different message. In applying his historical-dialectical approach to *tierra*, Sommers concludes: "The boy's discovery of self in the experience and the suffering of others is the antithesis of individualism and the affirmation of the value of collective identity" (74).

The observation that specifically descriptive or psychological readings of Rivera's work would yield a negative message concerning the Chicano community is a valuable insight. In either case, the critical approach is more of an imposition on the literary text than an active analysis based on cumulative evidence. As the present study has shown with other ethnic works, often Eurocentric ways of approaching literature simply do not apply to ethnic American writers. This is not, however, due to the fact that ethnic writers do not write "literature." Rather, it has more to do with the cultural assumptions that the reader brings to the ethnic work. By taking a dialectical and/or multiple approach, in which meaning is reconstructed through an accumulation and processing of culturally specific evidence in the text, critics are more likely to avoid the pitfall of inappropriate self-projection.

As outlined so far in this discussion on literary form, Rivera's narrative technique tends to decenter the child protagonist even when an episode seems to be *about* him. If we consider *tierra* a coming-of-age story, as most critics have, then how do we interpret the active deconstructing of the boy's consciousness in the text? Perhaps the answer can be found in a different understanding of the traditional bildungsroman.

In an article on ritual process in the Chicano novel Thomas Vallejos clearly demonstrates the rite-of-passage structure in *tierra* ("Ritual Process"). According to Vallejos, the three stages in the puberty ritual that the child protagonist undergoes—separation, transition, and reintegration—have one-on-one correlations with the novel's fourteen narratives. Rivera does not use a linear arrangement, however, in which the first narratives indicate separation, the second transition, and so on. Instead, the narratives overlap and must be read cumulatively as well as ritually. The "liminal phase," or transitional period, has identifiable characteristics: "the initiate is ambivalent, confused" and exhibits patterns of "immobility, passivity, guilt, and humiliation" (6). Within this framework, of major significance is "the connection of the individual rite of passage with that of the collective" in the novel (10).

This analysis of *tierra*'s ritual structure provides the key to our understanding of the tension between the individual and the communal in the novel. While classic bildungsromans in the Eurocentric tradition assume an individual rite of passage—in which the child becomes an adult when he or she is able to separate from his or her community—in Rivera's coming-of-age story the maturing child must find an appropriate connection to his community and the community must mature along with the child. In this sense the characters in *tierra* undergo a group ritual, and it is this ritual process that provides textual cohesion. At the same time, because "process" means "change," the novel's cyclical structure suggests an ongoing pattern of struggle and resolution beyond the symbolic one-year migrant cycle. At the end of the novel the boy reflects on what has been accomplished and thinks: "*Y tengo tanto en que pensar y me faltan tantos años. . . . Tendré que venir aquí para recordar los demás*" (*And I have so much to think about and I'm missing so many years. . . . I'll have to come here to recall all of the other years*) (102, 205). In this way the child does not really "come of age" by the end of the novel. The fact that he has found one lost year indicates that the process has just begun. Unlike the European bildungsroman, in which a final resolution is assumed, he and his people must continue the ritual to regain all the lost years.

As this study has argued, the critical approach of locating ethnic cultural assumptions embedded in the text can yield a worldview that is significantly different from the contemporary European American one. Through our understanding of the stages involved in a rite of passage, in which there can be a prolonged period of confusion and passivity, and with clear evidence that the boy is a part of the group undergoing the ritual, we are able to read *tierra* in a different light. The "simplicity" and "passivity" of the people, for example, have more to do with a transitional stage in the ritual process than the genetic makeup of Mexican Americans. Critics who find the self-made man myth in Rivera's novel are isolating the boy protagonist, pitting him *against* his community, and concluding that the author looks down on his people. By consulting Rivera's own critical position as documented in interviews and essays, as well as by examining other aspects of the literary text, I will offer additional evidence for a culturally informed reading of *tierra*.

In a 1977 interview Rivera attributed his own awakening as a Chicano writer to his discovery, in 1958, of Américo Paredes's study of *corridos* (border ballads) about Gregorio Cortez. According to Rivera, this find basically gave him permission to write *as* a Chicano *about* Chicanos (Bruce-Novoa, *Chicano Authors*, 150). Similar to the experiences of other writers in the present study, this momentous event was one in which the American writer "broke silence" and began to write from his or her ethnic reality.[9] "I felt that I had to document the migrant worker para siempre [forever]," says Rivera, "para que no se olvidará ese espíritu tan fuerte de resistir y continuar under the worst of conditions [so that their very strong spirit of endurance and will to go on under the worst of conditions should not be forgotten], because they were worse than slaves" (150–51).

As noted the concept of "endurance," if understood in terms of romanticizing the downtrodden who "grin and bear" their lot, can be considered patronizing in a racist way. Thus, William Faulkner's characterization of Dilsey (in *The Sound and the Fury* [1929]) as one who "endures" has been the subject of critical controversy over the years. It is important, therefore, to understand Rivera's comment within its appropriate context. First, the word Rivera used, *resistir*, was translated into *endurance* by the interviewer, Juan Bruce-Novoa. This is unfortunate because Rivera's active term is rendered passive through an act of translation. The interviewee's meaning is absolutely clear as he elaborates on the strength of the migrants he knew: "They may be economically deprived, politically deprived, socially deprived, but they kept moving, never staying in one place to suffer or be subdued" (qtd. in Bruce-Novoa, *Chicano Authors*, 151). Rivera's concept of migrants as "searchers" provides a clue to his point of view toward his people:

> I've written a poem called "The Searchers." Para mí era gente que buscaba [To me they were people who searched], and that's an *important metaphor in the Americas*. My grandfather was a searcher; my father was a searcher; I hope I can also be a searcher. That's the spirit I seek.
>
> Now . . . this is a positive image of the migrant as opposed to the negative one of him as lost in the stream of labor. Well, that's the point: to be able to document his strength, to show that he really was not lost. (151; emphasis added)

The writer did not see migrant workers—people whom he had grown up among and worked alongside of for a number of years—as "backward, superstitious, primitive, and simple" (J. Rodríguez, "Problematic," 136). As a writer and a Chicano, the highest compliment Rivera can pay to his people is that they are searchers. By explaining this concept as an "important metaphor in the Americas," he is claiming a place of dignity and respect for a hitherto invisible ethnic group.

It is important to remember that having communal values is not synonymous with the negative concept of a stagnant and repressive community. In the novel the child protagonist must learn to think for himself if he is to help forge a positive sense of community among his people. Key phrases in the prologue—"perdían las palabras" (words failed him), "se le olvidaba" (he forgot), "le entró miedo" (he became afraid)—provide clues to the initial problem. Basically, the boy is in a limbo state of isolation and confusion due to the demands of his subhuman migrant existence as well as specific cultural practices and beliefs that help to maintain the status quo. The word *el miedo* (fear), which appears frequently in the novel, explains the immobilization of the people.

As an oppressed, powerless labor force, reality for Chicanos seems centered on fear and intimidation. In such an environment parents are often unable to protect their children. On his first day of school, for example, the child must face the intimidating institution alone. He asks the parent, "But why don't you help me?" and gets the response, "You'll do just fine, don't be afraid" (123). Until he understands the nature of his oppression he also feels alienated from his parents for their lack of support. *El miedo* is not only an individual problem, though; it looms large in the community and seems to permeate the environment. From the migrant perspective even clouds suffer from this emotion. In a dialogue between two workers (the main words are attributed to the protagonist) one of them states: "ya aplanándose el sol ni una nubita se le aparece de puro miedo" (once the sun bears down like this not even one little cloud dares to appear out of fear) (44, 148). Such personification suggests that the problem is larger than the will of the individual. Thus, three key words—*el miedo, el asusto* (fright), and *loco* (crazy)—suggest a limbo state of entrapment and helplessness. The people are victimized by forces beyond their control.

Contrasted with this passivity in the text, however, is also the opposite emotion. Throughout the individual and group narratives, juxtaposed to the word *miedo* is *coraje* (anger), which, as one critic notes, represents "una toma de conciencia (an awareness)" (Rodríguez del Pino, *La novela chicana*, 17-18). In identifying the leitmotif of *miedo* (always associated with oppression) and *coraje* (always associated with consciousness) in the narrative units, the critic identifies an important dialectic operating in the text. Rather than interpreting experiences of *miedo*/oppression as stagnant descriptions of helpless victims, the reader should be interpreting the dialectic between *miedo* and *coraje*, between the initial passive response and its active transformation into anger and individual or group consciousness. Thus, in the episode in which the boy curses God he moves from *miedo* to *coraje*, and, since the earth does not open up to swallow him, he finds peace and a new self-confidence. Appearing halfway through the novel, this act of defiance and subsequent self-realization parallels the collective resolution at the end of the book. Thus, the two units must be read dialectically as well.

Throughout the novel the exploitative system of migratory labor with its accompanying social and economic injustices are clearly identified. As noted, this is accomplished through narrative point of view—usually through the voices of the people rather than through omniscient commentary. What makes this strategy convincing is, as one critic puts it, "instead of relying on a blatantly political statement, [Rivera] has incorporated those conditions of economic hardship into a total rhythm and pattern of life" (Testa, "Narrative Technique," 87). Social criticism, in the form of ironic ambiguity, implicates the reader when it is presented from the migrants' perspective in the novel. In "Es Que Duele" (It's That It Hurts) the boy's anxiety over whether he was really expelled from school (due to a racist encounter) is ironic because, as a result of language barrier, he is not even sure whether he is really in trouble. Thus, his debate with himself cannot be resolved: "Pero, a lo mejor no me expulsaron, n'ombre, sí a lo mejor no, n'ombre, sí" (But maybe they didn't expel me, *sure they did*, maybe not, *sure they did*) (23, 127). Being expelled from school means, in this migrant child's life, not attaining the aspiration his father has for him of becoming a telephone operator. The modesty of the aspiration as well as the boy's anxiety and misery more effectively tap our social conscience than a direct political statement would have done.

While Anglo greed and insensitivity are sources of oppression in *tierra*, ruthless exploiters, such as doña Bone and the portrait salesmen, can also be found among *el pueblo*. Thus, the novel neither glamorizes nor unjustly blames the migrant workers for their condition. The anonymous child protagonist, as a specific representation of the community, must regain a sense of continuity and connectedness through *remembering* the collective history of the people, *discovering* the strength of this group experience, and *willing* an active, constructive existence as the final step toward positive change. In an important essay describing how these key concepts operate through the literary imagination, Rivera states: "Remembering and discovery of oneself lead to volition, notwithstanding the structures which are imposed on it." The "American structures," the writer explains, were not able to disrupt the Chicano imagination; rather, such an unnatural imposition only served to intensify these "imaginative processes" ("Recuerdo," 75).

The imagination, then, is the connective link that enables a people to move beyond their oppression. In the same essay Rivera locates this exercising of the imagination in the oral tradition. To him oral storytelling means that, through words, the migrant workers of his youth were able to "escaparse a otros mundos, e inventarse también" (escape to other worlds as well as to invent them) (70). This brief account of his exposure to storytellers, or "narradores del pueblo," acknowledges the literary tradition that nurtured the Chicano writer. There is no condescension here toward the imaginative skills and what the writer calls the "inner sensitivity" of his people (71). In fact, this account, as corroborated by his other writings, identifies the ethnic culture as a major source of Rivera's respect for words. To a writer raised in such a communal tradition language, as filtered through the creative imagination and expressed either orally or in written form, can invent worlds.

It is the connective power of language that the child protagonist understands by the end of the novel. Hiding under a neighbor's house, his mind replays fragments of the migrant workers' lives as they were narrated in the text. While during the separation and liminal stages of his rite of passage he challenged and rejected specific customs and beliefs, such as his mother's faith in an all-powerful God, this does not mean that he therefore rejects his people or that they reject him. It is precisely *with* and *through* the people that the boy makes a crucial discovery: namely, that making connections is what counts in life ("Relacionar esto con esto, eso con aquello, todo con todo" [103]). The desire to round up everyone—all the characters in the book or all the people in the migrant community—so that he could hug the whole lot suggests that the individual has no intention of separating from the community.

In fact, the child protagonist's revelation leads to an act of volition. Perched on his tree back home, he *imagines* seeing a person in a distant tree, so he waves—thus, symbolically connecting with someone outside himself. This ending, although by no means a revolutionary act, suggests the beginnings of a new consciousness that locates a people's strength in group solidarity. It is important to note that, while the awareness is "new" and suggests the possibility of change within the community, the model of group solidarity is drawn from a preexistent heritage—the "mestizaje" culture of the Mexican borderlands,[10] which, through the historical dialectics of imperialism and oppression, became the North American Southwest. For a "narrador del pueblo" of this specifically Chicano identity language is a prominent issue.

In ethnic literary works the writer's specific linguistic choices disclose a great deal about the implied author's point of view in the text. Literature that focuses on a visibly ethnic group in the United States must be sensitive to the race and class biases built into European American English. *Tierra* was revolutionary for its day precisely because of this linguistic sensitivity. According to a major study on the commitment that five Chicano writers made to *la raza* (Mexican Americans) in the 1970s by writing in Spanish, not only is Rivera's novel the first in contemporary Chicano literature to have been written in Spanish, but its language is consistently and specifically in the vernacular: "Rivera ha empleado con acierto la forma de expresión popular con la cual el grupo social novelado se expresa. La realidad documental-social ha sido transportada a la estética literaria" (Rivera has accurately used the form of popular expression with which the social group in the novel express themselves. Documentary-social reality has been converted to the literary aesthetic; my translation) (Rodríguez del Pino, *La novela chicana*, 19).

Such faithfulness to the language of the people reflects a conscious artistic choice. Like Bartolo the poet, it validates the communal voice without distinguishing between the "intellectual" child protagonist and the other migrant workers. The child's thought processes, which include bilingual usages as well as the built-in ambiguities of colloquial speech (e.g., "No, pos sí"), are in no way more sophisticated, intellectual, or "educated" than those of his people. This indicates that the implied author does not view him as above the other characters in the novel. Rather, he is simply one representative from the collective. By narrating the entire novel in the vernacular, in "the everyday speech of the Chicanos who share the *compadrazco relationship*" (Kanellos, "Language and Dialog," 58), Rivera reveals the communal ethic in his novel.

According to a scholar of Chicano theater, there are major dramatic techniques in *tierra*, techniques that resemble the folk drama of the *teatro chicano*: "Some of the sketches or miniatures in . . . *tierra* are similar in format, content and language to Chicano theater *actos*.

They are dramatic capsules that present typical scenes and archetypal characters of Chicano life with humor, pathos and social satire" (Kanellos, "Language and Dialog," 57). While the art of understatement is common in twentieth-century literature, the specific folk slant in *tierra* renders it true to the 1950s Chicano migrant experience and clearly contrasts it with works such as Hemingway's *In Our Time* (1925), even though both works utilize spare narrative forms and colloquial speech. The difference between the two works offers a good example of a communal versus an individualist point of view.

Hemingway's Nick Adams functions as a controlling, dominant center of consciousness. The reader sees things through his eyes, and other characters serve as backdrop. His alienation and suppressed violence are presented as an individual will that is superimposed on everything—including humans and nature. The protagonist's maturation process points to a growing sense of isolation and nonengagement. The formed adult is an individual who, in "Big Two-Hearted River," thrives only in nature, away from other people. When we think of the child protagonist in *tierra*, however, the situation is quite different.

In Rivera's novel the child is at best a filter through whom the community is seen, felt, and experienced. Outside his confused psychological state and the attempts to make sense of his world he has no personal characteristics. He is part of an environment, part of a group experience taking place in historical time. In the next to the last episode, "Cuando lleguemos" (When We Arrive), for example, we enter the minds of several migrant workers through interior monologues. Inside a broken-down truck en route to the beet fields of Minnesota the travelers exhibit thought patterns that range from the mundane to the poetic, from the hostile to the philosophical. The expression *cuando lleguemos* is presented as ironic commentary through the voice of one traveler—who thinks the truth is that they never arrive—as well as an expression of hope lodged in the subjunctive form of the verb *llegar* (to arrive). The refrain "cuando lleguemos, cuando lleguemos . . . " is used to fade out the monologues, leaving the thought open-ended. Given the harsh conditions of the journey (in which many travelers, including children, have to ride standing for twenty-four hours), the collective "we" becomes the source of comfort and group strength. The sense of community in this sequence of multiple narratives is overwhelming.

This analysis of . . . *y no se lo tragó la tierra* leads to the conclusion that Rivera's art reflects a communal ethos. Given the opportunity to write a Chicano bildungsroman, Rivera turned the nineteenth-century European genre into a collective rite of passage built on communal memories and humanistic values. Far from being an elitist intellectual who despised Chicano migrant workers, the writer based his art on his people. His communal assumptions as an artist are apparent when he states in an interview: "If you want to write, I think there is one common thing: you have to have a love for people; otherwise you wouldn't write" (qtd. in Bruce-Novoa, *Chicano Authors*, 154). As a critic, his attitude is more revealing. In the same interview Rivera mentions that, at times, he had seen some grotesque things in Chicano theater. He points out, however, that "they're so damn human. They have substance." His humanistic approach, which gives people the benefit of the doubt, is reflected in the following statement about seemingly "grotesque" literature: "At one time there was one individual who thought he was saying something beautiful. The fact that he thought about it that hard, to me makes it beautiful" (160). In these words one finds complete acceptance of the other's reality without a superficially imposed standard. In Rivera's own writing it is the ability to present grotesque life in a humane light that makes *tierra* a valuable work of art.

"Home in the Heart": Sandra Cisneros's *The House on Mango Street*

> Yet in leaving home I did not lose touch with my origins because *lo mexicano* is in my system. I am a turtle, wherever I go I carry "home" on my back.
> —Gloria Anzaldúa, *Borderlands/La Frontera*

The witch woman Elenita says to young Esperanza, "I see a home in the heart. . . . A new house, a house made of heart." Disappointed with such a cryptic vision, Esperanza complains, "All this for five dollars I give her" (Cisneros, *Mango Street*, 60–61). In its function as *Mango Street*'s unifying trope, the metaphor of house/home serves as a nexus for the theme of individualism and community. Does the protagonist's desire for a "real house" imply an individualistic value system operating in the text? Although the materialism of owning a house might indicate such an outlook, the symbolic meaning of having a "home in the heart" suggests otherwise. Elenita's ambiguous message provides a key to understanding the house/home motif in relation to the theme of community as seen through the Chicana urban experience. By consulting interviews with the author, reviewing relevant historical background, and analyzing the fictional text, I will explore how this theme is developed in the novel.

Recipient of the 1985 Before Columbus American Book Award, Cisneros's first full-length work enjoys a popularity among readers that is unusual for the publication of a small regional press. This limited success, however, has not been matched by the kind of critical attention it deserves. In a 1990 article-length survey of Chicano literature the work is named "the most widely known Chicana novel" (Eysturoy and Gurpegui, "Chicano Literature," 59). Contradicting this statement is another scholar's report: "Difficult to find in most libraries and bookstores, it is well known among Chicano critics and scholars, but virtually unheard of in larger academic and critical circles" (McCracken, "Sandra Cisneros's *House*," 63). One of the first critical articles on the book (written in Spanish) urges readers not to limit the novel to the genre of children's literature (Gutiérrez-Revuelta, "Género e ideología," 48–49)—thus raising the issue of categorizing a sophisticated, adult-level ethnic work as "juvenile" due to its deceptively simple language and adolescent narrative point of view. These issues regarding the book's initial reception and critical standing have become moot, however, since a major publishing house has begun publishing Cisneros's fiction. Keeping in mind that this study deals mostly with writers in progress, I believe that Cisneros is an important emerging writer whose work must be taken seriously.

The pairing of Rivera and Cisneros has a certain symmetry. Both . . . *y no se lo tragó la tierra* and *The House on Mango Street* utilize, for example, narrative structures that render them difficult to classify in traditional generic terms: namely, each is a collection of "stories" and "vignettes" that are at once independent units and, when read together, offer additional and multiple meanings. Thus, we resort to the term *novel* for these texts simply to be able to refer to the work as a whole—which is greater than its individual narrative units. In addition, both texts fall under the rubric of the bildungsroman, even if they do not conform to European American standards. A third area of similarity is the theme of being uprooted: whether in a rural or urban setting, the characters in both novels have to move constantly—suggesting that there is no "home," as understood in middle-class European American terms. In the present study I have generally avoided direct one-on-one comparison in favor of encouraging readers to make connections among the analyses of the various ethnic texts. In this case, however, it is necessary to acknowledge the parallels between the two works within the context of Chicano/a literature.

The previous discussion of Rivera's novel locates it in its appropriate time and place. *Tierra* heralds an emerging group consciousness and solidarity as it documents pre-1960s Chicano migrant workers' lives. As mentioned earlier, the literature of the 1970s, whether written in Spanish, English, or interlingually, reflects a communal ethos that supports the Chicano Movement as expressly stated in the 1969 *El Plan Espiritual de Aztlán*. This first stage of solidarity utilized a cultural and historical image, the mythic land of Aztlán (the region of the American Southwest from which the Aztecs are said to have originated), to declare a people's freedom and nationhood. Thus, Aztlán crops up in Chicano/a literature as the people's mythic homeland. This consciously forged image gives the idea of community political, geographical, and spiritual specificity. Even though Rivera's novel does not use the term *Aztlán*, it is located in this literary space. Cisneros's text, on the other hand, both parallels and departs from this social and historical context.

Until the 1980s anthologies of Chicano literature barely included women writers.[11] This fact is registered in a previously mentioned critical study as: "Reasons for the continued exclusion of women writers from the history of Chicano narrative are as complex as are the reasons for the sexism of any other literary tradition" (R. Saldívar, *Chicano Narrative*, 172). Gender restrictions via patriarchal strictures thus have not, similar to the Black Aesthetics of the 1960s, afforded women an equal share of the legitimation garnered in the early years of the Movement. Reflecting this pattern is the public image of Rivera versus Cisneros. One might say that what Rivera represents for Chicano literature in the 1970s is parallel to what Cisneros and other Chicana writers accomplish in the 1980s. Thus, pairing Rivera and Cisneros is especially apt in terms of offering comparable texts viewed in their appropriate sociopolitical environments. The fourteen years separating Rivera's novel from Cisneros's first major work register the changing climate in terms of an evolving feminist consciousness. In relation to the topic of this investigation the woman-centered

Chicana voice of the 1980s offers a radical feminist critique of what "Chicano community" really means.

In Mexican/Chicano mythology Malintzin (also known as La Malinche and Doña Marina) is the prototypical whore who betrayed her own people by sleeping with the enemy. According to the legend, as Cortés's mistress, interpreter/liaison, and advisor, Malintzin used her multicultural/multilingual knowledge to ensure Cortés's conquest of the Aztec Empire (from 1519 to 1527). The beginning of the *mestizo* race (Malintzin bore Cortés a son) is thus attributed to a people's initial experience of betrayal at the hands of an "evil" woman. While Malintzin can be compared to Eve in Christian mythology, her historicity makes her legacy especially problematic for the Chicano community. As one Chicana scholar explains:

> Unlike Eve whose primeval reality is not historically documentable and who supposedly existed in some past edenic time, Malintzin's betrayal of our supposed pre-Columbian paradise is recent and hence almost palpable. This almost-within-reach past heightens romantic nostalgia and as a consequence hatred for Malintzin and women becomes as vitriolic as the American Puritans' loathing of witches-women. (Alarcón, "Chicana's Feminist Literature," 182)

Reevaluations of Malintzin by Chicana scholars today seek to separate myth from reality. By consulting and analyzing early accounts of the Conquest, feminist scholars now offer a different image of the historical figure—one that views her as brilliant, highly respected by the natives, and, given that she was sold by her Aztec mother into slavery, a resourceful slave rather than a traitor. In fact, one well-researched essay concludes that La Malinche was the "prototypical Chicana feminist" (Candelaria, "La Malinche," 6).

Nevertheless, according to Chicana writers, the fear of female betrayal runs deep in the male psyche. The "sullied whore who gave herself to the white conquistador," says María Herrera-Sobek, "has been and still is reiterated by modern intellectuals" (*Beyond Stereotyping,* 18). As the counterpart to La Malinche, the Virgin of Guadalupe seems to enjoy male patronage in Chicano literature. Norma Alarcón makes the useful observation that there is a "telling absence of poems by women to the Virgin . . . , while poems by men to her are plentiful" ("Chicana's Feminist Literature," 187). Due to the continued use of such specific cultural symbols, the dichotomization of women into virgins and prostitutes requires Chicana writers to work through such stigmatization in the fictional text. It is against this cultural backdrop that we can begin to understand Cisneros's treatment of the dialectic between the Chicana self and her ethnic community.

The House on Mango Street is dedicated "A las Mujeres/To the Women." Throughout the forty-four interrelated stories that constitute the novel, Esperanza, the young narrator/protagonist, comes in contact with a number of women in the neighborhood. From this cast of female characters, especially the ones like Rafaela and Sally who are "too beautiful to look at," one learns that female sexuality is a major liability in the Chicago barrio where the collective story takes place. *Mango Street* offers no rosy picture of barrio life. In an interview Cisneros demystifies the romanticized notion of "quaint" ethnic ghettos: "I was writing about it in the most real sense that I knew, as a person walking those neighborhoods with a vagina. I saw it a lot differently than all those 'chingones' that are writing all those bullshit pieces about their barrios" ("Solitary Fate," 69).

Part of the difference between Cisneros's stated position as this is translated into literature and that of the *chingones* (something like "tough guys" or "big shots") in real life is the text's narrative point of view. In the novel the childhood barrio is consistently seen through the eyes of a naive, impressionable young Chicana. From this vantage point an "unprotected" female *is* vulnerable. Having "protection," however, in the form of male dominance—that is, a "daddy's house"—can be even more deadly. The novel presents several examples of how some husbands, fathers, etc., watch over their women. At best women are locked indoors "sit[ting] their sadness on an elbow" (12); otherwise, they are beaten and/or raped. How could this bleak picture of a male-dominated, or "macho," culture engender in women anything but the desire for escape? Thus, Esperanza's yearning for a house of her own—suggesting financial, physical, and emotional independence—is a recurrent motif in the novel.

How one interprets this motif is of major importance to a reading of the novel. In the opening title story "house" is introduced in terms of family stability and the American Dream. The aspiration of a white house with trees and a large backyard is the promise of America, the "land of the beautiful and free." It is the image that immigrants and ethnics see on televisions and billboards, the photograph conjured up every time the last dollar is spent on a lottery ticket. To the young protagonist who has yet to experience life the small red house on Mango Street with "tight little steps" and "windows so small you'd think they were holding their breath" (8) does not bode well for her future. Instead of freedom from homelessness ("a real house . . . so that we wouldn't have to move each year" [8]), the dilapidated red house confirms the ethnic reality of the narrator's name, Esperanza, which, as she sees it, means "hope" in English but "sadness" and "waiting" in Spanish. Following Boelhower's semiotic terminology, we might say that the house on Mango Street is an "ethnic sign" that can easily close off the future for the young protagonist. That is, as a house that falls short of the American Dream, it can be viewed as a symbol of Anglo oppression. As such, Esperanza's attitude toward this house is all-important. If she accepts it as her lot in life, then she is conforming to the dominant culture's definition of who she is. Her refusal to accept this house as home, however, indicates that she has the capacity to look beyond her present conditions and continue to dream.

In several places in the text the house motif is associated with the feeling of shame. The first time the narrator mentions being made to feel ashamed is in reference to her home. She tells us that when a nun had said of her family's previous dwelling, "You live *there*?" she knew then that she had to have a real house someday. Thus, the first story in the novel establishes the dialectic between American Dream and Ethnic Reality, which, on a personal, psychological level, is the difference between self-respect and self-hatred.

Three-quarters through the novel the theme of shame is clearly stated. Out of the wisdom of her years Esperanza's mother tells her daughter: "Shame is a bad thing, you know. It keeps you down" (83). The desire for a "real" house reflects Esperanza's refusal to feel ashamed. It indicates that she has a solid sense of self-worth and cannot be bought off with an inferior substitute. Moreover, it insists that *if* Americans are entitled to adequate food and shelter—and, as a Chicana, Esperanza *is* an American—then she will not settle for what European American society identifies as her lot. This ethnically charged spirit of resistance contrasts sharply with several of her passive female friends.

In the novel, while male sexism poses a major threat to a healthy, viable community, ingrained female attitudes are also exposed as destructive. For example, Marin, the girl from Puerto Rico who sells Avon and babysits her cousins, lives in a fantasy world. Appearing early in the novel, Marin's story is used to pinpoint where young women like her go wrong: "What matters, Marin says, is for the boys to see us and for us to see them" (28). This dictum introduces the theme of female sexuality in the text. Marin's point of view is narrated by the naive Esperanza without value judgment: "Marin says that if she stays here next year, she's going to get a real job downtown because that's where the best jobs are, since you always get to look beautiful and get to wear nice clothes and can meet someone in the subway who might marry and take you to live in a big house far away" (27).

Esperanza tells us twice that "Marin is already older than us in many ways" (28). When she innocently adds that she looks up to Marin, the reader understands that this is a trap. Marin's story offers a classic case of "the Cinderella complex."[12] The expectation that one will be saved by Prince Charming riding on a white horse—even if the working-class version rides on the subway—keeps young women passive and helpless. In the text, while Esperanza the naive narrator/ protagonist merely describes Marin without value judgment, the implied author offers a critique through the vivid capsule image that ends Marin's story: "Marin, under the streetlight, dancing by herself, is singing the same song somewhere. I know. Is waiting for a car to stop, a star to fall, someone to change her life" (28). The "I know" posits an older, more mature narrator than Esperanza appears to be in the first part of this two-page narrative. The retrospective viewpoint of this closing lends it a quality of transcendence and universality, suggesting that women who wait are doomed to wait a long time. This single-image technique not only serves as social critique but also controls the distance between the naive narrator and Marin. While the implied author condones a certain amount of empathy between Esperanza and Marin, she is also telling us that Esperanza is *not* another Marin.

The critique is reduced to one sentence in a much later piece, which plays off the princess in the tower, or the Rapunzel, fairy tale. In the story of Rafaela, who gets locked in by her husband and who "escapes" by having tropical drinks delivered through the window on a clothesline, the critical voice concludes: "And always there is someone offering sweeter drinks, someone promising to keep them on a silver string" (76). Women who are lulled by "sweeter drinks" are kept on "silver strings" and made to remain docile and dependent. And again, like the Mamacita in another story who moves to America to join her husband and finds herself trapped, pining away for "home," women who do marry and attain Marin's dream—at least metaphorically—of living in a big house far away *are not saved!* In this way the fairy tale of Cinderella is exposed as a dangerous lie. The selection and narration of these women's stories around the theme of house/home suggests a textual deconstructing of the concept of home as safe female domain.

In *Mango Street* individual words such as *house* and *home* carry so much thematic weight that it would be helpful to consider how Cisneros thinks about and handles her choice of words. For this we can consult the writer's own statements regarding her art. In a 1988 interview in which she discusses her art in relation to her actual life after the publication of *Mango Street* the language Cisneros uses resonates with key figures and symbols also found in the novel. Such use of language suggests that we are privy to the writer's symbolic universe through the interviewing process. As a jumping-off point, it is worth noting that Cisneros says she later *did* find the "home in the heart" which the witch woman Elenita predicts in the novel. She insists, however, that she did not know where the expression came from when she wrote it. It simply popped into her head and seemed to match the other cryptic, ambiguous things Elenita says ("Solitary Fate," 73). The strange expression "anchor of arms," for example, matches "home in the heart" (in the text, Elenita says, "And did you lose an anchor of arms" [60]).

Another important clue from the interview is that Cisneros says she likes to dance at home alone. Keeping in mind the image of Marin dancing alone under the streetlight, which we interpreted as criticism of the Cinderella complex, how does the real-life information relate to the textual meaning? The writer herself provides the clue when she talks about her new book of poetry: "Like there is a poem called 'New Tango,' it's about how I like to dance alone. But the tango that I'm dancing is not a man over a woman, but a 'new' tango that I dance by myself" (79). The evolution from Marin's dancing under the streetlight in *Mango Street* to the poem "New Tango," from a young woman's dreamily awaiting Prince Charming to a woman who no longer needs to wait, reflects the personal development of the artist via the creative process. In other words progress (in terms of female liberation) occurs from literature to real life to a new understanding revealed in literature. One might say that the criticism of female dependency, which the implied author directs at Marin and others in *Mango Street*, is taken to heart by the historical author. Thus, the trope of dancing alone is transformed into something positive and "new" in the poem. It is important to note here that the movement is *away from* male domination (in Cisneros's words, "a man over a woman") *toward* a new way of being.

The newfound self is celebrated in a third book of poetry, the title of which is rich in personal symbolism. Whereas a previous collection, written mostly prior to *Mango Street*, is entitled *My Wicked, Wicked Ways*, the new volume is called *Loose Woman*. The writer states: "They're loose poems. But they're loose 'women' poems. You see? I'm reinventing the word 'loose.' I really feel that I'm the loose [*sic*] and I've cut free from a lot of things that anchored me. So, playing on that, the collection is called *Loose Woman*" ("Solitary Fate," 79). What this passage reveals is how Cisneros is actively engaged in reclaiming her space as a Chicana and a writer. An adjective like *loose* for woman—which in a sexist society means "bad," "wicked," "fallen," or simply a prostitute—is here reclaimed and reinvented to mean "carefree" and "independent." This declaration of independence through art is significant in that it enables the artist, especially one who comes from an oppressively patriarchal and religious culture,[13] to tell the truth. The witch woman's question, "And did you lose an anchor of arms," foreshadows this development in Cisneros's life. In the above quote note that the writer uses the same word, *anchor*, in her conversation outside the literary text. In this way life and art are connected through the symbolic imagination and the creative use of language.

Cisneros is also illuminating when talking about her approach to narrative and audience. When asked about her views on art she says: "To me, the definition of a story is something that someone wants to listen to. If someone doesn't want to listen to you, then it's not a story" ("Solitary Fate," 76). This position reflects a specific cultural assumption. The idea that a story must have an audience, that stories must be shared to be stories, situates her within the oral tradition of Chicano/a literature. The assumption that a story *by defini-tion* is communal tells us a great deal about her art.

Given this assumption, it is important to understand the writer's personal liberation through art as part of a process leading toward community. As a poet, Cisneros views writing as digging "to a real subterranean level, to get at that core of truth." This is a frightening venture because "you don't even know what the truth is!" ("Solitary Fate," 75). Thus, the poetic self must be courageous and willing to confront—to face the uncensored center. This is necessarily a solitary process. From this hard-won core the writer then builds props and creates fiction. When Cisneros says, "Poetry is the art of telling the truth, and fiction is the art of lying" ("Solitary Fate," 75), what she means by "lying" are the props used in fiction in order to tell the story. This understanding of the creative process suggests that Cisneros, who started off as a poet and moved to fiction to enhance her ability to communicate, is reaching outward through her art. In other words the journey inward is a prelude to the movement out-ward to others, or the individual necessarily precedes the communal. But, while storytelling implies community in Cisneros's view, does the novel itself actually exhibit a communal ethos? That community is the ultimate value in *Mango Street* requires further investigation.

In a study on contemporary Chicana poetry Marta Sánchez states: "Writing within and against these two [Anglo and Mexican-Chicano] traditions, the Chicana poets of this generation created a cultural discourse responding primarily to issues of ethnicity and gender" (*Contemporary Chicana Poetry*, 6). Our discussion so far cor-roborates this statement in relation to Cisneros's art. In addressing issues of ethnicity *and* gender, however, ethnic women writers (espe-cially African American, Asian American, and Latina) are often read as individualistic since they seem to find their extant ethnic commu-nities unacceptable. This, I contend, is a simplistic interpretation of ethnic women's literatures. As other sections of this study have shown, it is possible to be community-oriented while offering a radi-cal critique of negative traits, such as sexism and classism, operating within the community. The ethnic woman should not have to choose between ethnic solidarity and gender loyalty. The charge of "betray-ing one's culture" all too often means "don't rock the boat." Cultures, however, need to change and grow. In challenging certain cultural dictates, as *Mango Street* shows, the ethnic woman writer is not turning her back on her culture. Cisneros makes this point for herself and other Chicana writers: "None of us wants to abandon our culture. We're very Mexican, we're all very Chicanas. Part of being Mexicana is that love and that afinity [sic] we have for our *cultura*. We're very family centered, and that family extends to the whole Raza. We don't want to be exiled from our people" ("Solitary Fate," 66).

Mango Street epitomizes the seeming contradiction between loving one's culture and people on the one hand and insisting on self-definition and critiquing the culture on the other. As discussed elsewhere in this study this double positioning *is* part of the ethnic woman's reality. Gloria Anzaldúa locates the Chicana reality at the borderlands between cultures: "The new *mestiza* [of mixed cultures] copes by developing a tolerance for contradictions, a tolerance for ambiguity" (*Borderlands*, 79). The both/and position necessarily involves ambivalence, ambiguity, and tension. These are not, as the rationalist elements of European American culture assume, negative traits. Furthermore, unlike T. S. Eliot's Prufrock and similar protagonists, Esperanza is hardly a tormented soul wallowing in resentment and self-hatred. Instead, negative experiences seem to make her stronger, more flexible. A closer look at one section of the text will show that, due to her ability to tolerate contradictions, as Esperanza gets older, she does not draw simplistic conclusions based on her negative childhood experiences.

In the novel the protagonist's tolerance for the ambiguities of human relationships is illustrated with specific literary techniques. In "The First Job" Esperanza experiences sexual molestation on her first day of work. The story ends with an image of male aggression and an old man's betrayal of a young girl's trust. On the next page there is a story about Papa, who "crumples like a coat and cries" because his father had just died in Mexico. Instead of describing her own reaction to Papa's crying, the girl narrator offers us an image ("My Papa, his thick hands and thick shoes, who wakes up tired in the dark"), a thought ("And I think if my own Papa died what would I do"), and an action ("I hold my Papa in my arms. I hold and hold and hold him") (53). By juxtaposing the two stories—one of violation and betrayal, the other of tenderness and empathy—Cisneros demonstrates that Esperanza is able to differentiate between male figures and not allow her negative experience with an old man to color her compassion for her father.

The above example also supports what one critic identifies as the "dialectic of inside and outside" in the text (Olivares, "Sandra Cisneros's *House*," 161). It is important to note that nothing in the novel is one-sided. Cisneros says in an essay that she found her ethnic literary voice from a classroom discussion of Gaston Bachelard's *Poetics of Space* (1969), during which the metaphor of the house first clicked in her consciousness ("Writer's Notebook," 72–73). The idea of house from *her* experience, as opposed to Bachelard's, triggered "third-floor flats, and fear of rats, and drunk husbands sending rocks through windows" (73). Thus, the critic is correct in pointing out that Cisneros "inverts Bachelard's pronouncement on the poetics of space" (Olivares, "Sandra Cisneros's *House*," 161) by showing that *inside* means, for several of the women in the novel, confinement and/or personal harm (rocks, beatings) rather than comfort and a safe haven for daydreaming. From the Papa example, however, the inside/outside dialectic works the other way as well. The molestation incident occurs "outside," and the father/ daughter moment of sympathy and comfort occurs "inside." The tension of inside versus outside, then, is maintained as a two-way street.

A superficial reading of this tension, and one in which the protagonist Esperanza is equated with the author Cisneros either overtly or by implication, might draw the conclusion that the implied author advocates individualistic values (by rejecting her insider status) since the protagonist intends to leave her barrio (by going outside). The theme of desiring a "house of one's own" has led some critics to judge the work in this way.[14] The present discussion shows, however, that, while *Mango Street* does not endorse certain culturally sanctioned patterns of behavior—namely, those that are restrictive and abusive to women—its orientation and message are clearly communal.

To arrive at this conclusion the forty-four stories must be read individually *and* collectively. Since fiction operates on the level of figurative language, it is necessary to connect allusions, images, symbols, etc., in a cumulative way in order to interpret the overall meaning of the text. No single line or individual story in the collection is

the story or contains *the* message. For every time there is an "individualistic" statement in the text, such as "I would like to baptize
myself under a new name, a name more like the real me, the one
nobody sees" (13), there is also a communal counterpart, as in the
story "Our Good Day": "Down, down Mango Street we go. Rachel,
Lucy, me. Our new bicycle [a bicycle that the kids decide is "three
ways ours"]. Laughing the crooked ride back" (18) Thus, it is misleading to pull out any single sentence—such as "A house all my
own" (100) or "One day I will go away" (101)—and conclude that
Esperanza represents and Cisneros advocates individualistic values.

One critical study of *Mango Street* offers an interpretation based
on the novel's fuller sociopolitical context. Ellen McCracken considers
Esperanza's desire for a house a "chance to redress humiliation"
("Sandra Cisneros's *House*," 65) and attributes this desire to the community as a whole. In calling Cisneros's novel "community-oriented
introspection," she clearly distinguishes between introspection that
"correspond[s] to the ideological emphasis on individualism under
capitalism"—in which the self is aggrandized and "accorded exaggerated importance"—and Esperanza's brand of self-awareness, in
which the individual self is rooted in the "broader socio-political reality of the Chicano community" (62–64).

By locating Cisneros's work within its ethnic cultural context,
McCracken usefully points out the important difference between the
myth of the self-made individual, with its accompanying emphasis
on private property, and the metaphoric significance of a house
"quiet as snow, a space for myself to go" (*Mango Street*, 100). A more
complete understanding of the house/home motif in relation to the
theme of community requires further attention to the symbolism contained in the witch woman's prophecy of a "home in the heart."

Before engaging in this final analysis, however, we might pause
to consider the important part that the creative process of writing
itself plays in forming new patterns of thought. In discussing the
fortune-telling episode in the text, Cisneros tells her interviewer:
"The story impressed me very much because it is exactly what I found
out, years after I'd written the book, that the house in essence becomes you. You are the house. But I didn't know that when I wrote
it" ("Solitary Fate," 73). This statement suggests that the writer herself was not conscious of all that *house* signified for her when she
wrote the novel. According to Mark Schorer's thesis of "technique

as discovery," sometimes the use of a particular literary technique helps the artist "discover" his or her unconscious thoughts. Further, the literary work provides the reader with an opportunity to reflect on and partly create the fuller meanings of the words in the text.

Regarding the house/home motif and the theme of community in *Mango Street*, this study concludes that it is exactly the tension between individualism and community—the dialectic between the young protagonist's yearning for separation/individuation and other women's messages to her of communal responsibility—that reveals the communal ethos of the novel. A few short passages from the text will help to corroborate the conclusion that the novel ultimately endorses the connectedness, however uneasy the relationship may be, between the individual Chicana and her community.

In the last pages of the book, juxtaposed to demonstrations of rebellion ("I have begun my own quiet war" [82]), possessiveness ("A house all my own. With my porch . . ." [100]), and escapism ("One day I will go away" [101]), are opposite messages of love, loyalty, and personal responsibility toward the community. Individual women serve as role models for the young narrator. In "The Three Sisters" one of the women says to Esperanza: "When you leave you must remember to come back for the others. A circle, understand?" (98). While the narrator tells us that she is "a little confused" by this advice, the story on the following page indicates that she is finally getting the message:

> No, Alicia says. Like it or not you are Mango Street and one day you'll come back too.
> Not me. Not until somebody makes it better.
> Who's going to do it? The mayor?
> And the thought of the mayor coming to Mango Street makes me laugh out loud.
> Who's going to do it? Not the mayor.
>
> (99)

Perhaps more than anywhere else in this study, the final line of this exchange reflects the text's communal ethic and sense of ethnic solidarity. The realization that the mayor is certainly not going to show up in the barrio and "make it better" means that members of the community need to save themselves. To do this individuals who find a way out have the obligation to return, as the final lines in the text reassure us: "They will not know I have gone away to come back. For the ones I left behind. For the ones who cannot out [*sic*]" (102). This ending shows that Esperanza *has* absorbed the three sisters' message. Thus, the circle mentioned by them serves as a metaphor of return and a symbol of wholeness.

At this point, if we match what Cisneros says in the interview ("You are the house") with Alicia's words in the above exchange ("Like it or not *you are Mango Street*" [emphasis added]), the fullest meaning of *home in the heart* becomes clear. The metaphor serves a double meaning of *both* self-sufficiency (as in, wherever you are, that is your home) *and* group solidarity (if we equate *heart* with the barrio, which Mango Street represents, thus suggesting that Esperanza is part of a collective entity that can never be erased). This understanding of the house/home motif indicates that the house on Mango Street serves as the vehicle of Esperanza's liberation while simultaneously including her in its group identity.

In finding her home in the heart Cisneros is using her strength as an artist to serve her people. She need not physically return to the barrio—if this requires her to remain, as the saying goes, "barefoot and pregnant"—to express her communal values. The writer herself says, "There's no luxury or leisure in our [Chicana writers'] lives for us to write of landscapes and sunsets and tulips in a vase" ("Solitary Fate," 73). By choosing to write about Mango Street, Cisneros shows that she is not abandoning her people. Instead, she is working toward a new sense of community through her art, and solidarity among women seems to be her starting point. After all, *Mango Street* is dedicated "a las mujeres."

In pointing out the sense of collectivity in the novels of a major Chicano writer, a recent essay contrasts the "broad scope" of these works' titles with "the scores of Chicano titles which reveal a reduced, particularistic, often individualistic, primary focus." The critic goes on to say that, "where these works do include community, it is filtered through the experiences of the protagonist" (Broyles, "Hinojosa's *Klail City*," 110). Appearing in the essay under the subtitle "Community in 'Klail City,'" this statement gives the impression that

Chicano/a literature is generally individualistic. The present analyses of Rivera's and Cisneros's texts conclude, however, that, even though both use the narrative strategy of filtering communal experiences through the protagonist's consciousness, this is not an indication of individualistic assumptions or values. One Chicano work that does advocate individualism—and which the critic does not name—is the controversial autobiography *Hunger of Memory* (1982) by Richard Rodriguez. Given the work's popularity among Anglo educators and media critics, and given the relevancy of the work to the present study topic, it is important to situate the text within the broader framework of Chicano/a literary productions.

Since the publication of Rodriguez's book and its subsequent popularity in the United States, numerous articles by Chicano/a scholars have been published refuting Rodriguez's characterization of "The Chicano Experience."[15] Unfortunately, such scholarly articles do not enjoy wide circulation. Therefore, the author's version of *his* story is often taken as typical or normative. The following discussion will briefly examine Rodriguez's text as well as three other Chicano/a works in order to substantiate the belief that the individualistic ideology found in Rodriguez is the exception rather than the rule. Tomás Rivera's critique of *Hunger* can serve as a starting point.

In the essay "Richard Rodriguez's *Hunger of Memory* as Humanistic Antithesis" Rivera identifies Rodriguez's opting for his English-speaking public self as an illustration of "a colonized mind" (32). This, says Rivera, is reflected in the false dichotomization of the Mexican versus the American world: "Richard Rodriguez exists between two cultures, but he believes it more important to participate in one world than the other. But it is possible to participate in many worlds profoundly and without losing, but rather gaining, perception and appreciation from all" (32). The difference between Rivera and Rodriguez as (Chicano) writers is the difference between an either/or versus a both/and view of the world. In *Hunger* Rodriguez presents what becomes a titanic struggle between two worlds: on the one hand, the private, Spanish-speaking, "naive" Mexican childhood of his past; on the other, the public, English-speaking, "mature" American adulthood of his present. The firm belief that the two worlds are incompatible—and that he has to choose the latter if he seeks success in American society—forces him to assimilate into the Anglo world, which has no place for his private, ethnic self. In this rigid formulation maturation means assimilation. In describing his loneliness as a writer, for example, Rodriguez says: "Many days I feared I had stopped living by committing myself to remember the past. I feared that my absorption with events in my past amounted to an immature refusal to live in the present" (175). From Rivera's point of view, however, "a writer is lonely only if he has lost the sense of his community's aspirations and the integrative values" (33). To Rivera, Rodriguez's "loneliness" is due to his writing in a vacuum, without the benefit of a people to write for or about.

In comparing Ernesto Galarza's *Barrio Boy* (1971) to *Hunger* Ramón Saldívar makes a similar observation regarding Rodriguez. Galarza deals with the same "contradictory impulses" in his autobiography, says Saldívar, but, unlike Rodriguez, "he handles this turmoil not by rejecting his Mexican world as he develops a public self, but by 'navigating' precariously between both worlds, inhabiting both in good faith, and finally by forging a span between his original Mexican and his acquired American enculturations" (*Chicano Narrative*, 168). This dialectic approach enables the bicultural person to pick and choose during the maturation process, thereby creating a new, hybrid ethnic American self.

While both autobiographies are "success" stories of Mexican Americans, the way in which each author presents and interprets his experiences reveals his specific understanding of the self in society. When speaking of his acculturation process in America, the I-narrator in *Barrio Boy* includes a running critique of American capitalism. He points out, for example, the difference between "trust" and "credit" in describing the helping tradition among people in the barrio:

> Beds and meals . . . were provided . . . on trust, until the new *chicano* [unskilled newcomer from Mexico] found a job. On trust and not on credit, for trust was something between people who had plenty of nothing, and credit was between people who had something of plenty. It was not charity or social welfare but something my mother called *asistencia*, a helping given and received on trust, to be repaid because those who had given it were themselves in need of what they had given. (201)

In this passage, "credit," "charity," and "social welfare"—concepts that imply hierarchy and class difference—are contrasted with "trust," a folk value that assumes equality and communal sharing. Appearing three-fourths of the way through the book, this distinction reinforces folk traditions from the narrator's Mexican past (e.g., "Out of the forest a man took out only what he and his family could use" [57]) and suggests that Americanization need not preclude such values.

For Richard Rodriguez, on the other hand, Americanization means that the educated Chicano writer necessarily relinquishes his communal self in exchange for his public identity. This position is illustrated in the text through binary opposition. "There are things so deeply personal that they can be revealed only to strangers," we are informed. In direct contrast to this truism are the mother's old-world views. "For my mother that which is personal can only be said to a relative—her only intimates." Here Galarza's point about trust in human relationships is relegated to the parents' world and negatively assessed: "Of those matters too jaggedly personal to reveal to intimates, my parents will never speak. And that seems to me an extraordinary oppression" (185). Rodriguez's sense that the personal "can be revealed only to strangers" posits an isolated, estranged individual who can only "reveal" himself (notice that he does not "share" or "communicate," which would mean a two-way street) to an anonymous audience. This understanding of the task of writing assumes that the writer, operating in a vacuum, can thrust himself on the public without responsibilities or consequences; he can unburden himself by breaking silence on the printed page. Such an outlook indicates—in contrast to Rivera and Galarza—an "uncritical celebration of the autonomous individual" (R. Saldívar, *Chicano Narrative*, 169) and places ultimate value on the self-made man.

Rodriguez's belief that the novel form is for representing a "solitary existence set against a large social background" and that Chicano novels fail to capture communal life because of this mismatch ("Going Home," 24) has been disproven by my analyses of Rivera's and Cisneros's works. The assumption that the novel is necessarily an instrument of bourgeois individualism merely reflects Rodriguez's adoption of dominant cultural norms. In this respect, Rodriguez is not writing from within his ethnic culture; instead, he has assumed an elitist posture toward his people and uses the genre of autobiography, which seems to mirror his definition of the novel, for depicting his own solitary existence against a human backdrop. As the present

study has shown, this approach, whether practiced by artists or critics, stems from European American literary practices that are most
at odds with contemporary ethnic literatures. Unfortunately, Rodriguez himself as well as both the media and the academy have
considered *Hunger of Memory* the representative Chicano text. As one
critic puts it, "By fetishizing the efficacy of his single, unitary, homogeneous voice he, in effect, denies the harmony, discord and plural-
ity of other Latino voices" (Nericcio, "Autobiographies," 179).

As a post–Chicano Movement writer, Rodriguez is one example
of an academic of Mexican descent whose status as a "Chicano"
writer is open to question. Once again it is important to keep in mind
that, when we talk about Chicano/a writers, we are talking about
more than birthright and geographical background. The conscious
forging of a Chicano/a group identity in and through literature, as
many writers, critics, and promoters inform us, indicates a specific
(political) agenda behind the term *Chicano/a literature*. Whether individual writers see their work as political is beside the point.[16] In fact,
consciously propagandistic works that are weak artistically usually
do not survive their particular historical moment. When writers
choose to write from within their ethnic cultures, however, and call
themselves Chicanos or Chicanas, then they are part of the contemporary Chicano literary movement. Ideologically, this means that
they are working toward improved conditions for their (colonized)
people. In this light the ubiquity of Rodriguez's work in school text-
books suggests that, even though "cultural diversity" is purportedly
in vogue, it is filtered through a cultural hegemony that seeks to find
its own reflection. Because Rodriguez is a fine writer stylistically (by
traditional Western literary standards), he is considered an accept-
able Chicano spokesman. This travesty is named by one Chicano
critic: "*Hunger of Memory* is a perfect example of our tendency to
disguise the force of ideology behind the mask of aesthetics" (R.
Saldívar, *Chicano Narrative*, 170).

The agenda of the hegemonic order aside, it is my contention
that some of the most notable writings by Chicano/as of recent times
clearly reflect a communal ethos. Besides the works already discussed, there are other strong, well-crafted narratives that, in their
content and/or form, insist on valuing the collective above the isolated individual. As Juan Bruce-Novoa accurately states in his article
on the Chicano canon, both Rudolfo Anaya and Rolando Hinojosa

have produced major works that are communally oriented in theme and structure. Since these writers have received more critical attention than a host of others and, at this point, the value of collectivity and interconnectedness in their novels seems obvious, I will briefly touch upon two works by less studied Chicana writers to expand my thesis.

Perhaps one of the most clearly spelled out positions of solidarity can be found in Cherríe Moraga's 1983 autobiographical collection, *Loving in the War Years*. The dream poem that opens the book describes a couple in a prison camp. A soldier informs them that they will be executed. The I-narrator thinks about escape; this, however, would mean leaving her lover behind. The narrator concludes: "But immediately I understand that we must, at all costs, remain with each other. Even unto death. That it is our being together that makes the pain, even our dying, human" (i). This introduction, which conveys a universal message of allegiance—of throwing in one's lot with the oppressed versus the pursuit of self-interest—serves as a paradigm for human relationships throughout the book.

More specifically, the introduction, or prologue, states the textual premise. "The only way to write for la comunidad is to write so completely from your heart what is your own personal truth," a friend informs the narrator (vi). Telling the truth to ensure everyone's survival, as well as one's own, is the prime motivation for writing. Among a collage of poems, stories, and essays Moraga names specific oppressions, including the faultline in the concept of "Chicano community": "There is a deeper love between and amongst our people that lies buried between the lines of the roles we play with each other." She points out that true community is not based on hierarchal gender roles: "Family is *not* by definition the man in a dominant position over women and children. Familia is cross-generational bonding, deep emotional ties. . . . The strength of our families never came from domination. It has only endured in spite of it—like our women" (111).

In *Loving in the War Years* Moraga grapples with the risky parts of the self that she has kept hidden: her lesbianism and her ethnicity. In "coming out" on these two points, she is finally able to *own* her mother, the brown woman who speaks with her hands. "I am a white girl gone brown to the blood color of my mother" (60) serves as the refrain of a poem that first appeared in the 1981 women of color collection edited by Cherríe Moraga and Gloria Anzaldúa, *This Bridge Called My Back*. Moraga's critique of the Chicanos' major blind spot—namely, their attitudes toward female sexuality—reflects, like the writings of Gloria Anzaldúa, Ana Castillo, Sandra Cisneros, and a host of other Chicanas, the sincere desire for a viable, nonoppressive human community. In the essay "La Güera" Moraga states: "When I finally lifted the lid to my lesbianism, a profound connection with my mother reawakened in me" (*Loving*, 52). The family or community that she and other women of color are working toward is made up of those who are willing to "lift the lid" and "not settl[e] for less than freedom. . . . A total vision" (Preface, *This Bridge*, xix).

While Moraga's literary voice might be categorized as "radical Third World feminist"—a voice that conveys urgency, desperation, and absolute honesty—Denise Chávez promotes communal values through a different strategy. As a "performance writer" who has written and produced numerous plays over a twenty-year span, Chávez's debut as a fiction writer comes with her first Arte Público Press edition of *The Last of the Menu Girls* (1986). In seven interrelated stories, or "dramatic vignettes,"[17] narrated through the protagonist, Rocío Esquibel, Chávez portrays the interior and exterior worlds of clerks, gardeners, nurse's aids, hunchbacked dieticians—and manages to capture the essence of humanity in such everyday people.

Like Rivera's and Cisneros's texts, *Menu Girls* explores human relationships through characterization. In the title story the seventeen-year-old Rocío, working as a menu girl at the local hospital, finds it impossible to distance herself from the patients' lives: "My heart reached out to every person, dragged itself through the hallways with the patients, cried when they did, laughed when they did. I had no business in the job. I was too emotional" (35). The characters are both mundane and special. In the menu girl story and subsequent stories we come to understand that what makes these people interesting is precisely that Rocío is "too emotional." The moments of connection and misconnection that the protagonist experiences, ponders over, and dreams about are our moments as well. At the hospital, for example, a beautiful woman in a cream-colored gown screams at Rocío to go away. It is this woman "in her solitary anguish," Rocío tells us, who affects her the most deeply. The protagonist's own anguish is her inability to reach out and get through to the suffering woman: "Instead, I shrank back into myself and trembled behind the door" (27).

In the final story, "Compadre," Chávez draws on her cultural traditions to bridge the gap introduced in the title story. Here the practice of *compadrazgo* is explained and demonstrated cross-generationally. Rocío and her sister Mercy are the critical, dreamy, and disinterested younger generation who consider extended family obligations a nuisance. This gives the mother the opportunity to teach about loyalty, patience, and commitment, the qualities required in *compadrazgo:* "To be a compadre is to be unrelated and yet related, and yet willingly to allow the relationless relation absolute freedom within limits" (168). To willingly choose this "higher law," as the mother terms the Latino/a practice, is to be able to connect with strangers in mutual support and absolute trust. Thus, the mother values and honors her *compadre* Regino Saurez even though he is only the local handyman. "Compadre?" is the question that ends the book. In having the adult Rocío, on a visit back home, utter this one word, the author is suggesting that there *is* a way to bridge the gap between strangers. The mature Rocío now understands *how* to get through to others by drawing from communal models found in her ethnic roots. This conclusion refers the ending of the book back to the beginning, rendering the narrative circular rather than linear. Thus, the work can be considered a novel rather than a series of dramatic vignettes, or stories.

A 1988 interview with Chávez reveals the extent of her commitment to the people. "I think that writers need to train themselves to 'hit the streets,'" she states ("Interview," 3). Even in high school she used to write on slips of paper, staple them together, and pass them out as gifts. "Sometimes when I write a play I take it to the local senior center or the prison and share it." Chávez's purpose for writing—to communicate, to share—seems a direct antithesis to Richard Rodriguez's view of art. Perhaps the best contrast one can make is the difference, in terms of one critic's formulation cited elsewhere in the present study (see Clements, "Folk Historical Sense"), between having a folk versus an elitist historical sense in ethnic literature. *Folk art* in this sense (contrary to European American biases only now being corrected by revisions in "the canon") means a communal art different from, but not inferior to, other artistic forms. Praised for its stylistic polish, the work of Rodriguez is more widely accepted because it reinforces, among other things, an elitist view of the purposes of art. The more meaningful difference between Rodriguez and the other equally accomplished writers here, however, is precisely the difference between having an individualistic outlook and a communal one.

Chapter 6

The "First Language"
of Ethnic Community

In an interview entitled "Going Home," John Wideman offers the following image of cultural pluralism: "Culture is a house of cards. The parts are more tangible than the whole. A house of cards is dependent on the relationships among the cards. Its existence depends on the individual cards" (49). The writers and their works examined here are cards that form a significant portion of the "house" of American culture. The point is that *every* one is needed for the house to be a house. We cannot talk about "the first language of *American* individualism," therefore, without including the perspectives of ethnic writers on the issue of the primacy of the individual self.

Contemporary ethnic literatures exhibit commonalities as well as differences concerning the issue of individualism and community in America. A prominent similarity among the works discussed is that all the writers present the individual within a communal context. Unlike Eurocentric literary heroes, the individual alone is never viewed as a model of success. This does not mean, however, that every ethnic writer has the same degree of optimism toward the possibility of community in contemporary society. The variety of viewpoints range from the tragic in *The Year of the Dragon* to the new vision of community in *The Color Purple* and the long, time-honored perspective offered in *Ceremony*. The books in between these extremes affirm connection in a metaphoric and symbolic way (e.g., the protagonist might dance, sing, or participate in ritualized communal behavior in other ways).

The contrasts found between ethnic visions of life and individualist values, which Bellah and his associates and many other commentators attribute to American "habits of the heart," occur at the level of literary discourse. Elements borrowed from oral traditions convey a sense of community in ethnic literature that, as critics tell us, is rare in postmodernist European American fiction. At this point it is helpful to clarify the communal perspectives found in the texts discussed here by relating them to elements shared by one or more works. At the risk of oversimplifying I will begin by briefly situating these texts in the larger framework of American literature.

The 1975 collection of essays entitled *Individual and Community: Variations on a Theme in American Fiction* includes a critical study of Thomas Pynchon that credits the writer with an interest in the "connectedness of the world" after his first novel, *V*. The critic, however, considers this a deviation from other writers: "Pynchon's search for a new mode of indicative fiction is a lonely and isolated one, but it leads to a place where fiction can become less lonely, less isolated than it has been for many years" (Mendelson, "Sacred," 219). Had the study taken into consideration literatures by ethnic writers, even those published in the late 1960s and early 1970s, then this critic might not have found Pynchon unique. With the exclusion of ethnic American writers, however, the critic might be justified in claiming that "*Gravity's Rainbow* cataclysmically alters the landscape of recent fiction, and it alters the landscape of our moral knowledge as well" (221). A limited notion of what constitutes American literature stands behind this statement—the same limited perspective that enables some critics wrongly to assume that Momaday's 1968 novel has a nihilistic ending.

In the literature of Pynchon and other canonical European American writers the world is often an alienating, incoherent place. From this starting point characters seek to connect with or create some form of community. European and European American existentialist writings (e.g., from the late 1930s, such works as Jean Paul Sartre's *La Nausée* or Nathanael West's *The Day of the Locust*) have shown the difficulty of the enterprise. In these works lonely souls cross one another's paths, attempt and miss making real connections, then fade into a state of hopelessness. Compared to these alienated characters, Pynchon's Oedipa Maas can be considered "less lonely" when she relinquishes her indifference and the "exitlessness" of her life as a California housewife and stumbles upon hidden connections—upon networks of the outcast. This is a far cry, however, from the *affirmation* of community that can be found in contemporary ethnic literature. While the literary selections here are not unconditional celebrations of community, they do suggest worldviews that differ significantly from the modern Eurocentric one. A primary difference is the writers' attitudes toward family, culture, and society.

As noted at the beginning of this study, the standard for contemporary American literature, however much that standard is currently being challenged, was formalized by literary critics of the post–World War II era. The conformist and paranoid climate of the 1950s (with McCarthyism and the cold war) was not conducive to communitarian values. Middle American conformity—in the sense of complying with the "patriotic," suburban, "good-life" status quo of the era—isolated individuals and families. The emphasis on consumerism and "keeping up with the Joneses" promoted individualistic competition rather than communal sharing. Thus, Ralph Ellison's *Invisible Man*, a modernist "ethnic" work from this era, toys with the idea that individualism is the only worthwhile value. In the novel the protagonist concludes: "I've come a long way from those days when, full of illusion, I lived a public life and attempted to function under the assumption that the world was solid and all the relationships therein. Now I know men are different and that all life is divided and that only in division is there true health" (563).

Quoting the invisible man out of context is dangerous, since Ellison usually covers multiple sides of any issue. Nevertheless, throughout the novel the narrator speaks from a hole in the ground, and his final decision to come out is presented as an act of individual heroism and sacrifice rather than an affirmation of community. There is a "possibility," he says, "that even an invisible man has a socially responsible role to play" (568). There is both commitment and reservation in this statement. When we think of the narrator—who claims he will remain invisible—going above ground, we might also recall the first image offered in the prologue of the "invisible" black man beating up a white man who probably does not *see* him. This is hardly a positive model for human interaction. Even as Ellison resists the counterfeit illusions that present American culture as either white or "color-blind," the existential alternative he offers still leaves the individual alienated in society and disconnected from a divided black community.

The present investigation of a selection of ethnic works from the 1960s to the 1980s suggests a different literary emphasis. In these works alienation is not the result of impersonal societal forces but, rather, largely the result of specific social, political, and economic forms of oppression—primarily racism. Each protagonist's fate is determined by the degree of this oppression and by whether there remains a functioning, viable ethnic culture with which the individual can reconnect. When the ethnic culture is viewed as solely a negative reflection of white domination, as is the case with Frank Chin's San Francisco Chinatown, there is no alternative for the individual. From the playwright's viewpoint bourgeois individualism is not a viable solution: this is evident from the grotesque imagery at the end of the play. By forcing us to come to terms with our own destructive values, the tragedy is implicitly cathartic and offers an incentive for change. When, on the other hand, communal values are viewed as being sidetracked with "false" poses and behavior patterns—as in the case of Alice Walker's black rural South—then the negative aspects can be explicitly purged within the text, and a new model for community can be forged out of traditional values. Once again genuine connectedness is presented as the prerequisite for individual and societal health.

Whether the protagonist has access to a communal culture as well as whether he or she comprehends this culture appear to be crucial in these ethnic texts. Individuals left completely to their own devices—those who view themselves as ultimate arbiters of values—are presented by the ethnic writers as insensitive, self-centered, and harmful to others. The two Chinese American writers both present a parent who destroys or nearly destroys a child. Brave Orchid's treatment of her daughter in *The Woman Warrior* leaves the girl confused and fearing for her sanity. Pa's domination of Fred in *The Year of the Dragon* destroys the artistic, caring son and creates a monster. In either case the parent is a brave soul whose independent spirit in immigrating to America becomes entrenched and dogmatic when influenced by European American culture and affected by racism and classism. In order to gain a perspective on the ethnic culture that is more objective than the one offered by the individualist parent, therefore, the protagonist must leave home.

In the ethnic texts examined here leaving is not the permanent solution it often is in Eurocentric literature: even at a distance, the ethnic hero's energy is directed homeward. Thus, Chin's protagonist gives up his chance to be a writer and returns home, while Kingston's adult narrator reveals her psychic connection to her Chinese American heritage. That the ethnic protagonist is uncomfortable with the implications of absolute individualism is graphically depicted in Kingston's memoirs. "I could not understand 'I,'" the narrator tells us. "The Chinese 'I' has seven strokes, intricacies. How could the American 'I' . . . have only three strokes, the middle so straight?" (*Woman Warrior*, 193). As a literary trope, this example suggests that the Chinese American sense of personal identity is communal. The self-assertiveness in the English "I"—a linguistic sign that offers no communal support, no "intricacies"—is foreign and threatening to the ethnic child.

In claiming that the vitality of American literature resides in aggressive self-assertion bordering on "romantic nihilism, a poetry of force and darkness," Richard Chase and other Americanists obviously attribute an individualist ethic to American culture.[1] According to Chase's analysis, America's first language—as manifested in literature—is incontestably individualistic. In fact, American literary heroes turn their backs on culture altogether: "the sheer romantic exhilaration of escape from culture itself, into a world where nature is dire, terrible, and beautiful, where human virtues are personal, alien, and renunciatory, and where contradictions are to be resolved only by death" (*American Novel*, 7).

My examination of ethnic texts has not yielded this vision claimed for American literature. The yearning for the primal state of man (Chase could not have had women in mind!) described above seems essentially nostalgic and romantic. In contrast, ethnic literatures that reconnect with the past are generally confrontational, thematically grounded in a complex sense of historical reality, and less simplistic about culture. The ethnic community is not idealized; in fact, significant problems and conflicts within the culture are often closely scrutinized and, if possible, creatively resolved through art. Critics like Chase find literary value in works that express the "psychic wound" of the individual. An appropriate critique of ethnic American writing, on the other hand, understands that often the literary value in ethnic works is to be found in the literature's expression of the possibilities of communal healing.

In an article describing her experience with *The Woman Warrior*, a visiting professor from China writes: "Thanks to the Chinese-American Professor and the American students [from a course she audited], I could see the book in a different light. It is, after all, an

American story, not a Chinese one. Some of my assumptions were wrong from the very beginning because I am Chinese" (Zhang, "Chinese Woman's Response," 104). This candid testimonial can serve as a model for the present critical approach to ethnic literatures. As I have argued throughout this study, critics must examine their assumptions before they can effectively read an ethnic text. Until recent times the history of ethnic literary criticism has been largely one of misreading. Richard Wright's *Black Boy* (1937), for example, was read by white reviewers as proof that black people have no culture (Reilly, "Criticism," 10). As demonstrated in the present discussion, some critics have not progressed from such assumption-bound readings of ethnic literature. A major problem is that traditional theories regarding canonical American literature cannot be applied to literature by ethnic Americans without significant questioning of their informing ideology.

A parallel situation exists in the field of women's literature. Paul Lauter complains that, when he attended a panel discussion on women's literature, he found the panelists—all women scholars—taking turns offering close readings of one text ("Caste," 58). This approach to criticism—gleaned from New Critical theories—angered him, he says. Basically, he sensed the irrelevance of the critical methodology being imposed on the text:

> It seemed quite plain that significantly diverse experiences will produce significantly diverse cultural forms among men and women, just as among blacks and whites, working people and bourgeoisie. And that, therefore, the application to women's art of principles and standards derived almost exclusively from the study of men's art will tend to obscure, even hide, and certainly undervalue what women have created. (73)

New Critical methodology does not work well with ethnic and women's literature because it removes the text from its cultural-historical context. In ethnic literature such context is essential to the story. When the "environment" is ignored or insufficiently comprehended we are likely to misjudge the value of the work.

As seen in the present analysis, many contemporary ethnic writers are exploring aspects of their cultures' oral traditions. Whether as narrative structure, theme, or subject, the art of storytelling and mythmaking plays a prominent role in ethnic texts. Partly from the built-in structure of the oral performance and partly from the world-view these authors seek to convey through their medium, ethnic literatures tend to have a communal ethos. The writers in this study do not claim an individual "creative genius." There is the interesting phenomenon that, even as writers from ethnic American cultures are gaining ownership of their texts, in contrast to earlier white media-tion, these authors are assuming the posture of nonownership. The point is, oral performances *are* communal. Hence, literatures con-structed out of vernacular cultures do not usually have a single, con-trolling consciousness. *Vernacular* refers to "the people." For a story to retain a sense of the folk—that is, that the people are telling their own tales—writers must either find ways for the authorial voice to disappear into that of the oral storyteller or employ other strategies, such as ambiguity in *The Woman Warrior* and dramatic form in *The Year of the Dragon*, to achieve a similar end.

Beyond the evocation of group participation that can be found in contemporary ethnic texts there is a variety of approaches to the oral tradition among writers. Rivera, for example, uses the Chicano Spanish of the Texas-Mexico border to convey a sense of *el pueblo* (the people). The lives of Mexican American migrant workers are docu-mented, as he said, *para siempre* (forever) through this linguistic/cultural validation. Cisneros, on the other hand, evokes the child-hood of an inner-city Chicana through a combination of half-remem-bered and improvised songs, rhymes, and fairy tales and a variety of wordplay (the oxymoron *linoleum roses*, for example). Her accounts of children playing in the streets convey the creative, educational aspects of barrio culture.

Silko's insistence that, within the Laguna Pueblo culture, "no-body saves stories" (Silko, "Leslie Marmon Silko," 88) inserts tribal values into print culture. For Silko stories are sacred because they serve an important function: they save lives. In this context *sacred* does not mean, in contrast to scriptures and literary canons, "en-shrined" and "unchangeable." The idea that stories exist in a culture and are passed around—constantly being changed and updated by their tellers—until they are no longer needed indicates a completely communal attitude toward the "text." From his studies of mythology worldwide Joseph Campbell learned the same lesson. "Myths offer life models," he says. "But the models have to be appropriate to the time in which you are living. . . . The moral order has to catch up with the moral necessities of actual life in time, here and now" (*Power of Myth*, 13). In *Ceremony* Tayo's successful cure becomes a new myth to be shared within the Laguna Pueblo community. The story of sickness and recovery is placed into a contemporary, post–World War II context, which more effectively speaks to a younger generation.

Critics have hinted at "similarities" between the two Native American works discussed in the present study. In fact, novels by D'Arcy McNickle and James Welch—as well as the two by Momaday and Silko—have been tagged by at least one critic as "the mainstream tradition in Native American writing" (Silberman, "Opening the Text," 103), which bear "a striking family resemblance to one another" (101). As mentioned earlier, there does seem to be a homing-in pattern among Native American writers. From the analysis of Momaday's and Silko's texts strong parallels between the two are evident. It might even be said that Silko essentially repeats Momaday's story. *Ceremony* can be viewed as a tribal myth first recorded in print by Momaday. As Silko retells the story nine years later through Thought-Woman, this second literary performance both continues the tradition and updates/transforms the myth in significant ways. While it is not within the scope of this study to compare and contrast the two works, the connection between Silko's and Momaday's first novels needs to be stated. By Eurocentric literary standards Silko's novel might be considered "unoriginal" and plagiaristic.[2] Within the Native American oral and literary traditions, however, the text is a part of the community so that modern Eurocentric concepts of originality are meaningless. Silko's approach to storytelling is perfectly consistent in the tribal context. In fact, the Silko/Momaday example appropriately illustrates the American Indian belief that "the story belongs to everyone."

While Momaday shares Silko's sense of continuity, he also has a different agenda. In a previously cited article entitled "Folk Historical Sense" William Clements points out that "the concept of historical sense, folk or elite, must be applied pluralistically" (75). Both writers share a folk sense of their tribal cultures, says Clements, but Momaday's literary goal is preservation, while Silko's is perpetuation of the storytelling process. Clements's observation reminds us that, even among Native American writers, the general reliance upon communal memory to keep stories alive can be "Westernized" for a specific purpose. This is partially due to the different historical circumstances of the two writers' backgrounds. Preservation is crucial for Momaday because the Kiowa culture is essentially defunct, except in people's memories and residual rituals such as the Gourd Dance.[3] Silko, on the other hand, writes from a living oral culture—a traditional heritage that change and adaptation have not destroyed. This is to say that she can better afford to assume a less permanent and more experiential attitude toward the written word. Thus, historical and social factors play a significant role in an ethnic writer's approach to the literary act.

Even with variations in each writer's group historical experience, an interest in preservation as a literary theme seems more prevalent among the male writers in the study. This observation suggests that even male writers who are identifiably ethnic appear to have, similar to certain white male writers, a streak of the "lost paradise" attitude toward the concept of community. Once again no blanket statement can be made in this regard since the present sample is small and each writer's situation is unique. Nevertheless, a concern for the sacredness of the text—in terms of "monument" or "icon"—is more apparent among Momaday, Chin, Rivera, and Wideman than among the women authors. Feminist theorists would attribute this difference to "male" product orientation, which is generally equated with individualism, and "female" process orientation, which is considered communal. This implies that men are more individualistic, while women are more community oriented. My research indicates that this formulation is useful to an extent but should not be applied monolithically. Ethnicity, race, and class considerations—not to mention a writer's personal choice—significantly modify gender-based preferences that are, after all, socially acquired. The contrast between Chin and Kingston, for example, reflects each writer's specific approach to Chinese American culture.

Whatever his philosophical attitude toward Chinese tradition, Chin the playwright has chosen to dramatize the dilemma of a Chinese American family whose members are caught between a traditional set of values from a different culture and an untenable white-determined present in which they cannot maintain constructive relationships. Perhaps it is the insistence on the immutability of one's heritage that makes it difficult for the Eng family to find a viable solution to the alienation described in *The Year of the Dragon*. The protagonist's desire to be the filial son, for example, becomes self-defeating with a father who denies the reciprocal relationship behind the concept of filial piety. Chin's vision is tragic in its depiction of ethnic Americans who are unable to adapt traditional values to present conditions. As the playwright effectively demonstrates, rigidity and self-centeredness can ultimately destroy the ethnic family unit.

When she published *The Woman Warrior* Kingston seemed totally unconcerned with the accurate portrayal of her cultural heritage (its history and myths) in her art.[4] She once said, "I know all of these great heroes from the high tradition and they're not helping me in my American life. Such myths need to be changed and integrated into the peasant's life as well as into the Chinese American's life" ("Maxine Hong Kingston," 14). Her artistic rendering of Chinese legends enables her metaphorically to offer a vision of community that transcends the limitations of the "emigrant villagers." In this way culture is preserved by being made relevant to contemporary life.

Kingston's approach to oral tradition resembles Silko's in its emphasis on process and the need for change. The Chinese American writer departs from the Native American one, however, in her belief in the nonsacredness of myths. "Somehow," she says, "I think there's something wrong with oral histories. People are treating them like *sacred* material when what they are is *raw* material" ("This Is the Story," 6). This pragmatic viewpoint privileges poetic license and individual imagination. It enables the writer to maintain flexibility and ambiguity in the text. By utilizing a naive narrator who does not know what Chinese American culture is (as opposed to Chin's characters, who *think* they know and are subsequently trapped by their own constructs), the author is free to create meaning and "save" her protagonist from rigid cultural definitions. Given that this approach is not drawn directly from oral tradition, Kingston's artistic premise can be considered more "literary" than Silko's.

Silko draws from an ethnic culture that is grounded in this country, that is primarily oral, and that respects all life forms as sacred. Oral histories in such a culture are not just "raw material"; on the contrary, they exist and persist in spite of any individual influence. The myths, chants, etc., as well as the overall narrative structure in *Ceremony*, convey a sense of the sacredness of stories that is not found in Kingston's text. Silko is primarily an oral performer who is seeking ways to transmit the storytelling experience in written form.

There is also an observable difference between Walker's and Wideman's approaches to literature. Walker, along with other contemporary women writers, situates herself in a matrilineal storytelling tradition. This enables her to tell her "mothers'" stories as well as to update and contextualize them in the contemporary setting. In a way Walker's critical and artistic usage of Hurston's text—what Gates would call "Signifyin(g),"[5] or intertextuality—resembles what Silko does with Momaday's novel. Repetition with a difference—this basic strategy places the contemporary writer in a communal context as a link in the chain of an identifiable literary heritage. Once again the approach completely overturns the concept of individual originality. In reading *The Color Purple* one gets the sense that the women in the novel—and black women outside the novel—are telling a communal tale. We care about Celie and Shug as individuals, but we also hear other women's voices speaking through them. Walker conveys the sense of an ongoing community through her narrative strategy.

Wideman also generates a sense of collective existence in the semifictional black community of Homewood. Through vernacular elements such as blues piano music and tropic folk language the author situates the text within urban black culture. Juxtaposed to the open interaction among Homewood residents, however, are the memories, dreams, and nightmares of various characters. In these passages there is a lingering fear of loss—of a rich cultural past squandered by irresponsible individuals. More than once, for example, Carl wonders: "If he didn't wake up one morning, would there still be a Homewood?" (367). Nostalgia for an idealized black community, then, is part of the narrative structure as well as a literary theme in Wideman's *Sent for You Yesterday*.

Wideman's expression of the ephemeral nature of the world—that reality is created in our imaginations—resembles Momaday's interest in the same subject. In *House Made of Dawn* Abel's longing for an unnameable past is symbolically represented as a backward glance toward the land beyond the knoll. In Momaday's nonfictional *The Way to Rainy Mountain* and *The Names* the Kiowa past is relived and memorialized through the artistic imagination. Both the desire to capture and preserve in writing a specific reality—the Kiowa culture for Momaday and the black community of Homewood for Wideman—and the thematic treatment of rigid adherence to the past (as in Chin's work) contrasts with Silko's, Kingston's, Walker's, and Cisneros's attitudes toward literature. In *The House on Mango Street*, for example, the concept of "house" seems to operate on levels of cultural complexity—including the symbolically ambiguous—that contrast sharply with Momaday's identifiably mythic and spiritual "house made of dawn." Nevertheless, ultimately the intention of the writer shapes the product but does not change the result. That is, even if an artist like Silko is not primarily concerned with preserving the story through her writing, once committed to print the story is here to stay. Furthermore, in the last analysis the difference in emphasis between male and female ethnic writers regarding the immutability of the past can be attributed to artistic strategy as well as gender.

In taking a pluralistic approach, I have attempted to respect the cultural integrity of each text. The essential conclusion of this study is that ethnic literature does indeed offer an alternative discourse, a "first language" of community rather than individualism. The communal values promoted by the writers in this study reflect what one scholar has identified as the "local" in Hawai'i's multicultural environment: "The concept of the 'local' includes an intuitive grasp, at the very least, of family, reciprocity, and loyalty as fundamental values supposedly inherited from native Hawaiian and Asian immigrant communities" (Sumida, "Hawaii, the Northwest and Asia," 15). The shift in common discourse from the "melting pot," a Eurocentric concept in which ethnic diversity is neutralized, to the pluralistic idea of the "local" suggests that ethnic cultures are affirming communal values without giving up their identities. This idea of unity in diversity parallels what contemporary ethnic writers are inserting into American literary discourse.

As this discussion has shown, while the writers here approach their art from various perspectives, they also share significant common ground. One of the most prominent features is the use of vernacular elements in the narrative structure and language of the text. In the article "Theories of Ethnic Humor: How to Enter, Laughing" John Lowe informs us:

> Ethnic writers' pride in folkspeech stems from their joint aware-
> ness that dialect is rich, humorous, laden with metaphor, and
> therefore tactile and appealing. Since dialect, at least to the op-
> pressor, is part and parcel of the negative stereotype, pride in
> dialect constitutes inversion, transforming an oppressive signi-
> fier of otherness into a pride-inspiring prism, one which may be
> used for the critical inspection of "the other." At the same time,
> dialect writing is a kind of protective cloak that a critic can wear;
> the rustic satirist is less inclined to draw the immediate ire of the
> urbane reader. (448)

Obviously, linguistic control means power for a writer. This study
has found that it is through vernacular speech (including pidgin,
dialect, creole, and other versions of what are considered nonstandard English), cultural metaphors (such as a spider's web, a patch-
work quilt, and railroad ties), and cultural rituals (in the forms of
song, dance, and storytelling) that ethnic literature generates and
promotes a sense of community. As Lowe suggests, the use of vernacular language has the added advantage of enabling "cloaked"
criticism. Social commentary disguised as harmless dialect may be
one of the oldest "tricks" in the book. By utilizing the speech patterns
of the folk, writers are able to critique and challenge some prevalent
assumptions in American culture.

In contemporary ethnic American literature the use of folklore is
an alternative language that expresses an alternative vision. Folkloric
discourse, with its emphasis on rituals, myths, and vernacular
speech, offers a vision of society that affirms and celebrates community. Individuals in such a society are not isolated or narcissistic;
instead, they view themselves always in relation to others. For many
ethnic American cultures success, as Native American writers Louise
Erdrich and Paula Gunn Allen inform us, is measured by one's relationships—the size of and commitment to one's extended family, for
example—and not by material goods. Reciprocity rather than competition is the primary value, whether explicit or implied, that informs
these ethnic texts. Even from this limited exploration into literatures
from ethnic cultures, the "symbolic ethnicity" that Herbert Gans
found among white ethnics—with its implication of superficial values—certainly cannot be applied to these ethnic American cultures.

In a recent full-length study championing "middle American individualism," Gans faults Bellah and his associates for seeking a "quasi-religious community" in *Habits of the Heart*. "Thus," says Gans, "his [Bellah's] transcendentalism is his own. It is also utopian in the sense that it requires not only a different society but possibly another kind of human nature" (*Middle American Individualism*, 113). The ethnic writers here, who cannot be accused of being unduly "religious," would not agree with Gans's cynicism. The sense of community that they convey is not otherworldly but, rather, applies to the here and now among nonwhite ethnic peoples. The alternative vision contemporary ethnic American writers are promoting through their art can be viewed as a significant countercurrent to what Gans *and* Bellah assume are *American* "habits of the heart."

Notes

Chapter 1

1. Bellah et al.'s work is only a recent manifestation of a long line of canonized works on the "American national character" that emphasize American individualism. Consider, for example, Slotkin's *Regeneration through Violence*, Riesman et al.'s *The Lonely Crowd*, and Lasch's *The Culture of Narcissism*. In a twenty-page critique of *Habits*, Fredric Jameson identifies the researchers' "discourse analysis" concerning the "first language of individualism" as "one of the most remarkable features of the authors' work" ("On Habits," 556). For my purposes the value of the study resides mainly in its analysis of the *language* of individualism—a convenient starting point for discussing the use of language in ethnic literary texts.

2. While the Sapir-Whorf hypothesis has lost ground in the field of sociolinguistics, experts have not relinquished the connection between language and thought; they are just not willing to express the connection in absolute terms. As Trudgill explains, although the idea "that thought is actually constrained by language" is unacceptable, the conditioning of habitual thought by language is likely (*Sociolinguistics*, 26–28).

3. Baym cites Henry Nash Smith, Charles Feidelson, R. W. B. Lewis, Richard Chase, and Daniel G. Hoffman.

4. It is important to distinguish between the *recognition* of this literature in recent times and the existence of a literary tradition among specific ethnic groups. My contention is that ethnic literary traditions have existed for some time but have only been considered valid or worthwhile subjects of "serious" scholarly attention in academic circles since the late 1960s (with the possible exception of African American literature). This point is made by one critic and can be applied to other ethnic cultures: "There is a lingering impression given by some contemporary writers and critics that Afro-American (Black) writing (and Black consciousness) had an immaculate conception and a virgin birth one troubled night in the late-Sixties" (Everett, "'Tradition,'" 21).

5. Rivera makes the Chicano emphasis on community sound too recent. Significant sociological/cultural studies attribute familial and communal values to traditional Chicano culture. See, for example, Keefe and Padilla's *Chicano Ethnicity* (1987).

6. Schultz briefly discusses Leon Forrest, Charles Johnson, John Wideman, Albert Murray, Al Young, and John McCluskey.

Chapter 2

1. See Kitano and Daniels, *Asian Americans*, for the origin and coinage of the term *model minority*, pp. 48–50.
2. See Takaki's *Strangers*, chapter 12.
3. See Boelhower's *Through a Glass Darkly* for a definition and usage of this term.
4. In the preface to her recent study, *Between Two Worlds*, Ling identifies three anthologies published in the early 1970s (see pp. xii–xiii).
5. McDonald cites Chin's statement in a letter to Michael Kirby: "The Chinese used to say the Cantonese were so individualistic, they didn't get along with or trust anyone, not even each other. . . . EVERY CANTONESE IS WHOLE UNTO HIMSELF AS A PLANET and trusts no other living thing" (see McDonald Introduction, xxvi).
6. See, for example, Cawelti's *Apostles*.
7. The prose style of colloquial speech found among premodernist and modernist writers such as Twain, Stein, and Hemingway, which utilizes a syntax stressing individual word units rather than subordination as in compound-complex sentence structures. This has been identified as a distinctively American style by critics such as Harold Whitehall and Northrop Frye.
8. See the epigraph at the beginning of the discussion on Chin.
9. Among the attackers are Frank Chin, Benjamin R. Tong, and Jeffrey Paul Chan. See Kim's *Asian American Literature* (198–99) and accompanying notes for an introduction to the controversy.
10. Oscar Wilde once said, "Give a man a mask and he'll tell you the truth." Kingston could have published *Woman Warrior* under the mask of fiction in order to protect the truth she tells. However, her ethnicity and gender complicate the issue. Would her first work be taken as seriously if it were advertised as fiction? In effect, Kingston uses fictional techniques—the mask—in a nonfictional genre to tell the truth of her ethnic female experience. This strategy of expedience must be linked with audience expectations in a racist and sexist society.
11. Newman cites Nee's article, "See, Culture Is Made, Not Born . . . ," in her write-up of the 1978 Talk Story Conference in Hawaii (see "Hawaiian-American Literature Today," 53).
12. In Kingston's *China Men*, the narrator's ancestors find ingenious ways to combat this deprivation while working as laborers in mines and on the construction of railroads: they sing, recite poetry, and shout into empty spaces.
13. *China Men* lists immigration laws for eight straight pages as a frustrated response to this ignorance.
14. Kingston makes a point of not intruding and making connections of which her narrator is incapable. A child growing up in a multiethnic urban environment, for example, is bound to sort by color, if not by gender and class. The protagonist stresses the "Chinese" stories through the same lens—as that aspect of her reality that best captures her vivid imagination.
15. For example, according to Blinde, "It is as if the richness of a bi-cultural life experience cannot be contained within the limits of literary dictates and that a 'spill-over' from one form to another is the only justice that can be done in the rendition of such a life" ("Icicle," 53).

16. Since "talk-story" has become common vernacular in Hawai'i, Kingston picked up this term from living on the islands.

17. Historically, it was a male warrior, General Yueh Fei, who had his back tattooed (Lightfoot, "Hunting the Dragon," 65, n. 2).

18. In Giacomo Puccini's 1904 opera, *Madame Butterfly*, a U.S. naval officer (Pinkerton) buys a beautiful Japanese woman (known as Butterfly) for less than an American dollar. He makes her fall in love with him, uses her, then leaves. When she confirms that she has been abandoned, she kills herself. This is explained in the play (see Hwang, *M. Butterfly*, 4–5, 12–15).

19. In this context, *Issei* refers to the first-generation Japanese immigrants, while *Nisei* designates second-generation Japanese Americans who are actually born in America.

Chapter 3

1. The terms *black* and *African American* are used interchangeably in this study, although the suitability of either term within a specific context guides the usage.

2. Both have promoted the myth that African Americans have no culture (see Frazier, "Traditions and Patterns of Negro Family Life"; and Glazer and Moynihan, *Beyond the Melting Pot*).

3. According to Johnson, "It is probably the most commercially successful novel in the entire history of Afro-American letters . . . " (*Being and Race*, 105).

4. T. Harris faults Walker for the lack of verisimilitude in her characters. She exclaims, for example, "I couldn't imagine a Celie existing in any black community I knew or any that I could conceive of. What sane black woman, I asked, would sit around and take that crock of shit from all those folks?" ("On *The Color Purple*," 155). This type of criticism requires the author to depict only one type of character—someone who meets the critic's standard of a "sane black woman."

5. Pryse speaks of "a lately evolved tradition in literary history" in referring to writings by black women (see *Conjuring*, 22).

6. Willis calls this "the four-page formula" of storytelling in contemporary writings by black women (see *Specifying*, 14–15).

7. Martin and Martin make the significant point that some social scientists have confused the street ideology with black culture when street cool is actually "deviant from—the very antithesis of—legitimate black culture" (*Helping Tradition*, 74).

8. Hernton finds Nettie's letters too great a departure from the slave narrative genre and incongruous with Celie's narrative in "texture and substance." He observes that they "sound too much as if they were written during the nineteenth century by, say, Charlotte Forten Grimke" (*Sexual Mountain*, 29). Hernton does not take into account the *contrast* between black vernacular English and standard English. Nettie's educated language, especially since she is writing in a vacuum with no real audience, necessarily sounds textbookish. This language also reflects Nettie's movement away from Celie's trapped world.

9. As this study goes to press, the single edition of the three works called *Homewood Trilogy* has gone out of print. Each of the three works in the trilogy has been published separately by Random House. For our purposes, however, the single

edition is cited because of its importance in discussing the genesis and development of the whole trilogy as it was conceived.

10. This woman was Wideman's real ancestor, just as Homewood was the black community in which Wideman had spent his childhood. Fact and fiction cross a great deal in the trilogy.

11. Henry Louis Gates, Jr., had built his doctoral dissertation around this eye-opening issue. In his own words, "It remains difficult for me to believe that any human being would be demanded to write himself or herself into the human community" (see *Figures in Black*, xv–xxxii).

12. Framing is the practice of quoting in dialect or other forms of ethnic speech while narrating in "standard" English, thereby "framing" language that is considered "substandard" rather than "nonstandard." This is a common technique in nineteenth-century uses of colloquial language—one that writers like Mark Twain tried to break out of.

13. Wideman published all three books of the trilogy in original paperbacks to make them more accessible to the black community. He emphasizes that he is not "writing down" to a black audience ("because my people have had the full range of human experience"), but, rather, he is expanding his "own frames of reference" as a writer (see "Going Home," 43–44).

14. Wideman refers to this as "allow[ing] one person to get inside another person's skin." This is one way in which he conveys a sense of the collective unconscious (see "Going Home," 48).

15. I am borrowing Bell's terminology in *Afro-American Novel* (see pp. 307–15 on Wideman).

16. A great deal of energy has been spent in arguing whether the young woman Beloved is supposed to be a ghost or a lost runaway slave (see, for example, House's article). Apparently, some critics consider it unworthy of Morrison to be writing "Gothic tales." It is my opinion that critical energies would be better spent in interpreting other elements of the novel while taking a more relaxed approach toward the ghost-versus-human question. Once again a both/and approach yields a richer reading experience than would a reductionistic one. I believe that Western society's insistence on a concrete, black/white, nonspiritual world unnecessarily restricts the art of many ethnic American writers.

Chapter 4

1. This discussion utilizes the terms *Native American* and *Indian* synonymously, although the suitability of the term within a specific environment dictates the usage. Currently, many indigenous peoples prefer to be called "Indians" and refer to their respective tribes as "Indian nations."

2. Allen is not saying that only Indians can achieve this sense of timelessness in literature, however. According to her, James Joyce did it, and, "if it weren't for Joyce, we wouldn't have Momaday" ("MELUS Interview," 20).

3. This point will be discussed in the concluding chapter of this study.

4. Schubnell, Momaday's biographer, notes: "When the Pulitzer Prize jury for fic-

tion . . . selected *House Made of Dawn* for their award, they took the reading public as well as the author by surprise. Momaday at first refused to believe the news, and some of the senior editors at Harper and Row could not even remember the novel" (*N. Scott Momaday*, 93).

5. Momaday studied with Yvor Winters at Stanford University, during which time his authoritative research was instrumental in resurrecting the nineteenth-century antitranscendental poet Frederick Goddard Tuckerman.

6. For example, Captain Ahab, Jay Gatsby, Huck Finn, and Joe Christmas.

7. The American novel typically includes an element of romance, says Richard Chase in *The American Novel and Its Tradition*. This points to an identifiable "native tradition," which might be called the "American romance-novel" (viii).

8. So far I have seen this connection made only in Schubnell's analysis (*N. Scott Momaday*, 122).

9. Dearborn writes, "Indeed, many ethnic women's novels are not *by* ethnic women; they are 'as told to' stories, anthropological narratives, collections of letters, biographies" (*Pocahontas's Daughters*, 15).

10. It seems that, if an ethnic writer like Silko utilizes communal lore, she is evidencing, according to critics like Dearborn, "compromised authorship." If a canonical writer like Joyce or Eliot or the great Shakespeare does virtually the same, however, he is said to be "richly allusive" (see, for example, Eliot's "Tradition and the Individual Talent").

11. Concern with "original" material is post-Renaissance in the European literary tradition (it does not mark Chaucer or Shakespeare, for example) and is particularly reflected in Romantic notions regarding artistic genius.

12. See Tedlock, "Toward an Oral Poetics," for an understanding of this aspect of oral performance.

13. This observation comes from my classroom experiences in teaching this work.

14. In his introduction to *American Indian Literature* Velie points out that "traditional Indian literature was more functional than ours [meaning Eurocentric, or what he calls 'mainstream American literature']. Myths and tales were educational tools that taught the young tribal beliefs and values" (7). It is important to keep in mind the didactic purpose of stories in Native American cultures.

Chapter 5

1. See, for example, Lizárraga, "Patriarchal Ideology"; Fuente, "Invisible Women"; and Rascón, "La caracterización."

2. All future citations from *tierra* will be taken from the 1987 edition translated by Evangelina Vigil Piñon due to its ready availability.

3. Rivera served as chancellor at University of California at Riverside during the last five years of his life.

4. See José Saldívar's well-argued essay ("The Ideological and the Utopian"), which locates meaning in contemporary Chicano narratives, including Rivera's, within a dialectical analysis of the ideological and the utopian as defined in Fredric Jameson's *The Political Unconscious*. While the present analysis does not directly

utilize such a dialectic, Jameson's formulation that "dialectical thought [is] the anticipation of the logic of a collectivity which has not yet come into being" (286) can be productively kept in mind as this analysis proceeds.

5. Thus, placing the writer in the same assimilationist camp as Richard Rodriguez, whom Rivera himself has challenged in a critical essay (see Rivera's "Richard Rodriguez's *Hunger of Memory* as Human Antithesis").

6. While terminology for ethnic American groups continues to be problematic, this restrictive definition can be helpful in distinguishing between a specifically Chicano/a ethos versus the more neutral or broader Mexican American, Latino/a, and Hispanic designations.

7. Although Rivera saw himself as a "documenter" of the migrant workers he had known from 1945 to 1955 (see Bruce-Novoa's interview in *Chicano Authors*, 148–50), *tierra* is still a work of the imagination and, as such, cannot be read literally as straight history or sociology.

8. The author's original manuscript corroborates this reading. See n.7 of Olivares's article "Search for Being."

9. Ramón Saldívar's research indicates that the *corrido* traditionally has been a male domain, and, as such, "its symbolic value is decisively affected both in terms of performance and content by gender roles and specifically male values" (*Chicano Narrative*, 38). Therefore, while Rivera found Paredes's book liberating, gender restrictions would have made similar artistic and cultural identifications difficult for women writers.

10. Vallejos has written an informative dissertation on the "ancient Indian religious" elements in literature by contemporary Chicano writers, including Rivera and Anaya (see "Mestizaje," esp. chap. 3).

11. One exception is Quinto Sol's 1973 issue of *El Grito* entitled *Chicanas en la literatura y el arte/Chicanas in Literature and Art* (see Romano-V. and Ríos-C.) Critical studies of Chicano literature have included one or two female writers out of at least a dozen writers discussed. Bruce-Novoa's 1982 study of Chicano poets, for example, includes one Chicana (see *Chicano Poetry*).

12. See Dowling's *Cinderella Complex*.

13. Cisneros makes an interesting observation regarding her Chicano culture: "Part of it is our religion, because there's so much guilt. . . . it's in your blood. Mexican religion is half western and half pagan; European Catholicism and Precolumbian religion all mixed in. It's a very strange Catholicism like nowhere else on the planet and it does strange things to you. There's no one sitting on your shoulder but you have the worst censor of all, and that's yourself" ("Solitary Fate," 67). This comment corroborates Rivera's point in *tierra*, in which the child openly challenges his fear by cursing God and discovers that the earth does not really split open, as he had been taught, and devour the blasphemer. In this respect both Cisneros and Rivera were working toward the same liberation from cultural taboos through their art.

14. In his analysis of *Mango Street* Gutiérrez-Revuelta quotes Juan Rodríguez's judgment of Esperanza's leaving Mango Street as being "Anglicized" and "individualistic." While he considers this too harsh, he himself also falls into the trap of confusing Esperanza with Cisneros and indicting the author for the fictional character's

"escapism." As the critic states: " . . . olvidará Esperanza 'who she is?'. La única forma de respondernos a esta pregunta es estando pendientes de la nueva producción de Sandra Cisneros. (. . . will Esperanza forget 'who she is'? The only way to answer this question is to wait for Sandra Cisneros's new work; my translation)" ("Género e ideología," 56). Assuming that Cisneros will again write about Esperanza indicates that the critic thinks Esperanza *is* Cisneros.

15. See, for example, Ramón Saldívar's *Chicano Narrative*, chap. 7; Vallejos's "Ritual Process"; Nericcio's "Autobiographies"; and Villanueva-Collado's "Growing Up Hispanic."

16. See Mindiola, "Politics and Chicano Literature," for a brief comparison of several writers on the topic.

17. In the interview with Lynn Gray, Chávez uses this term to refer to *Menu Girls:* "It's like a series of scenes more than short stories; it's not a novel. Maybe dramatic vignettes is a better description" ("Interview," 2). Once again there is the problem of viewing the work as fragments rather than a complete whole. Since this text resembles those of Rivera's and Cisneros's in conceptual layout, it might be useful to consider it a novel made up of dramatic vignettes or stories.

Chapter 6

1. In fact, Chase and other canonical scholars of the 1950s—due to their influence in academia—probably helped to form the individualistic, white, middle-class language that researchers like Bellah and his associates encountered in the 1980s.

2. In my research I have not encountered any critic who directly addresses this issue. Perhaps the topic is taboo at the moment since critics suspect, but are unwilling to confront, what might be considered the ultimate sin by post-Romantic Eurocentric literary standards.

3. Momaday has a book of poems entitled *The Gourd Dancer.*

4. This attitude in Kingston's first work reflects the author's artistic approach as well as a lack of knowledge (intentional at the time) of her ethnic heritage. As Chin and others have charged, however, the uninformed reader tends to interpret *The Woman Warrior* as "static," as a faithful rendering of history and myth. Since the controversial publication of her book as "nonfiction," Kingston has shown a growing awareness and interest in Chinese American history and myth.

5. Gates's definition as used in this context can be found in *Figures in Black:* "Signifyin(g) is a uniquely black rhetorical concept, entirely textual or linguistic, by which a second statement or figure repeats, or tropes, or reverses the first. Its use as a figure for intertextuality allows us to understand literary revision without resource to thematic, biographical, or Oedipal slayings at the crossroads; rather, critical signification is tropic and rhetorical" (49); see also Gates's *Signifying Monkey.*

Works Cited

Acuña, Rodolfo. *Occupied America: A History of Chicanos*. 3d ed. New York: Harper and Row, 1988.

Alarcón, Norma. "Chicana's Feminist Literature: A Re-Vision through Malintzin/or Malintzin: Putting Flesh Back on the Object." In Moraga and Anzaldúa, *This Bridge Called My Back*, 182–90.

Allen, Paula Gunn. "Bringing Home the Fact: Tradition and Continuity in the Imagination." In Swann and Krupat, *Recovering the Word*, 563–79.

———. "A MELUS Interview: Paula Gunn Allen." With Franchot Ballinger and Brian Swann. *MELUS* 10, no. 2 (Summer 1983): 3–25.

———. "The Sacred Hoop: A Contemporary Indian Perspective on American Indian Literature." In Chapman, *Literature of the American Indians*, 111–36.

Anello, Ray, and Pamela Abramson. "Characters in Search of a Book." *Newsweek* 99, no. 25 (21 June 1982): 67.

Anzaldúa, Gloria. *Borderlands/La Frontera: The New Meztiza*. San Francisco: Spinsters/ Aunt Lute, 1987.

Bachelard, Gaston. *The Poetics of Space*. Translated by María Jolas. Boston: Beacon Press, 1969.

Baker, Houston A., Jr. *Blues, Ideology, and Afro-American Literature: A Vernacular Theory*. Chicago: University of Chicago Press, 1984.

Barth, Fredrik, ed. *Ethnic Groups and Boundaries: The Social Organization of Culture Difference*. Oslo, Norway: Universitetsforlaget, 1969.

Bassnett, Susan. "Bilingual Poetry: A Chicano Phenomenon." *Revista Chicano-Riqueña* 13 (1985): 3–4.

Baym, Nina. "Melodramas of Beset Manhood: How Theories of American Fiction Exclude Women Authors." In *The New Feminist Criticism: Essays on Women, Literature, and Theory*, edited by Elaine Showalter, 68–80. New York: Pantheon, 1985.

Bell, Bernard W. *The Afro-American Novel and Its Tradition*. Amherst: University of Massachusetts Press, 1987.

Bellah, Robert N., et al. *Habits of the Heart: Individualism and Commitment in American Life*. Berkeley and Los Angeles: University of California Press, 1985.

———, eds. *Individualism and Commitment in American Life: Readings on the Themes of Habits of the Heart*. New York: Harper and Row, 1987.

Bender, Thomas. *Community and Social Change in America*. Baltimore: Johns Hopkins University Press, 1978.

Bennion, John. "The Shape of Memory in John Edgar Wideman's *Sent for You Yester-day*." *Black American Literature Forum* 20 (Spring–Summer 1986): 143–50.

Bercovitch, Sacvan. *The American Jeremiad*. Madison: University of Wisconsin Press, 1978.

Bevis, William. "Native American Novels: Homing In." In Swann and Krupat, *Recovering the Word*, 580–620.

Black Elk. *Black Elk Speaks: Being the Life Story of a Holy Man of the Oglala Sioux*. As told through John G. Neihardt. 1932. Reprint. Lincoln: University of Nebraska Press, 1988.

Blinde, Patricia Lin. "The Icicle in the Desert: Perspective and Form in the Works of Two Chinese-American Women Writers." *MELUS* 6, no. 3 (Fall 1979): 51–71.

Blue, Adrianne. "From the Ghetto." *New Statesman* 108, no. 2802 (30 November 1984): 34.

Boelhower, William. *Through a Glass Darkly: Ethnic Semiosis in American Literature*. New York: Oxford University Press, 1987.

Broyles, Yolanda Julia. "Hinojosa's *Klail City y sus alrededores*: Oral Culture and Print Culture." In *The Rolando Hinojosa Reader*, edited by José David Saldívar, 109–32. Houston: Arte Público Press, 1985.

Bruce-Novoa, Juan. *Chicano Authors: Inquiry by Interview*. Austin: University of Texas Press, 1980.

———. *Chicano Poetry: A Response to Chaos*. Austin: University of Texas Press, 1982.

———. *Retrospace: Collected Essays on Chicano Literature, Theory, and History*. Houston: Arte Público Press, 1990.

Bruchac, Joseph. "Survival Comes This Way: Contemporary Native American Poetry." In Harris and Aguero, *A Gift of Tongues*, 196–205.

Campbell, Joseph. *The Power of Myth*. With Bill Moyers. New York: Doubleday/Anchor Books, 1988.

Candelaria, Cordelia. "La Malinche, Feminist Prototype." *Frontiers* 5, no. 2 (1980): 1–6.

Carter, Barbara L., and Dorothy K. Newman. "Perceptions about Black Americans." In *America in the Seventies: Some Social Indicators*, edited by Conrad Taeuber, 179–205. The Annals of the American Academy of Political and Social Science 435. Philadelphia: American Academy of Political and Social Science, 1978.

Cassirer, Ernst. *Language and Myth*. Translated by Susanne K. Langer. New York: Harper and Brothers, 1946.

Cawelti, John. *Apostles of the Self-Made Man*. Chicago: University of Chicago Press, 1965.

Chapman, Abraham, ed. *Literature of the American Indians: Views and Interpretations*. New York: NAL/Meridian Books, 1975.

Chase, Richard. *The American Novel and Its Tradition*. Baltimore: Johns Hopkins Press, 1957.

Chávez, Denise. "Interview with Denise Chávez." With Lynn Gray. *Short Story Review* 5, no. 4 (Fall 1988): 2–4.

———. *The Last of the Menu Girls*. Houston: Arte Público Press, 1986.

Chávez, John R. *The Lost Land: The Chicano Image of the Southwest*. Albuquerque: University of New Mexico Press, 1984.

Chin, Frank. *The Chickencoop Chinaman and The Year of the Dragon*. Seattle: University of Washington Press, 1981.

———. "Confessions of the Chinatown Cowboy." *Bulletin of Concerned Asian Scholars* 4, no. 3 (Fall 1972): 52–70.

Chin, Frank, et al., eds. *Aiiieeeee!: An Anthology of Asian-American Writers.* Washington: Howard University Press, 1983.

Christian, Barbara T. "Alice Walker." *Dictionary of Literary Biography* 33:258–71.

———. *Black Women Novelists: The Development of a Tradition, 1892–1976.* Westport, Conn.: Greenwood Press, 1980.

Cisneros, Sandra. "From a Writer's Notebook." *Americas Review* 15, no. 1 (Spring 1987): 69–79.

———. *The House on Mango Street.* Houston: Arte Público Press, 1985.

———. "On the Solitary Fate of Being Mexican, Female, Wicked and Thirty-Three: An Interview with Writer Sandra Cisneros." With Pilar E. Rodríguez Aranda. *Americas Review* 18, no. 1 (Spring 1990): 64–79.

Clements, William M. "Folk Historical Sense in Two Native American Authors." *MELUS* 12, no. 1 (Spring 1985): 65–78.

Clemons, Walter. "A Gravestone of Memories." *Newsweek* 110 (28 September 1987): 74–75.

Colburn, David R., and George E. Pozzetta, eds. *America and the New Ethnicity.* Port Washington, N.Y.: Kennikat Press, 1979.

Dearborn, Mary V. *Pocahontas's Daughters: Gender and Ethnicity in American Culture.* New York: Oxford University Press, 1986.

Deloria, Vine, Jr. *Custer Died for Your Sins: An Indian Manifesto.* New York: Avon Books, 1969.

DeVos, George, and Lola Romanucci-Ross, eds. *Ethnic Identity: Cultural Continuities and Change.* Palo Alto, Calif.: Mayfield, 1975.

Dillard, J. L. *Toward a Social History of American English.* Berlin: Mouton, 1985.

Doherty, Thomas P. "American Autobiography and Ideology." In Stone, *American Autobiography*, 95–108.

Dowling, Colette. *The Cinderella Complex: Women's Hidden Fear of Independence.* New York: Summit Books, 1981.

Du Bois, W. E. Burghardt. *The Souls of Black Folk.* New York: NAL/Signet Books, 1969.

Eakin, Paul John. *Fictions in Autobiography: Studies in the Art of Self-Invention.* Princeton: Princeton University Press, 1985.

Eliot, T. S. "Tradition and the Individual Talent." In *Critical Theory since Plato*, edited by Hazard Adams, 784–87. New York: Harcourt Brace Jovanovich, 1971.

Ellison, Ralph. *Invisible Man.* New York: Random House/Vintage Books, 1972.

———. *Shadow and Act.* 1953. New York: NAL/Signet Books, 1966.

Erdrich, Louise. *Tracks.* New York: Henry Holt, 1988.

Erdrich, Louise, and Michael Dorris. "An Interview with Louise Erdrich and Michael Dorris." With Kay Bonetti. *Missouri Review* 11, no. 2 (1988): 79–99.

Everett, Chestyn. "'Tradition' in Afro-American Literature." *Black World* (December 1975): 20–35.

Evers, Larry. "A Response: Going Along with the Story." In Sands, *Special Symposium Issue*, 71–76.

Eysturoy, Annie O., and José Antonio Gurpegui. "Chicano Literature: Introduction and Bibliography." *American Studies International* 28, no. 1 (April 1990): 48–82.

Faulkner, William. *The Sound and the Fury*. New York: Random House/Vintage Books, 1929.

Fisher, Dexter, ed. *The Third Woman: Minority Women Writers of the United States*. Boston: Houghton Mifflin, 1980.

Forkner, Ben. "Ernest J. Gaines." *Critical Survey of Short Fiction* 4:1429–36.

Frazier, E. Franklin. "Traditions and Patterns of Negro Family Life in the United States." In *Race and Culture Contacts*, edited by E. B. Reuter, 191–94. New York: McGraw-Hill, 1934.

Fryer, Judith. "Tending the Language: American Ethnic Women's Fictions." *American Quarterly* 38, no. 4 (Fall 1986): 661–67.

Fuente, Patricia de la. "Invisible Women in the Narrative of Tomás Rivera." *Revista Chicano-Riqueña* 13, nos. 3–4 (1985): 81–89.

Fuller, Hoyt W. "The New Black Literature: Protest or Affirmation." In *The Black Aesthetic*, edited by Addison Gayle, Jr., 346–69. New York: Doubleday/Anchor Books, 1972.

Gaines, Ernest J. *Bloodline*. 1968. Reprint. New York: W. W. Norton, 1976.

———. *A Gathering of Old Men*. 1983. Reprint. New York: Random House/Vintage Books, 1984.

———. "This Louisiana Thing That Drives Me." With Charles H. Rowell. *Callaloo* 1, no. 3 (May 1978): 39–51.

"Gaines, Ernest J. (1933–)." In *Modern Black Writers: A Library of Literary Criticism*, edited by Michael Popkin, 198–202. New York: Ungar, 1978.

Galarza, Ernesto. *Barrio Boy*. Notre Dame: University of Notre Dame Press, 1971.

Gans, Herbert J. *Middle American Individualism: The Future of Liberal Democracy*. New York: Free Press, 1988.

———. "Symbolic Ethnicity: The Future of Ethnic Groups and Cultures in America." In Gans et al., *On the Making of Americans*, 193–220.

Gans, Herbert J., et al., eds. *On the Making of Americans: Essays in Honor of David Riesman*. Philadelphia: University of Pennsylvania Press, 1979.

García, Reyes. "Sense of Place in *Ceremony*." *MELUS* 10, no. 4 (Winter 1983): 37–48.

Gates, Henry Louis, Jr. *Figures in Black: Words, Signs, and the "Racial" Self*. New York: Oxford University Press, 1987.

———. *The Signifying Monkey: A Theory of Afro-American Literary Criticism*. New York: Oxford University Press, 1988.

Genovese, Eugene D. *Roll, Jordan, Roll: The World the Slaves Made*. 1974. Reprint. New York: Random House, 1976.

Glazer, Nathan, and D. Moynihan. *Beyond the Melting Pot: The Negroes, Puerto Ricans, Jews, Italians, and Irish of New York City*. 1963. 2d ed. Cambridge: MIT Press, 1970.

———. Introduction to Glazer and Moynihan, *Ethnicity*, vii–xcv.

———, eds. *Ethnicity: Theory and Experience*. Cambridge: Harvard University Press, 1975.

Gordon, Milton M. *Assimilation in American Life: The Role of Race, Religion, and National Origins*. New York: Oxford University Press, 1964.

Gutiérrez-Revuelta, Pedro. "Género e ideología en el libro de Sandra Cisneros: *The House on Mango Street*." *Crítica: Journal of Critical Essays* 1, no. 3 (1986): 48–59.

Harris, Marie, and Kathleen Aguero, eds. *A Gift of Tongues: Critical Challenges in Contemporary American Poetry*. Athens: University of Georgia Press, 1987.

Harris, Trudier. "On *The Color Purple*, Stereotypes, and Silence." *Black American Literature Forum* 18, no. 4 (Winter 1984): 155–61.

Hemingway, Ernest. *In Our Time*. 1925. Reprint. New York: Charles Scribner's Sons, 1930.

Hernton, Calvin C. *The Sexual Mountain and Black Women Writers: Adventures in Sex, Literature, and Real Life*. New York: Doubleday/Anchor Books, 1987.

Herrera-Sobek, María, ed. Introduction to *Beyond Stereotyping: The Critical Analysis of Chicana Literature*, 9–28. Binghamton, N.Y.: Bilingual Press/Editorial Bilingüe, 1985.

Hogan, Linda. "Who Puts Together." In *Studies in American Indian Literature: Critical Essays and Course Designs*, edited by Paula Gunn Allen, 169–77. New York: MLA, 1983.

Hornstein, Lillian H., et al., eds. *The Reader's Companion to World Literature*. 2d ed. New York: NAL/Mentor Books, 1973.

House, Elizabeth B. "Toni Morrison's Ghost: The Beloved Who Is Not Beloved." *Studies in American Fiction* 18, no. 1 (Spring 1990): 17–26.

Howe, Irving. "The Limits of Ethnicity." *New Republic* 176, no. 26 (25 June 1977): 17–19.

———. *The World of Our Fathers*. 1976. Reprint. New York: Simon and Schuster/Touchstone Books, 1983.

Hsu, Francis L. K. *The Challenge of the American Dream: The Chinese in the United States*. Belmont, Calif.: Wadsworth, 1971.

Hwang, David Henry. *M. Butterfly*. New York: Penguin/Plume Books, 1989.

Jameson, Fredric. "On *Habits of the Heart*." *South Atlantic Quarterly* 86, no. 4 (Fall 1987): 545–65.

———. *The Political Unconscious: Narrative as a Socially Symbolic Act*. Ithaca, N.Y.: Cornell University Press, 1981.

Jencks, Christopher. "The Social Basis of Unselfishness." In Gans et al., *On the Making of Americans*, 63–86.

Jennings, Francis. *The Invasion of America: Indians, Colonialism, and the Cant of Conquest*. Chapel Hill: University of North Carolina Press, 1975.

Johnson, Charles. *Being and Race: Black Writing since 1970*. Bloomington: Indiana University Press, 1988.

Jones, LeRoi. *Blues People*. New York: Morrow Quill, 1963.

Kanellos, Nicolás. "Language and Dialog in . . . *y no se lo tragó la tierra*." *Revista Chicano-Riqueña* 13, nos. 3–4 (1985): 53–65.

Keefe, Susan E., and Amado M. Padilla. *Chicano Ethnicity*. Albuquerque: University of New Mexico Press, 1987.

Kilson, Martin. "Blacks and Neo-Ethnicity in American Political Life." In Glazer and Moynihan, *Ethnicity*, 236–66.

Kim, Elaine H. *Asian American Literature: An Introduction to the Writings and Their Social Context*. Philadelphia: Temple University Press, 1982.

———. Preface to Kim, *Asian American Literature*, xi–xix.

Kingston, Maxine Hong. *China Men*. New York: Alfred A. Knopf, 1980.

———. "Cultural Mis-readings by American Reviewers." In *Asian and Western Writers in Dialogue: New Cultural Identities*, edited by Guy Amirthanayagam, 55–65. London: Macmillan, 1982.

———. "Maxine Hong Kingston." With Arturo Islas. In *Women Writers of the West Coast:*

Speaking of Their Lives and Careers, edited by Marilyn Yalom, 11–20. Santa Barbara: Capra, 1983.

———. "Talk with Mrs. Kingston." With Timothy Pfaff. *New York Times Book Review* (18 June 1980): 1, 25–26.

———. "This Is the Story I Heard: A Conversation with Maxine Hong Kingston and Earll Kingston." With Phyllis Hoge Thompson. *Biography* 6, no. 1 (Winter 1983): 1–12.

———. *The Woman Warrior: Memoirs of a Girlhood among Ghosts*. New York: Random House/Vintage Books, 1977.

Kitano, Harry H. L., and Roger Daniels. *Asian Americans: Emerging Minorities*. Englewood Cliffs, N.J.: Prentice-Hall, 1988.

Krupat, Arnold. *For Those Who Come After: A Study of Native American Autobiography*. Berkeley and Los Angeles: University of California Press, 1985.

Lame Deer, John Fire, and Richard Erdoes. *Lame Deer: Seeker of Visions*. New York: Simon and Schuster, 1972.

Larson, Charles R. *American Indian Fiction*. Albuquerque: University of New Mexico Press, 1978.

Lasch, Christopher. *The Culture of Narcissism*. New York: W. W. Norton, 1978.

Lattin, Vernon E., ed. *Contemporary Chicano Fiction: A Critical Survey*. Binghamton, N.Y.: Bilingual Press/Editorial Bilingüe, 1986.

Lattin, Vernon E., et al., eds. *Tomás Rivera, 1935–1984: The Man and His Work*. Tempe, Ariz.: Bilingual Review/Press, 1988.

Lauter, Paul. "Caste, Class, and Canon." In Harris and Aguero, *A Gift of Tongues*, 57–82.

Lawrence, D. H. *Studies in Classic American Literature*. New York: Doubleday/Anchor Books, 1955.

Lightfoot, Marjorie. "Hunting the Dragon in Kingston's *The Woman Warrior*." *MELUS* 13, nos. 3–4 (Fall–Winter 1986): 55–66.

Lincoln, Kenneth. *Native American Renaissance*. Berkeley and Los Angeles: University of California Press, 1983.

Ling, Amy. *Between Two Worlds: Women Writers of Chinese Ancestry*. New York: Pergamon Press, 1990.

Lizárraga, Sylvia. "The Patriarchal Ideology in 'La noche que apagaron las luces.'" *Revista Chicano-Riqueña* 13, nos. 3–4 (1985): 90–95.

Lorde, Audre. *Sister Outsider*. New York: Crossing Press, 1984.

Lowe, John. "Theories of Ethnic Humor: How to Enter, Laughing." *American Quarterly* 38, no. 3 (September 1986): 439–60.

Martin, Joanne M., and Elmer P. Martin. *The Helping Tradition in the Black Family and Community*. Silver Springs, Md.: National Association of Social Workers, 1985.

McCracken, Ellen. "Sandra Cisneros's *The House on Mango Street*: Community-oriented Introspection and the Demystification of Patriarchal Violence." In *Breaking Boundaries: Latina Writings and Critical Readings*, edited by Asunción Horno-Delgado et al., 62–71. Amherst: University of Massachusetts Press, 1989.

McDonald, Dorothy Ritsuko. Introduction to Chin, *Chickencoop Chinaman*, ix–xxix.

Mendelson, Edward. "The Sacred, the Profane, and *The Crying of Lot 49*." In *Individual and Community: Variations on a Theme in American Fiction,* edited by Kenneth H. Baldwin and David K. Kirby, 182–222. Durham, N.C.: Duke University Press, 1975.

Mindiola, Tatcho, Jr. "Politics and Chicano Literature: The Views of Chicano Writers." In *Understanding the Chicano Experience through Literature,* edited by Nicolás Kanellos, 15–27. Houston: Mexican American Studies, University of Houston, 1981.

Minh-ha, Trinh T. *Woman, Native, Other: Writing Postcoloniality and Feminism.* Bloomington: Indiana University Press, 1989.

Momaday, N. Scott. *The Gourd Dancer.* New York: Harper and Row, 1976.

———. *House Made of Dawn.* New York: Harper and Row, 1977.

———. "The Man Made of Words." In Chapman, *Literature,* 96–110.

———. "A MELUS Interview: N. Scott Momaday—Literature and the Native Writer." With Tom King. *MELUS* 10, no. 4 (Winter 1983): 66–72.

———. *The Names: A Memoir.* New York: Harper and Row, 1976.

———. *The Way to Rainy Mountain.* 1969. Reprint. Albuquerque: University of New Mexico Press, 1976.

Moore, R. Laurence. "Insiders and Outsiders in American Historical Narrative and American History." *AHR Forum* 87 (1982): 390–412.

Mora, Pat. "Tomás Rivera." *Borders.* Houston: Arte Público Press, 1986.

Moraga, Cherríe. *Loving in the War Years: Lo que nunca pasó por sus labios.* Boston: South End Press, 1983.

———. Preface to Moraga and Anzaldúa, *This Bridge Called My Back,* xiii–xix.

Moraga, Cherríe, and Gloria Anzaldúa, eds. *This Bridge Called My Back: Writings by Radical Women of Color.* Watertown, Mass.: Persephone Press, 1981.

Morrison, Toni. *Beloved.* New York: Alfred A. Knopf, 1987.

———. *The Bluest Eye.* 1970. New York: Bantam, 1972.

———. "In the Realm of Responsibility: A Conversation with Toni Morrison." With Marsha Darling. *Women's Review of Books* 5, no. 6 (March 1988): 5–6.

Mukherjee, Bharati. *The Middleman and Other Stories.* 1988. Reprint. New York: Ballantine/Fawcett Crest, 1989.

Murayama, Milton. *All I Asking for Is My Body.* 1959. Reprint. Honolulu: University of Hawaii Press, 1975.

Myrdal, Gunnar. *An American Dilemma: The Negro Problem and Modern Democracy.* 1944. 20th anniv. ed. New York: Harper and Row, 1962.

Nee, Dale Yu. "See, Culture Is Made, Not Born . . . ." *Bridge, an Asian-American Perspective* 3, no. 6 (1975): 42–48.

Nericcio, William Anthony. "Autobiographies at *La Frontera:* The Quest for Mexican-American Narrative." *Americas Review* 16, nos. 3–4 (Winter 1988): 165–87.

Newman, Katharine. "Hawaiian-American Literature Today: The Cultivation of Mangoes." *MELUS* 6, no. 2 (Summer 1979): 47–77.

Novak, Michael. "The New Ethnicity." *Center Magazine* 7 (1974): 18–25.

———. *The Rise of the Unmeltable Ethnics: Politics and Culture in the Seventies.* New York: Macmillan, 1972.

Olivares, Julián. "Sandra Cisneros's *The House on Mango Street* and the Poetics of Space." In *Chicana Creativity and Criticism: Charting New Frontiers in American Litera-*

ture, edited by María Herrera-Sobek and Helena María Viramontes, 160–70. Houston: Arte Público Press, 1988.

———. "The Search for Being, Identity and Form in the Work of Tomás Rivera." *Revista Chicano-Riqueña* 13, nos. 3–4 (1985): 66–80.

Ong, Walter J., S.J. "Oral Culture and the Literate Mind." In *Minority Language and Literature: Retrospective and Perspective,* edited by Dexter Fisher, 134–49. New York: MLA, 1977.

Paredes, Américo. *"With His Pistol in His Hand": A Border Ballad and Its Hero.* 1958. Reprint. Austin: University of Texas Press, 1988.

Parsons, Talcott. "Some Theoretical Considerations on the Nature and Trends of Change of Ethnicity." In Glazer and Moynihan, *Ethnicity,* 53–83.

Pryse, Marjorie, and Hortense J. Spillers, eds. *Conjuring: Black Women, Fiction, and Literary Tradition.* Bloomington: Indiana University Press, 1985.

Rabine, Leslie W. "No Lost Paradise: Social Gender and Symbolic Gender in the Writings of Maxine Hong Kingston." *Signs* 12, no. 3 (1987): 471–92.

Rankin, Mary Backus. "The Emergence of Women at the End of the Ch'ing." In *Women in Chinese Society,* edited by Margery Wolf and Roxane Witke, 39–66. Palo Alto, Calif.: Stanford University Press, 1975.

Rascón, Francisca. "La caracterización de los personajes femeninos en '. . . y no se lo tragó la tierra.'" In Lattin, *Contemporary Chicano Fiction,* 141–48.

Reilly, John M. "Criticism of Ethnic Literature: Seeing the Whole Story." *MELUS* 5, no. 1 (Spring 1978): 2–13.

Riesman, David. "Some Observations on Intellectual Freedom." *American Scholar* 23 (Winter 1953–54): 9–25.

Riesman, David, et al. *The Lonely Crowd: A Study of the Changing American Character.* New Haven, Conn.: Yale University Press, 1950.

Rivera, Tomás. "Chicano Literature: The Establishment of Community." In *A Decade of Chicano Literature (1970–1979): Critical Essays and Bibliography,* edited by Luis Leal et al., 9–17. Santa Barbara, Calif.: Editorial La Causa, 1982.

———. "Chicano Literature: Fiesta of the Living." In *The Identification and Analysis of Chicano Literature,* edited by Francisco Jiménez, 19–35. Binghamton, N.Y.: Bilingual Press/Editorial Bilingüe, 1979.

———. "Into the Labyrinth: The Chicano in Literature." *Southwestern American Literature* 11, no. 2 (1972): 90–97.

———. "Recuerdo, Descubrimiento, y Voluntad en el Proceso Imaginativo Literario" (Remembering, Discovery and Volition in the Literary Imaginative Process). Translated by Gustavo Valadez. *Atisbos: Journal of Chicano Research* 1 (Summer 1975): 66–77.

———. "Richard Rodriguez's *Hunger of Memory* as Humanistic Antithesis." In Lattin et al., *Tomás Rivera,* 28–33.

———. "The Searchers." In Lattin et al., *Tomás Rivera,* 15–20.

———. *. . . y no se lo tragó la tierra / . . . and the earth did not devour him.* Translated by Evangelina Vigil-Piñon. Houston: Arte Público Press, 1987.

———. *. . . y no se lo tragó la tierra / . . . and the earth did not part.* Translated by Herminio Ríos-C. Houston: Arte Público Press, 1971.

Rodríguez del Pino, Salvador. *La novela chicana escrita en español: cinco autores comprometidos*. Ypsilanti, Mich.: Bilingual Press/Editorial Bilingüe, 1982.

Rodríguez, Alfonso. "Tomás Rivera: The Creation of the Chicano Experience in Fiction." In Lattin et al., *Tomás Rivera*, 77–82.

Rodríguez, Juan. "The Problematic in Tomás Rivera's *. . . and the earth did not part.*" In Lattin, *Contemporary Chicano Fiction*, 131–40.

Rodriguez, Richard. "Going Home Again: The New American Scholarship Boy." *American Scholar* 44, no. 1 (Winter 1974–75): 15–28.

———. *Hunger of Memory: The Education of Richard Rodriguez*. New York: Bantam Books, 1982.

Romano-V., Octavio I., and Herminio Ríos-C., eds. *Chicanas en la literatura y el arte/ Chicanas in Literature and Art*. Special issue of *El Grito*, year 7, no. 1. Berkeley: Quinto Sol, 1973.

Rowell, Charles H. "The Quarters: Ernest Gaines and the Sense of Place." In *Afro-American Writing Today*, edited by James Olney, 146–63. Special issue of *Southern Review*. Baton Rouge: Louisiana State University Press, 1985.

Royster, Philip M. "In Search of Our Fathers' Arms: Alice Walker's Persona of the Alienated Darling." *Black American Literature Forum* 20, no. 4 (Winter 1986): 347–70.

Saldívar, José David. "The Ideological and the Utopian in Tomás Rivera's *y no se lo tragó la tierra* and Ron Arias's *The Road to Tamazunchale*." *Crítica: Journal of Critical Essays* 1, no. 2: 100–114.

Saldívar, Ramón. *Chicano Narrative: The Dialectics of Difference*. Madison: University of Wisconsin Press, 1990.

Samuels, Wilfred D. "John Edgar Wideman." *Dictionary of Literary Biography* 33:271–88.

Sánchez, Marta Ester. *Contemporary Chicana Poetry: A Critical Approach to an Emerging Literature*. Berkeley and Los Angeles: University of California Press, 1985.

Sands, Kathleen M., guest ed. *A Special Symposium Issue on Leslie Marmon Silko's "Ceremony."* *American Indian Quarterly* 5, no. 1 (1979): 1–76.

Schneider, David M. *American Kinship: A Cultural Account*. 1968. 2d ed. Chicago and London: University of Chicago Press, 1980.

Schor, Naomi. "Fiction as Interpretation/Interpretation as Fiction." In *The Reader in the Text: Essays on Audience and Interpretation*, edited by Susan R. Suleiman and Inge Crosman, 165–82. Princeton: Princeton University Press, 1980.

Schorer, Mark. "Technique as Discovery." *The World We Imagine: Selected Essays by Mark Schorer*, 3–23. New York: Farrar, Straus, and Giroux, 1948.

Schubnell, Matthias. *N. Scott Momaday: The Cultural and Literary Background*. Norman: University of Oklahoma Press, 1985.

Schultz, Elizabeth A. "The Heirs of Ralph Ellison: Patterns of Individualism in the Contemporary Afro-American Novel." *College Language Association Journal* (December 1978): 101–22.

———. "The Insistence upon Community in the Contemporary Afro-American Novel." *College English* (October 1979): 170–84.

Silberman, Robert. "Opening the Text: *Love Medicine* and the Return of the Native American Woman." In *Narrative Chance: Postmodern Discourse on Native American Indian Literatures*, edited by Gerald Vizenor, 101–20. Albuquerque: University of New Mexico Press, 1989.

Silko, Leslie Marmon. *Ceremony*. New York: Signet Books, 1977.

————. "Language and Literature from a Pueblo Indian Perspective." In *English Literature: Opening Up the Canon, Selected Papers from the English Institute, 1979*, edited by Leslie A. Fiedler and Houston A. Baker, Jr., 54–72. Baltimore: Johns Hopkins University Press, 1981.

————. "A Leslie Marmon Silko Interview." With Kim Barnes. *Journal of Ethnic Studies* (Winter 1986): 83–105.

————. "Stories and Their Tellers—A Conversation with Leslie Marmon Silko." With Dexter Fisher. In Fisher, *Third Woman*, 18–23.

Slotkin, Richard. *Regeneration through Violence: The Mythology of the American Frontier, 1600–1860*. Middletown, Conn.: Wesleyan University Press, 1973.

Smith, Anthony D. *The Ethnic Revival*. Cambridge: Cambridge University Press, 1981.

Smith, Sidonie. *A Poetics of Women's Autobiography: Marginality and the Fictions of Self-Representation*. Bloomington: Indiana University Press, 1987.

Sollors, Werner. *Beyond Ethnicity: Consent and Descent in American Culture*. New York: Oxford University Press, 1986.

Sommers, Joseph. "From the Critical Premise to the Product: Critical Modes and Their Applications to a Chicano Literary Text." *New Scholar* 6 (1977): 51–80.

Steinberg, Stephen. *The Ethnic Myth: Race, Ethnicity, and Class in America*. New York: Atheneum, 1981.

Stone, Albert E. "Introduction: American Autobiographies as Individual Stories and Cultural Narratives." In Stone, *American Autobiography*, 1–9.

————, ed. *The American Autobiography: A Collection of Critical Essays*. Englewood Cliffs, N.J.: Prentice-Hall, 1981.

Sumida, Stephen H. *And the View from the Shore: Literary Traditions of Hawai'i*. Seattle: University of Washington Press, 1991.

————. "Hawaii, the Northwest and Asia: Localism and Local Literary Developments in the Creation of an Asian Immigrants' Sensitivity." *Seattle Review* 11, no. 1 (Spring–Summer 1988): 9–18.

Swann, Brian, and Arnold Krupat, eds. *Recovering the Word: Essays on Native American Literature*. Berkeley and Los Angeles: University of California Press, 1987.

Takaki, Ronald. *Strangers from a Different Shore: A History of Asian Americans*. New York: Penguin, 1989.

Tan, Amy. *The Joy Luck Club*. 1989. Reprint. New York: Ballantine/Ivy Books, 1990.

Tedlock, Dennis. "Toward an Oral Poetics." *New Literary History* 8 (Spring 1977): 507–19.

Testa, Daniel P. "Narrative Technique and Human Experience in Tomás Rivera." In *Modern Chicano Writers: A Collection of Critical Essays*, edited by Joseph Sommers and Tomás Ybarra-Frausto, 86–93. Englewood Cliffs, N.J.: Prentice-Hall, 1979.

Tocqueville, Alexis de. *Democracy in America*, vol. 2. Edited by J. P. Mayer and Max Lerner. Translated by George Lawrence. 2 vols. New York: Doubleday/Anchor Books, 1969.

Tönnies, Ferdinand. *Community and Society*. 1887. Reprint. Translated by Charles P. Loomis. New York: Harper and Row, 1963.

Trudgill, Peter. *Sociolinguistics: An Introduction to Language and Society*. New York: Penguin, 1974.

Tsai, Shih-Shan Henry. *The Chinese Experience in America*. Bloomington: Indiana University Press, 1986.

Vallejos, Thomas. "Mestizaje: The Transformation of Ancient Indian Religious Thought in Contemporary Chicano Fiction." Ph.D. diss., University of Colorado, 1980.

———. "Ritual Process and the Family in the Chicano Novel." *MELUS* 10, no. 4 (Winter 1983): 5–15.

Van den Berghe, Pierre L. Preface to *The Ethnic Phenomenon*, ix–xii. New York: Elsevier, 1981.

Velie, Alan R., ed. *American Indian Literature: An Anthology*. Rev. ed. Norman: University of Oklahoma Press, 1991.

"Vernacular." *American Heritage Dictionary*. 2d ed. 1985.

Villanueva-Collado, Alfredo. "Growing Up Hispanic: Discourse and Ideology in *Hunger of Memory* and *Family Installments*." *Americas Review* 16, nos. 3–4 (Fall–Winter 1988): 75–90.

Walker, Alice. *The Color Purple*. New York: WSP, 1982.

———. "*One* Child of One's Own: A Meaningful Digression within the Work(s)." In *The Writer on Her Work*, edited by Janet Sternburg, 121–40. New York: W. W. Norton, 1980.

———. *In Search of Our Mothers' Gardens*. San Diego: Harcourt Brace Jovanovich, 1983.

Walters, Anna Lee. *The Sun Is Not Merciful*. Ithaca, N.Y.: Firebrand Books, 1985.

Ward, John William. "Who Was Benjamin Franklin?" In *Retracing the Past: Readings in the History of the American People*, edited by Gary B. Nash: 90–97. 2 vols. New York: Harper and Row, 1986.

Wideman, John Edgar. "The Black Writer and the Magic of the Word." *New York Times Book Review* (24 January 1988): 1, 28–29.

———. "Defining the Black Voice in Fiction." *Black American Literature Forum* 2, no. 3 (Fall 1977): 79–82.

———. "Going Home: A Conversation with John Edgar Wideman." With Wilfred D. Samuels. *Callaloo* 6, no. 1 (1983): 40–59.

———. *The Homewood Trilogy: Damballah, Hiding Place, Sent for You Yesterday*. New York: Avon Books, 1985.

———. *The Lynchers*. New York: Harcourt Brace Jovanovich, 1973.

———. "Playing, Not Joking, with Language." Review of *The Signifying Monkey*, by Henry Louis Gates, Jr. *New York Times Book Review* (14 August 1988): 3.

Willis, Susan. *Specifying: Black Women Writing the American Experience*. Madison: University of Wisconsin Press, 1987.

Woolbright, Louie A., and David J. Hartmann. "The New Segregation: Asians and Hispanics." In *Divided Neighborhoods: Changing Patterns of Racial Segregation*, edited by Gary A. Tobin, 138–57. Urban Affairs Annual Reviews 32. Newbury Park, Calif.: Sage Publications, 1987.

Wright, Anne, ed. *The Delicacy and Strength of Lace: Letters between Leslie Marmon Silko and James Wright*. Saint Paul, Minn.: Graywolf Press, 1986.

Wright, Richard. *Black Boy*. 1937. Reprint. New York: Harper and Row, 1989.

Zhang, Ya-jie. "A Chinese Woman's Response to Maxine Hong Kingston's *The Woman Warrior*." *MELUS* 13, nos. 3–4 (Fall–Winter 1986): 103–8.

Index